W9-BZI-159

NUCLEAR WAR IN THE 1980's?

Contributors:
Compiled by Christopher Chant and Ian Hogg.
Illustrators: Peter Sarson & Tony Bryan, Phil Jacobs'
Studio. Additional artwork by Janos Marffy, Mike
Saunders, Gillian Burgess Artists.
Transparencies supplied by Frank Spooner Pictures Ltd.

This book has been designed by Phil Jacobs' Studio.
Filmset by Words & Pictures, London SE19
Color separations by RCS Graphics Ltd.
Printed and bound in Italy by Poligrafici Editoriale.
Nuclear War in the 1980's?
Created and Produced by
Nomad Publishers Ltd.

Nuclear War in the 1980's?
Copyright ©1983 by Nomad Publishers Ltd.

All rights reserved. Printed in Italy. No part of this book
may be used or reproduced in any manner
whatsoever without written permission except in the
case of brief quotations embodied in critical articles
and reviews. For information address Harper & Row
Publishers, Inc., 10 East 53rd Street, New York,
N.Y. 10022.
Published simultaneously in Canada by Fitzhenry & Whiteside
Limited, Toronto.

First U.S. Edition

LIBRARY OF CONGRESS CATALOG CARD NUMBER: 83-47534

ISBN 0-06-105196-X   83 84 85 86 87 10 9 8 7 6 5 4 3 2 1

ISBN 0-06-091079-8 (pbk.) 83 84 85 86 87 10 9 8 7 6 5 4 3 2 1

NUCLEAR WAR IN THE 1980's?

Compiled by Christopher Chant and Ian Hogg
with an Introduction by Professor Laurence Martin

A Nomad Book

HARPER & ROW, PUBLISHERS, New York
Cambridge, Philadelphia, San Francisco,
London, Mexico City, Sao Paulo, Sydney

1817

Contents

Nuclear weapons present the world with several deadly paradoxes. The most destructive military instruments ever devised, they have remained unused for decades despite the constant warfare since their debut at Hiroshima and Nagasaki nearly forty years ago. Nevertheless, unused in battle and often declared to be unusable, they dominate strategic thought and ensure that military questions preoccupy the great powers more persistently than ever before in peacetime.

The root of this paradox lies in the fact that the nuclear weapon constitutes an increase in military potential that is unprecedented and almost certainly unsurpassable whatever technological surprises the future may have to offer us. For in its thermonuclear or fusion form — the hydrogen or 'H-bomb' — the new weapon offers virtually unlimited destructive power. Destruction is inherently easier than construction, but in previous periods of military history the limited destructive power afforded by conventional or chemical explosives, especially when compounded with limits on the capccity to deliver that power to the target, set physical bounds to warfare even when the political will for limitation broke down. Thus, terrible though the damage caused by bombing in the Second World War was, especially when the fire-raid was perfected, the modest payload of manned aircraft and their relative inability to penetrate to or even find and hit their target ensured that the more horrifying prophecies of 'war in the air' that fascinated the thirties were far from fulfilled.

Thermonuclear warheads with explosive yields measured in the equivalent to millions of tons of TNT — megatons or MT — when married to accurate and as yet relatively irresistible ballistic missiles, afford every promise of belatedly vindicating those earlier prophecies. To the immense damage wreaked by the blast, prompt radiation and short-term fall-out of a full scale nuclear war would be added literally incalculable ecological and genetic ill-effects. The novel element of radiation adds, indeed, that extra degree of horror that has always accompanied the 'poison' weapons.

Against destructive forces on this scale and delivered in such a manner, no satisfactory active or passive defence offers itself. If there were an adequate defence along the lines envisaged, amongst others, by President Reagan's 'Starwars' project for anti-missile defences, and assuming aircraft, cruise missiles or other alternative delivery systems could also be mastered, the world would return to the possibilities of more conventional warfare but now enhanced by all the many non-nuclear refinements of technology. It seems doubtful in principle, however, whether any such defence is practicable, for the destructive power of even a few thermonuclear warheads is so great, that the performance of a defensive system would have to be impossibly perfect if damage were to be reduced to 'tolerable' levels.

This is the essential and probably irreversible significance of the nuclear revolution: that mutual holocaust between nuclear powers henceforth remains forever a technological possibility — a possibility that no new methods of mass destruction could take to politically significant higher levels.

We live, therefore, in an age of decisive strategic revolution and as this revolution is at most a few decades old, first fully realised perhaps only in the sixties when fusion warheads were first really successfully married to ballistic missiles, we need to be extremely cautious in believing that we have yet divined the military and political consequences. Precisely because there are no previous periods of nuclear strategic thought against which to measure the current orthodoxy, we need to assess the important contemporary facts and issues presented in this book against some examination of how the problem has evolved since the atomic bombs first fell on Japan.

The consequences of a large scale nuclear war being so horrendous and in many ways unpredictable, the supreme aim for all the military powers, however divided on other issues, must be to prevent such a war occurring. This aim, common though it may be, is however a very narrow and limited purpose and we continue to live in a world of deep political conflict. Even Pope John Paul II, reflecting on military issues, has remarked that "a totally and permanently peaceful human society is unfortunately a Utopia." A realistic nuclear strategy must therefore embrace the art of pursuing conflicts of interest without destroying the world.

Some farsighted thinkers perceived this problem as soon as the atomic bomb proved practical — indeed a few of the scientists in the know had turned their minds, however cursorarily, to the problems of a nuclear balance before the first fission device was proved in the desert at Alamagordo. The alleged pre-war aphorism of the British Prime Minister Stanley Baldwin, that "the bomber will always get through", somewhat falsified by the experience of the subsequent World War, seemed about to be vindicated for all practical purposes by this new scale of destructive power. There would now, it seemed, truly be no defence.

Those who saw this prospect came to an early and significant conclusion: if there can be no defence in the traditional sense of warding off the enemy attack, security must be sought in presenting the would-be aggressor with the certain prospect of suffering the same intolerable damage in reply. It seemed reasonable to assume that the worse the damage threatened, the more effective would be the deterrent. This theoretical assumption combined with practical experience in the recent World War to suggest the mutual 'city-busting' attacks that still constitute the popular image of nuclear war.

The basic principle that bombing targets should be of military significance, as it could certainly be argued was required by international law, was never wholly abandoned during the German 'blitz' and the Allied air assaults on Germany and Japan. But the limitations of bombing techniques contributed to the virtual irrelevance of this distinction so far as urban populations were concerned. While bombers might ostensibly have munitions factories and railway marshalling yards as aiming points,

the gross errors in target identification and the crudity of delivery systems resulted in much more widespread devastation than effect on the target; in other words, what we would now call 'collateral damage' dominated intended military effects. At one stage the RAF made a virtue of this by stretching the notion of a military target to the utmost by undertaking to destroy German workers' housing and thus indirectly incapccitate war industry. There can be no doubt — and there is a lesson for today to learn — that by that time mutual suffering had introduced an element of sheer revenge and morale breaking into the equation. Only toward the end of the war, especially in American daylight raids, did more precise concepts of what is now termed 'microtargetting' effectively re-enter the field of strategic bombing.

It was therefore only to be expected that when bombs of immensely greater destructive potential became available, they were initially thought of as intended for large and important targets situated in or around cities. Moreover, the new radii of devastation feasible with single weapons offered an obvious way to compensate for continued inaccuracy of delivery and this, deliberately or not, meant that collateral damage reigned more dominant than ever over intended effects. Thus while it is true that bombing cities for its own sake seems never to have played an explicit part in Soviet nuclear strategic theory, and that the United States Air Force never abandoned the selection of targets justifiable by a military rationale, the difference it would have made for urban populations was little, given the consequences that would have followed attacking those target lists with the weapons available.

These underlying technical reasons for not finding a real alternative to the devastation of cities at times became a consciously articulated policy. When, in the fifties, the Eisenhower Administration reacted against the frustrations of fighting a limited conventional war in Korea and enunciated the doctrine of Massive Retaliation — the notion that lesser wars might be met by a response against the main aggressor — the idea was generally associated with the bombing of Soviet cities, even though this was never officially specified. Similarly the doctrine of retaliation adopted by the United Kingdom and later by France, implied attacks on cities as such, given the small scale of the force available.

Moreover a strategy of attacking cities had certain paradoxical advantages to recommend it even to those with the opposite of a blood thirsty turn of mind. Cities constitute a finite set of targets, readily located and easily destroyed. Designing a force to discharge that mission therefore seemed relatively easy, whereas attacks on military and military-industrial targets might require increasingly sophisticated weapons and a number of such weapons partly dictated by how large the enemy's forces had become. There were therefore the seeds of an active arms race in anti-military or 'counterforce' targetting. Furthermore, while there might be argument about how successful counterforce attacks would be and about how much of them the enemy might regard as an unacceptable price to pay, it hardly seemed to need arguing that no nation could willingly incur the destruction of its major cities. Thus not only did a massive threat against cities seem to promise 'stability' in the absence of an active arms race, but also 'crisis stability', in that powers so deterred would be cautious in promoting and pursuing conflict to the point of hostilities.

It seems to have been predominantly a desire to limit the demands of his military services for increased forces that led the American Secretary of Defense, Robert McNamara, to abandon a previously declared intention to seek 'damage limitation' and base his policy firmly on the deterrent idea of 'assured destruction': that is, an obvious and reliable capacity to retaliate for a Soviet attack and destroy the Soviet Union as a 'twentieth century society'. By overtly declaring what high levels of destruction of Soviet industry and fatalities among the Soviet population would constitute an adequate deterrent, Mr. McNamara, whatever the actual targetting plans of his strategic forces, put nuclear deterrence at the 'declaratory' level clearly onto the basis of destroying Soviet society rather than Soviet military power. Moreover, in the hope of stabilising what might otherwise still become an arms race or a condition in which the Soviet Union might be tempted to strike first in desperation, Mr. McNamara made it clear that it would be reasonable, indeed desirable, for the Soviet Union to have an 'assured destruction' capability against the United States. Assured Destruction would be Mutual Assured Destruction, thus coining the well-known acronym MAD.

It soon became apparent, however, that there were serious inherent flaws in the MAD doctrine. In the first place, leaving on one side the disturbing moral implications of such a policy and the questionable permanent stability of a strategy that required great and technologically powerful nations to live forever more under the constant threat of rapid annihilation, the threat of actually executing the retaliatory strike seemed to derive such credibility as it might enjoy from the prospect of a devastating nuclear attack on the proprietor of the force in question. Where then did this leave the allies of the United States, hitherto sheltering reasonably comfortably under the American nuclear 'umbrella', now that American strategy had begun to adjust so overtly to the inability of the United States to defend itself or even try to defend itself against a Soviet nuclear attack? From this

doubt, already raised by sceptics about the credibility of Eisenhower's Massive Retaliation, flowed the evolution of President de Gaulle's 'force de frappe', new rationales for the British nuclear force, and increased anxiety in the Federal Republic of Germany for which, after such abortive schemes for collective nuclear forces such as the Multilateral Force (MLF), new schemes of joint planning were instituted as a palliative. A new ingredient had clearly been added to the incentives for nuclear proliferation.

At the same time, the technical tasks of meeting the requirements of assured destruction were seen to be more demanding than at first realised. Studies made in the mid- fifties had illuminated the problem of maintaining a 'secure second-strike'; for while there might be no adequate defence against a powerful nuclear force once launched, it could of course be negated if destroyed on the ground. The vulnerability of aircraft in this respect had stimulated development of the hardened missile silo and the submarine-launched ballistic missile. If a second-strike force could probably still be maintained, it would only be at the price of considerable effort. By the late fifties systems for intercepting missiles in flight were appearing and though their performance was quite inadequate to afford a tight defence, the concept of active defence combined with the notion of counterforce to discredit the early assumption of deterrence theory, that there was no possibility of defending oneself. This was now true only at certain states of the balance of power and the idea that stability could be based on building a finite force against cities and leaving it at that could no longer be sustained. If anti-submarine warfare (ASW) were to make major advances the problem of maintaining a second-strike would be further aggravated.

While efforts to perfect ASW have continued to frustrate technologists, immense improvements in guidance systems have so increased the accuracy of both ballistic and air-breathing cruise-missiles that the hardened silo no longer affords a safe refuge for second-strike missiles. New measures of protection thus have to be considered and these include both mobility — which increases the problem of ascertaining the strength of rival forces — and the use of active, anti-ballistic missile devices. All these trends further destroy the one-time illusion that nuclear missiles offered a simple way to assure an adequate retaliatory force irrespective of the efforts of others. Thus nuclear strategy is driven back, like previous military generations, to the anxious calculation of orders of battle and the potential for arms racing remains.

From this dilemma has arisen the great interest in nuclear arms control: if technology does not give rise spontaneously to a stable strategic balance at reasonable cost, perhaps nuclear powers can design a mutually acceptable balance and agree not to go beyond it. By good fortune satellite and other technology has greatly eased the problem of verification, if only for a certain range of weapons. But because strategic nuclear forces have now to be measured for their potential to destroy enemy forces as well as cities, the design of a stable balance is an intricate and frustrating task, even assuming mutual goodwill. When it is recalled, however, that the urge for agreement arises solely from fear of annihilation and not from mutual trust, and when, indeed, not merely conventional military forces but the very fear of nuclear weapons can be used as coercive instruments in a world of conflict, it is not surprising that progress in strategic arms control is slow and even becomes itself a source of friction.

Nor, of course, would putting the strategic nuclear balance on an agreed and stable foundation solve the problem of relating deterrence to lesser threats and aggressions, especially those perpetrated against the allies of nuclear powers. Faced with the superior conventional forces of the Soviet Union and having failed to fulfil early plans to match these in kind, the North Atlantic Alliance had come to rely, in the Massive Retaliation era of the late fifties, on the early use of nuclear weapons. The increasing availability of once scarce fissile material and the development of smaller nuclear devices capable of being packaged in even such small vehicles as 155 mm artillery shells had permitted plans to use nuclear weapons 'tactically' on the battlefield as well as in strategic strikes. These weapons, of which the United States enjoyed an initial monopoly, were introduced without much clear thinking about their function. It was never explicitly decided whether they were added firepower to redress the tactical balance in a war short of a 'strategic exchange', an adjunct to such an exchange or, perhaps, an 'escalatory' signal that such an exchange was imminent barring a rapid political settlement. Whatever the rationale, the deterrent effectiveness of a strategy requiring 'first use' of nuclear weapons fell into increasing doubt as the vulnerability of the United States to Soviet retaliation became more obvious.

While the French solution was to develop a national nuclear force to exercise deterrence solely against an attack on France, on de Gaulle's well-known theory that a threat of suicide was credible only on behalf of the nation possessing the power to execute it, NATO adopted a strategy of 'flexible response'. This strategy entailed increasing the capacity to mount an initial conventional defence. But it retained the ultimate threat of nuclear escalation and, as the alliance still failed to provide conventional forces adequate to sustain prolonged resistance against the Warsaw Pact, the problem of first use and credibility was postponed or alleviated rather than

solved. When, in the seventies, the Soviet Union deployed a vastly improved array of tactical or 'theatre' nuclear weapons of its own, including the notorious SS-20 intermediate-range missile, NATO found itself entangled once again in a debate about the validity of nuclear guarantees, the problem of first use and escalation, and about the place of the various categories of nuclear weapons in these strategic relationships. The intermediate nuclear forces (INF) being the ones most obviously forming a link between the local European battle and the intercontinental strategic balance, it was only to be expected that as the eighties began, INF became the key issue in both East-West and intra-Western strategic debates.

The theoretical possibility of a war involving nuclear weapons confined to the battlefield does not exhaust the conceivable forms of limited nuclear war. As early as the mid-fifties, the same realisation that retaliatory forces might be subject to 'pre-emptive' attack that bred concern with the technological requirements of maintaining a secure second strike, naturally implied that cities were not the only possible targets for strategic nuclear weapons. Increasing accuracy and controllability of missiles has made it possible to think of attacks on military targets, not necessarily including the enemy's nuclear forces, conducted in such a way as to minimize casualties and thereby give the enemy an incentive not to respond with the retaliatory all-out attack on cities envisaged in the classical doctrine of deterrence. Thus various concepts of limited nuclear war or 'limited strategic options' have emerged in recent years. From a technological perspective these encourage development of accurate missiles with small warheads — indeed long-range attacks with conventional explosives become practicable now that accuracies of some thirty metres are attainable at intercontinental ranges — and elaboration of sophisticated systems for target identification and damage assessment. From the political viewpoint, for an alliance like NATO, the feasibility of less than total nuclear war might restore the credibility of the United States initiating nuclear action on behalf of its allies, whereas the mutually suicidal war of assured destruction is credible if at all only in self-defence.

There are, however, obviously grave difficulties about the idea of limited nuclear war and these underlie much of the strategic debate in the eighties. In the first place there are those who fear the notion makes nuclear war seem 'acceptable' without providing any real assurance that it would in fact stay limited. Such a war would obviously strain political self-control to the limits; moreover it is far from clear that the technical pre-requisites for limitation can be met — in particular the survival of the means of command and control under conditions of nuclear war and the sufficiently perfect performance of weapons to keep the intended limits mutually perceptible. On the other hand, if no efforts are made to provide the concepts and mechanisms for control, any nuclear war that does occur will almost certainly be an unmitigated disaster and the problem of extending nuclear guarantees remains unsolved.

As the French demonstrated by the development of their national ' force de dissuasion ', one answer to the inadequacy of third party nuclear guarantees for a nation that feels threatened and possesses appropriate technological capability, is nuclear proliferation. So far in the nuclear age it is fair to say that proliferation has proceeded much more slowly than was once commonly feared. Forty years after Hiroshima there are still only five fully declared nuclear powers and two, Israel and India, in twilight zones of their own making. But as the charts later in this book clearly indicate, the capability for making nuclear weapons is rapidly spreading.

It was once generally believed that the secret of controlling nuclear proliferation lay in restricting this physical capacity to manufacture bombs: thus the earliest schemes for control envisaged international ownership of nuclear industry and all powers with nuclear knowledge imposed severe and elaborate measures to preserve secrecy. Over the years it has become clear that the secret cannot be kept and the way to design a weapon is known to any competent nuclear physicist. This does not mean that secrets are not valuable; there are many tricks to making effective weapons economically. But any reasonably advanced nation could make a serviceable weapon if it chose to devote the necessary resources. Securing enough fissile material presents problems to the majority without indigenous uranium and the efforts of the leading nuclear nations — which for this purpose must include those such as Canada, with advanced peaceful nuclear industries — to restrict material and equipment undoubtedly hampers several would-be military-nuclear powers. In the long run, however, the pluralism of the nuclear market, the political and commercial rivalry among the 'haves', make denial of the physical capability to construct nuclear weapons at best a partial constraint on proliferation.

Probably more important are the political constraints. The fact that such powers as Canada have long enjoyed the full wherewithal to make nuclear weapons but have not done so demonstrates that capability is by no means equivalent to execution where proliferation is concerned. Making a bomb is expensive and can be dangerous, depending on the reaction of other states. Moreover it is by no means necessarily the best answer to security problems even where serious threats exist. Thus unlike France, most European members of NATO have not 'gone

nuclear' — Britain did so in a rather different climate in the momentum of the World War II effort in which it had participated so vigorously. Israel, if virtually nuclear, has thought the danger to its ties with the United States and the possible repercussions amongst Arab states — not certainly denied Soviet nuclear aid — sufficient to recommend abstention at least from overt declaration of nuclear status. South Korea has been successfully threatened with loss of American military aid when contemplating major steps toward a nuclear capability. Pakistan, by contrast, may feel too isolated to refrain from matching India's progress, dangerous though such a competition must undoubtedly be.

It would seem, therefore, as though the efforts to control the flow of nuclear knowledge and facilities are only an element in a much broader and more complex network of influences determining the decision to go nuclear. In this network the pressures and incentives brought to bear by allies, guarantors and enemies on specific candidate nations are probably more important than the general system of prohibition and disapproval embodied in the Non-Proliferation Treaty. That Treaty and the consequent safeguards imposed and inspected under the auspices of the International Atomic Energy Authority are by no means negligible, however, for they provide a framework of information and legitimacy within which the more powerful but less formal political pressures work.

Given the importance that the evolution of the nuclear balance between the existing nuclear powers has placed upon such considerations as the safe design and custody of nuclear weapons, the prospect of those weapons spreading throughout the Third World should perhaps arouse more acute concern than the progress of the so-called arms race between the Superpowers. For although the Non-Proliferation Treaty links the pledge of non-acquisition with a parallel undertaking by the existing nuclear signatories to pursue disarmament, the latter are, if dangerously well-armed, locked in a balance that has so far proved stable, and possess highly developed internal systems of political control. In the Third World, however, the would-be nuclear powers are typically urged in that direction precisely by severe security problems and are more often than not domestically unstable and faction-ridden. Moreover the process of proliferation itself would in all probability greatly enhance regional tensions. Thus, as a speculative scenario in this volume suggests, it may well be that the greatest risk of the world's second warlike use of nuclear weapons lies not in the great nuclear arsenals that so preoccupy us but in some lesser, newly fledged, nuclear power. Tragic and dangerous in itself, such an event might have an even more serious consequence, for it would breach the taboo on actually using nuclear weapons that the early nuclear states have successfully observed since Japan surrendered.

Whether nuclear instruments could descend yet further down the chain of political elements into the hands of terrorists remains to be seen. There are several reasons for believing this unlikely; certainly a terrorist use or threat to use a nuclear device would not have the same impact on the assumptions underlying interstate relations as a small scale nuclear war. But the possibilities offer added reasons for efforts to keep nuclear weapons out of the hands of unstable and inefficient states; indeed under circumstances not hard to imagine in some contemporary cases, the distinction between turbulent state and terrorist might not be easy to maintain. Indirect action by a 'rogue' government may be the most plausible route by which terrorists might overcome the otherwise formidable obstacles in their path.

The nuclear era, still in its infancy, has nevertheless seen the most intensive and by most measures the most successful effort in history to pursue disarmament and what is nowadays called arms control. While the international agreements reached and ratified are perhaps modest when set against the scale of the problem, they are far from negligible whether judged against the achievements of previous ages or the complexity of the contemporary military and diplomatic scene. Probably more impressive, however, if easily overlooked, is the intellectual progress that has been made in comprehending what disarmament requires and in evolving the parallel concept of 'arms control' to correct some of the flaws in the classical notion of disarmament. Put briefly, arms control sets as its goal not the elimination or even necessarily a reduction in armaments, but the avoidance of war and, should that effort fail, the minimisation of its destructive effects.

From this perspective a great deal of the modern military scene, particularly the nuclear aspect, can be viewed as a contribution to arms control, even though apparently far removed from the process of negotiating and observing explicit agreements. Thus the efforts of the nuclear powers to maintain forces that are not vulnerable to a first strike, that can therefore avoid the compulsion to precipitate use on the 'use it or lose it' principle, probably do more than anything else to stabilize the balance in crisis. The fact that the nuclear powers are conscious of this mutual dependence and take great pains to communicate such restraint to each other, if often in oblique form, is a tribute to the modification that fear of nuclear war has engendered in international conduct. A more specific illustration is provided by the willingness of even such a secretive power as the Soviet Union to co-operate in the surveillance of its strategic forces

by American satellites within the framework of the Strategic Arms Limitation Agreements.

While the common appreciation of an interest in avoiding nuclear war is a fundamental source of international security, the task of converting this appreciation into explicit arms control agreements that might reinforce this stabilising influence, if possible at lower levels of expenditure, is inherently difficult. Two emerging complexities well exemplified in the chapters that follow make it uncertain whether the remarkable achievements of the SALT treaties constitute the beginning of a cumulative process.

The first complexity arises from the increased variety of weapons relevant to the nuclear balance. At the outset of the SALT process only intercontinental and submarine launched missiles were counted; by the time of the unratified but mutually observed SALT II it was no longer possible to ignore long-range bombers or the existence of multiple warheads (MIRVs). The subsequent negotiations, called by the Americans START, for Strategic Arms Reduction Talks, tried to embrace warheads and missile payload more explicitly. But by that time, the blurred frontier between intercontinental and intermediate systems had come to complicate matters. It became clear that the first SALT treaty had been a crude affair and that any agreement fully comprehending the nuclear balance would either be extremely complex or have to be very flexible. Either solution would inevitably greatly exacerbate the problem of verification, hitherto solved by the remarkable but nevertheless very constrained reconnaissance capability of satellites and electronic eavesdropping.

The intrusion of the intermediate nuclear forces into the negotiations between the Superpowers also exemplified the second new complexity: the need to take more than two nuclear powers into account. Soviet demands that British and French nuclear forces be explicitly entered into the calculation was a significant difficulty in the negotiations. It was far more ominous as a reminder that in a world of many nuclear powers, deterrence as well as arms control is immensely complicated. So far the problem has been confined by the disparity in scale between the two Superpowers and the other nuclear states and by the fact that two of the lesser are linked by alliance to the United States. If and when the powers become more commensurate in size — and, ironically, any limitation of Superpower armament may make it easier for third party nuclear forces to appear a threat — or when the lesser nuclear powers become embroiled in adversary balances between themselves, the task of calculating let alone regulating balances will become much more difficult. The fact that an apparent surplus of nuclear power or more graduated nuclear strategies along the lines of 'limited strategic options' might facilitate nuclear guarantees and thereby reduce the incentive for proliferation or enhancement of existing lesser nuclear forces indicates how paradoxical the nuclear balance of power can be.

Whether arms control, narrowly or broadly conceived, unilateral or multilateral, can save us from the potential disaster of nuclear warfare thus remains uncertain. What is not in doubt is that with the secret of the nuclear weapon forever unlocked from the mysteries of physics and loose in the minds of men, the world is fated to wrestle with these paradoxes for ever more. Solutions evade the experts scarcely less than the man in the street. If there are to be solutions, however, they must surely arise from a wider and deeper public understanding of the issues that are presented as dispassionately and as simply as possible in the chapters that follow.

Laurence Martin
University of Newcastle Upon Tyne
July 1983

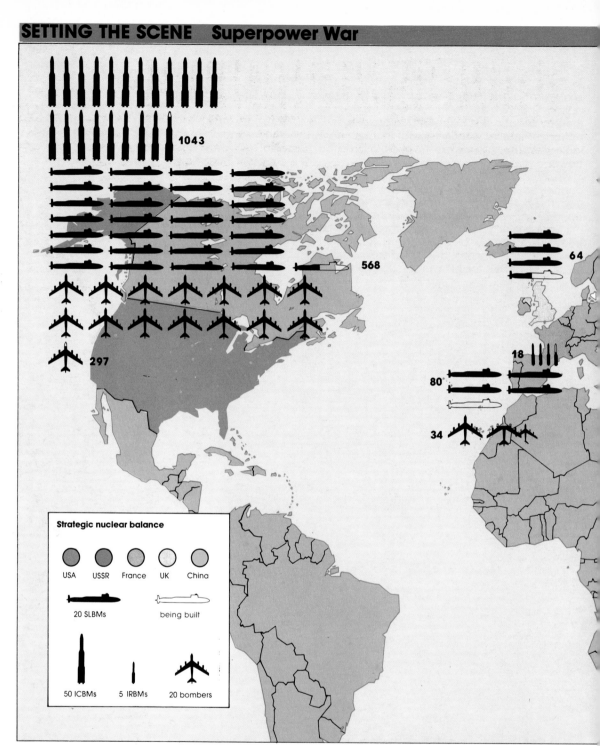

1043

568

64

297

18

80

34

Strategic nuclear balance

USA USSR France UK China

20 SLBMs   being built

50 ICBMs   5 IRBMs   20 bombers

The antagonism between the USA and USSR is one of the most significant factors on the current world stage, for it conditions to an incalculable degree the political, economic, military and social life of the powers directly involved, of their allies, and satellites, and of those countries whose strategic position, raw material resources or markets are coveted by the superpowers.

The root of this antagonism, given concrete form in the vast nuclear arsenals depicted above, is clearly related to ideological differences between the United States and the Soviet Union. The relationship between this antagonism and more traditional nationalistic and geopolitical conflicts is much debated, but whatever its origins the mutual hostility is of long standing, first manifested in the American 'intervention' in Russia at the close of World War I and developing (despite the rapprochement of World War II) into the current 'cold war' by way of the Russian blockade of Berlin, the

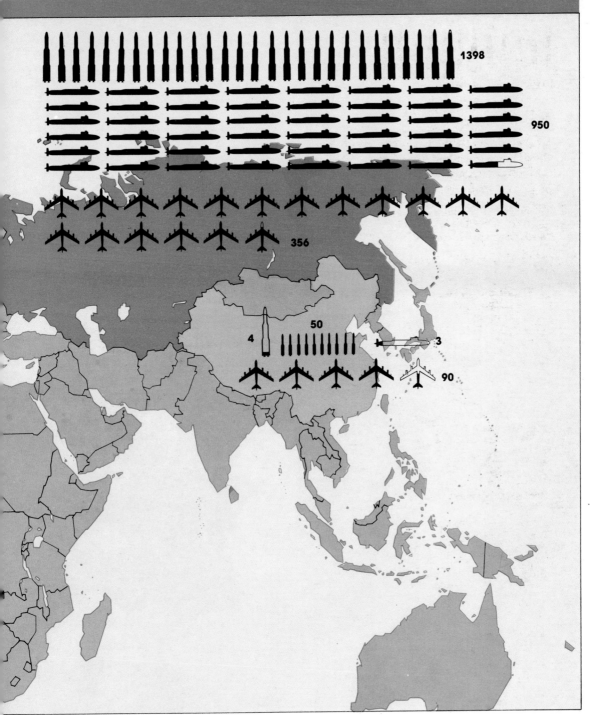

1398

950

356

4   50   3

90

development of the Korean War, the nuclear competition, conflicts on decolonisation, especially in Asia and the Middle East, the Cuban missile crisis, the Vietnam War, regional conflicts in Africa, Central America and elsewhere, and a constant jockeying within the third world to secure strategic and economic advantage.

At the same time, the situation is made more complicated by the later appearance of other lesser nuclear powers, France and the UK broadly aligned with the USA, and China representing an independent communist nuclear force capable of threatening the Soviet Union and soon, the United States as well.

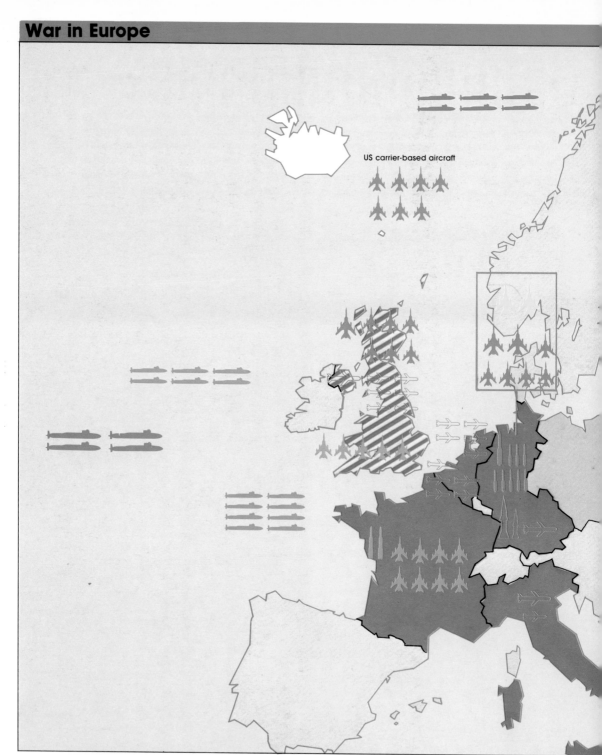

US carrier-based aircraft

The USA and USSR face each other at shortest range over the Arctic ocean, and for this reason each superpower's ICBM deployments are north-facing. But the USSR must also take into account her flanks, exposed to military action from China in the east and the NATO powers in the west. As the latter include the USA, which has powerful conventional and nuclear forces in Europe this is clearly a potential threat which cannot safely be ignored by the USSR.

Thus Europe plays a central part in Russian strategic thinking, as is evident from the map, for while the nuclear threat from the USA is massive, the threat posed in Europe by the physical confrontation with the NATO countries and the states of the Warsaw Pact is complex in the extreme, and fraught with the possibility of escalation from conventional to nuclear warfare. For this reason,

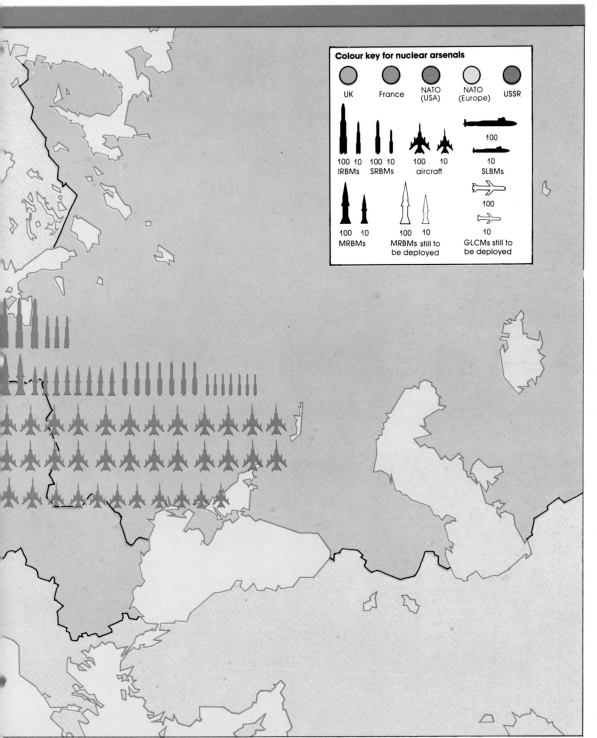

Colour key for nuclear arsenals

| UK | France | NATO (USA) | NATO (Europe) | USSR |

100 10 IRBMs | 100 10 SRBMs | 100 10 aircraft | 100 10 SLBMs

100 10 MRBMs | 100 10 MRBMs still to be deployed | 100 10 GLCMs still to be deployed

therefore, Europe plays a more important part in Russian political and military thinking than would otherwise be the case.

This threat might impel the Russians into a nuclear strike against Europe in the event of hostilities with the USA, for only thus could American nuclear forces in several European states be neutralised. However, also of deep concern to the Russians are the independent nuclear powers of Europe, France and the UK, which are aligned with or committed to NATO but could be used independently of American forces in circumstances of supreme national interests.

Neighbourhood Wars

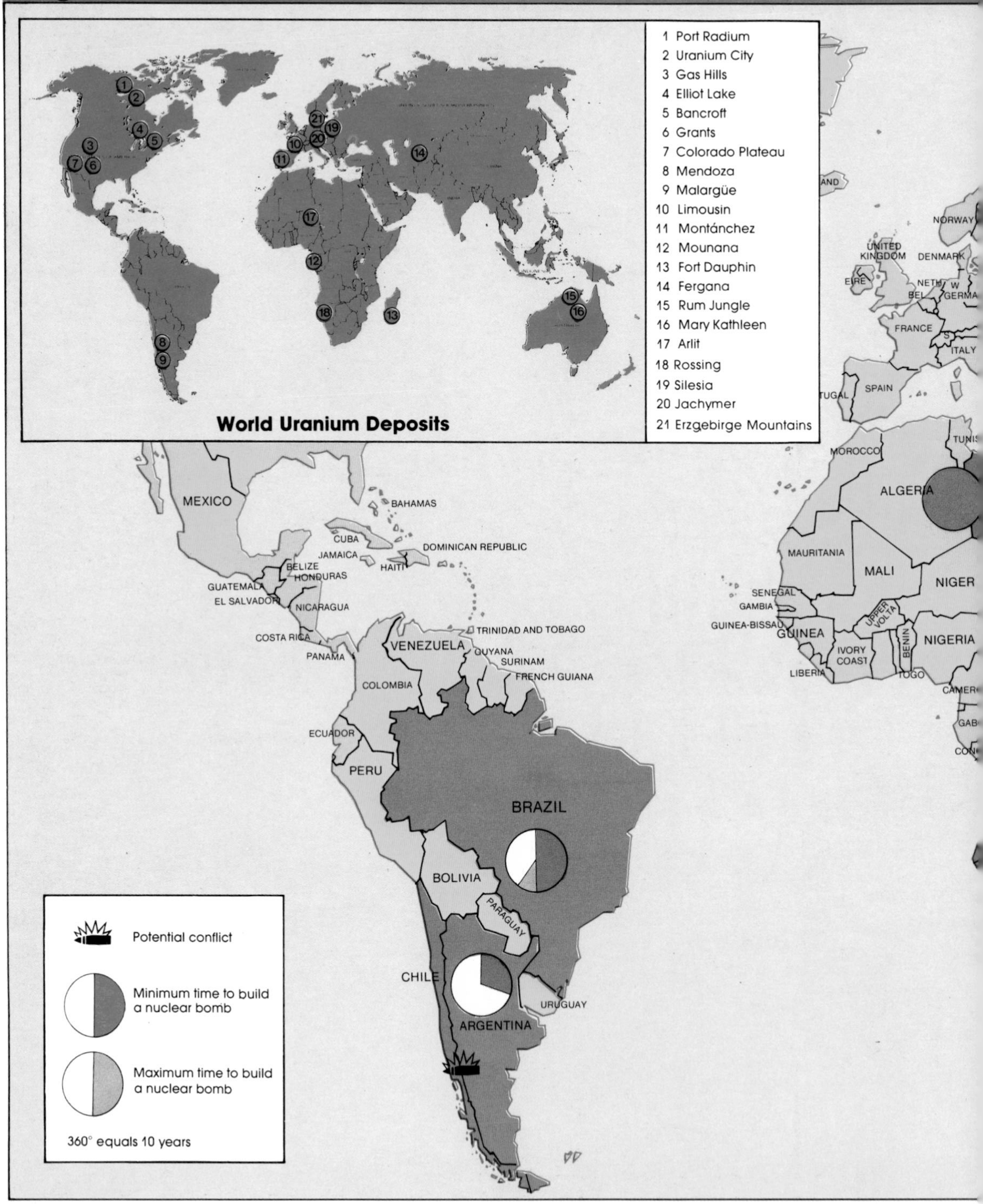
1 Port Radium
2 Uranium City
3 Gas Hills
4 Elliot Lake
5 Bancroft
6 Grants
7 Colorado Plateau
8 Mendoza
9 Malargüe
10 Limousin
11 Montánchez
12 Mounana
13 Fort Dauphin
14 Fergana
15 Rum Jungle
16 Mary Kathleen
17 Arlit
18 Rossing
19 Silesia
20 Jachymer
21 Erzgebirge Mountains
World Uranium Deposits
Potential conflict
Minimum time to build a nuclear bomb
Maximum time to build a nuclear bomb
360° equals 10 years
MEXICO
BAHAMAS
CUBA
JAMAICA
HAITI
DOMINICAN REPUBLIC
BELIZE
HONDURAS
GUATEMALA
EL SALVADOR
NICARAGUA
COSTA RICA
PANAMA
TRINIDAD AND TOBAGO
VENEZUELA
GUYANA
SURINAM
FRENCH GUIANA
COLOMBIA
ECUADOR
PERU
BRAZIL
BOLIVIA
PARAGUAY
CHILE
ARGENTINA
URUGUAY
NORWAY
UNITED KINGDOM
DENMARK
EIRE
NETH
BEL
FRANCE
ITALY
SPAIN
MOROCCO
ALGERIA
MAURITANIA
MALI
NIGER
SENEGAL
GAMBIA
GUINEA-BISSAU
GUINEA
UPPER VOLTA
BENIN
NIGERIA
IVORY COAST
LIBERIA
TOGO

Five countries currently admit to the possession of nuclear weapons. However, the proliferation of nuclear power reactors for generating electricity has put the technology for simple atomic weapons almost within the grasp of several other countries. It is feared that the greater availability of such weapons may increase the likelihood of the weapons' use, and this danger is exacerbated by the relative instability of many of the countries involved, where conflict with neighbouring states and political and economic instability is a persistent feature of their contemporary history. In these circumstances such countries might wish to pursue the development of nuclear weapons as means of ensuring their security against stronger neighbours.

The countries capable of producing simple nuclear weapons within the next 10 years may have

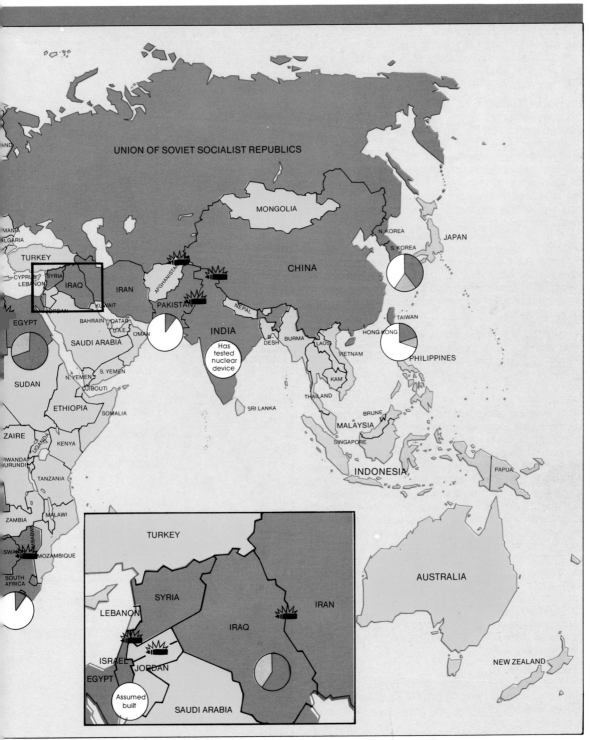

UNION OF SOVIET SOCIALIST REPUBLICS

MONGOLIA

CHINA

N. KOREA

JAPAN

S. KOREA

TURKEY

CYPRUS SYRIA
LEBANON IRAQ

IRAN

AFGHANISTAN

PAKISTAN

NEPAL

TAIWAN

EGYPT

SAUDI ARABIA

BAHRAIN QATAR
U.A.E.
OMAN

INDIA

Has tested nuclear device

B. DESH

BURMA

LAOS

HONG KONG

VIETNAM

PHILIPPINES

KUWAIT

SUDAN

N. YEMEN
DJIBOUTI

S. YEMEN

KAM

THAILAND

SRI LANKA

BRUNE

MALAYSIA

ETHIOPIA

SOMALIA

ZAIRE

KENYA

RWANDA
BURUNDI

UGANDA

TANZANIA

SINGAPORE

INDONESIA

PAPUA

ZAMBIA

MALAWI

ZIMBABWE

MOZAMBIQUE

SWA

SOUTH
AFRICA

AUSTRALIA

TURKEY

SYRIA

IRAN

LEBANON

IRAQ

ISRAEL
EGYPT

JORDAN

Assumed
built

SAUDI ARABIA

NEW ZEALAND

ample political reason for so doing; with the exception of Brazil, all of these countries have long standing disputes with close neighbours. And often these neighbours possess an overwhelming superiority in conventional arms, or have the capacity to threaten the security of the country in other ways. Thus countries such as South Africa (faced with hostile African states grouped to form the front line states to the north); Israel (which has fought wars with each of its neighbours, and whose existence is not completely accepted by them); and Pakistan (increasingly caught in a vice between India and the USSR) are typical of those who feel that the ultimate threat of nuclear retaliation against invasion may be necessary. Nuclear weapons are in themselves destabilising and their acquisition by many other countries may be disastrous for the world.

The deterrent triad concept calls for a trio of strategic delivery systems with different capabilities and operational characteristics to provide optimum survivability and offensive capability.

The Manned Bomber

The manned bomber is the oldest of the three elements, and despite some obsolescence still has a major part to play. On the credit side, the manned bomber has flexible range and payload, and can deliver with high accuracy and targetting flexibility right up to the last moment thanks to the availability of satellite communications. It also has two unique assets in that it can be recalled at short notice and can return for use in another strike. On the debit side, the manned bomber is vulnerable on the ground and in the air, (many aircraft will be lost to attacking interceptors and SAMs), has complex procedures for full alert generation, and is difficult to sustain at high levels of generated alert for protracted periods.

The ICBM

Second oldest of the triad elements, the inter-continental ballistic missile (ICBM) is a land based weapon system characterised by short flight times, ability to penetrate defences, and to accurately deliver nuclear weapons of high explosive yield onto targets. Other credit features of the ICBM are the fact that it can be retargetted rapidly, can be quickly generated to full alert, and when protected in underground silos has high pre-launch survivability (though the latter is diminishing due to the increasing accuracy available for strategic warheads designed to attack hardened point targets such as missile silos and command centres). The ICBM also possesses good command and control characteristics enabling the missiles to be flexibly managed in crisis and (it is anticipated) in war. On the debit side, the key vulnerability of the ICBM to emerge in recent years has been to a pre-emptive attack by an adversary's ICBM force equipped with ICBMs that provide a significant hard target kill probability. Such a vulnerability is considered as de-stabilising in periods of tension or crisis, even though two other elements of the triad would survive such a pre-emptive attack.

The SLBM

Most recent of the triad components, the sub-marine launched ballistic missile (SLBM) is a sea-based system offering its possessor the best combination of operational capability and survivability though at the expense of highly responsive command and control, and reduced accuracy of the missiles. On its credit side, the SLBM has extremely low vulnerability to pre-emptive attack, and is the strongest leg of the triad for assured retaliatory capability. On the debit side, however, there are a number of difficulties with the command, control and communication required for an SLBM force which greatly complicate the task of managing the force flexibly in crisis.

miles   1000

bombers scrambled to join those on routine patrol

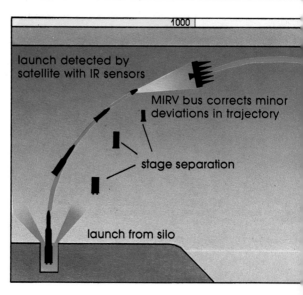

1000

launch detected by satellite with IR sensors

MIRV bus corrects minor deviations in trajectory

stage separation

launch from silo

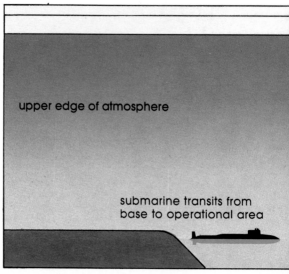

upper edge of atmosphere

submarine transits from base to operational area

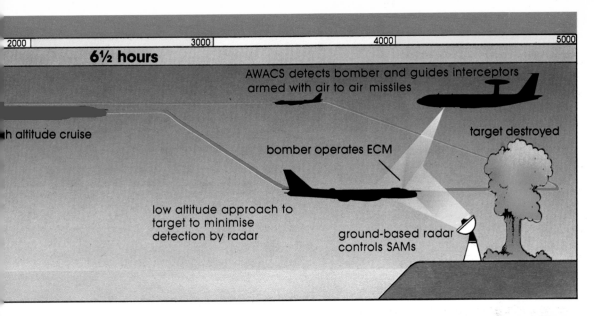

2000 | 3000 | 4000 | 5000

6½ hours

AWACS detects bomber and guides interceptors
armed with air to air missiles

h altitude cruise

target destroyed

bomber operates ECM

low altitude approach to
target to minimise
detection by radar

ground-based radar
controls SAMs

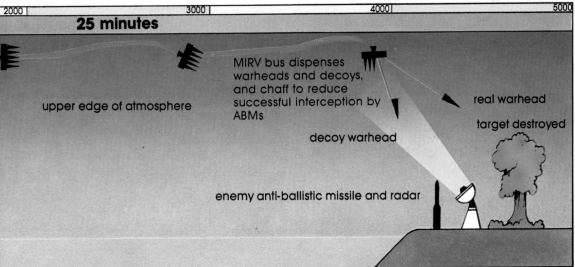

2000 | 3000 | 4000 | 5000

25 minutes

MIRV bus dispenses
warheads and decoys,
and chaff to reduce
successful interception by
ABMs

upper edge of atmosphere

real warhead

target destroyed

decoy warhead

enemy anti-ballistic missile and radar

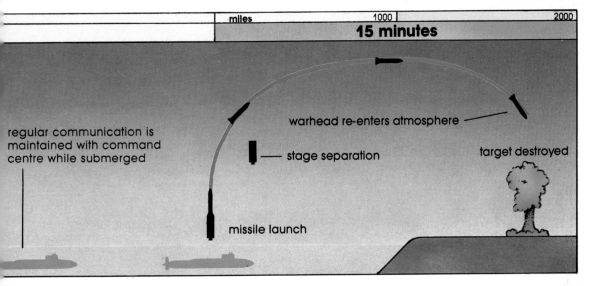

miles | 1000 | 2000

15 minutes

warhead re-enters atmosphere

regular communication is
maintained with command
centre while submerged

stage separation

target destroyed

missile launch

Early Warning System detects nuclear attack.

NORAD confirms a nuclear attack alert. Chiefs of Staff and President informed.

Strategic Air Command bomber crews, ICBMs and SCBMs on full nuclear alert.

Chiefs of Staff consult with President; final confirmation of nuclear attack.

ICBMs are launched from silos.

Surprise Attack

While America had exclusive possession of the atomic bomb the threat of its use was considered sufficient to deter the Soviet Union from initiating a conventional military attack against western European nations. Even though the American monopoly was short lived, the United States was able to maintain a technological lead over the Soviet Union in the design and manufacture of nuclear weapons. American strategic war plans of this period have been declassified, but Soviet ones are generally assumed to have been similar. That is, both powers sought to deter the use of nuclear weapons against themselves by maintaining the capability to inflict a wholly unacceptable level of destruction upon the power initiating nuclear war. The selection of predominantly urban and industrial targets was derived from the technical constraints imposed by the design, manufacture, performance and operational characteristics of the weapon and its delivery system.

The development of the intercontinental ballistic missile initiated a major re-evaluation of nuclear strategy. It was recognised that the principal purpose of maintaining nuclear weapons was to deter the prospect of their use and the most important influence on the design of a nuclear force was survivability against surprise attack.

A policy to launch on warning is considered the most vulnerable to instability during crisis, especially as there have been a number of false alarms. To maintain a policy of only launching a retaliatory attack after first absorbing the effects of an enemy attack is militarily risky, technically expensive to implement, and politically difficult; even though the assured ability to retaliate after first absorbing a full scale attack is very well suited to maintaining deterrence.

As a consequence each component of the triad is exploited to provide the optimum insurance against surprise attack. SLBMs are most suited to assured retaliation by virtue of their high survivability, and ICBMs to launch-on-warning and launch under attack because of their quick reaction time. Bombers share many of the response characteristics of ICBMs but are difficult to maintain at high levels of alert for long periods and have questionable capability to reach their targets without being destroyed.

Sophisticated early warning systems are used to detect preparations for, and execution of, a surprise attack. These systems utilise satellites and specialised radars to enable the authorities to make timely evaluations of suspicious events. The command centres are buried deep underground to reduce the risk of early destruction, thus ensuring that a sufficient command structure would survive to ensure that a retaliatory attack could be made.

In the scenario depicted here it is assumed that a period of crisis has increased to the point where certain preparatory measures for a surprise attack have already been observed. The following sequence of events provides in encapsulated form the process by which a retaliatory strike might be implemented in response.

1200: Early warning systems detect launches of missiles. Computers at the headquarters of the North American Aerospace Defence Command (NORAD), Cheyenne Mountain, Colorado calculate trajectories of the missiles, identify their targets and estimate warhead arrival times.

1201: The nuclear attack alert procedures are initiated. At NORAD incoming data from early warning systems are analysed to confirm that detection is not a false alarm due to anomalous phenomena. These can range from a flock of migrating geese giving radar signatures similar to attacking bombers, to malfunctions within the NORAD computers.

Once the alert has been initiated and the evaluation process begun the Joint Chiefs of Staff and the President are informed immediately of the exact nature of the alert. In parallel a number of routine alert measures begin implementation including an assessment of defensive options.

1208: A large scale nuclear attack is confirmed and all strategic nuclear forces are brought to full alert. The bombers of Strategic Air Command are scrambled within seven minutes to join those already on routine patrol. ICBM crews begin launch-preparation procedures, and SLBMs are ordered to action stations.

1213: During the alert extensive political and military consultation has been taking place including the use of the "hotline" between Washington and Moscow and to other capitals. But a decision has shortly to be made either to wind down the alert or to continue and prepare for a retaliatory strike attack.

1220: If a decision to conduct a retaliatory strike is made coded executive orders are transmitted to the nuclear forces.

1222: The President is taken from the White House by helicopter to nearby Andrews Air Force Base where E-4 airborne command post aircraft would be already prepared. With the President and command staff aboard the aircraft takes off and flies a course calculated to maintain the maximum availability for communications and safety against the effects of the anticipated attack.

1230: The attacking missiles destroy their targets, and initial damage assessments are made using satellite collected data. But the retaliatory strike has been committed and would be underway. Thus a policy of Mutual Assured Destruction would have been implemented even though it had failed in its primary purpose of deterrence.

Strategic air command bombers, carrying nuclear bombs or nuclear-tipped missiles, fly to targets.

SLBMs are launched from submarines.

President rushes from helicopter to Airborne Command Post which immediately takes off.

Both nations will suffer devastating casualties and urban destruction.

Estimated Strategic Nuclear Warheads USA table 1

System	Number deployed	Total warheads
ICBM Minuteman II		
Minuteman III		
Titan		
SLBM Poseidon C-3		
Trident C-4		
Sub-total	1611	7674
Aircraft B-52G		
B-52H		
FB-111A		
TOTAL:	1908	9719

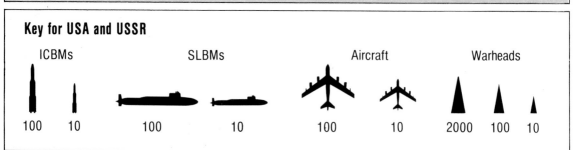

Key for USA and USSR

ICBMs	SLBMs	Aircraft	Warheads
100 10	100 10	100 10	2000 100 10

Exact figures for the numbers of missiles, bombs and other nuclear devices held by the various powers are, for obvious security reasons, impossible to determine with total accuracy. However, it is possible to work out with reasonable accuracy a superpower balance that provides a useful insight into the relative nuclear strengths of the Eastern and Western blocs.

There are several ways in which such information may be presented, the simplest and most obvious being the numbers of delivery systems and warheads available within each category of weapon fielded by the various powers (Table 1). Such a presentation has value, but it begs any indication of the systems' real military potential, which depends as much on destructiveness and accuracy as on overall numbers and warhead yield. There are two basic methods by which this military potential can be assessed: equivalent megatonnage (EMT) and counter-military potential (CMP).

EMT (see Table 2 overleaf) takes into account

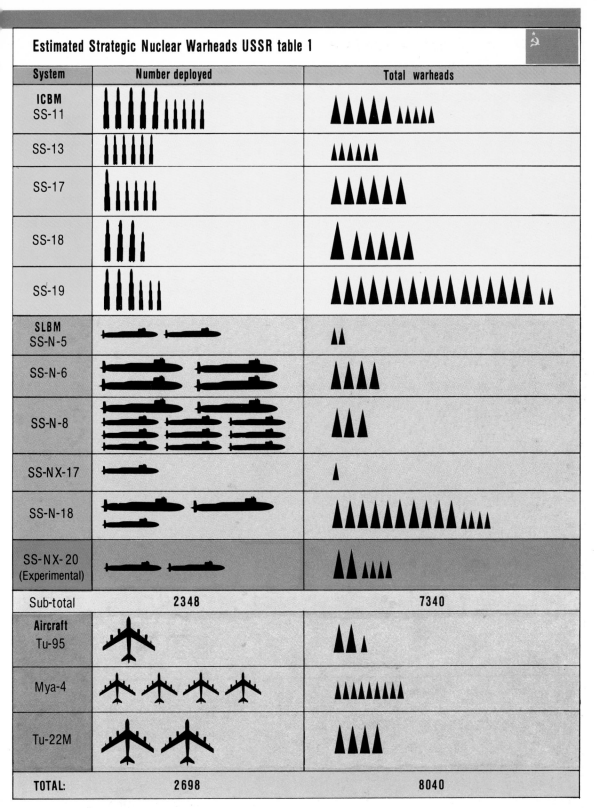

Estimated Strategic Nuclear Warheads USSR table 1

System	Number deployed	Total warheads
ICBM SS-11		
SS-13		
SS-17		
SS-18		
SS-19		
SLBM SS-N-5		
SS-N-6		
SS-N-8		
SS-NX-17		
SS-N-18		
SS-NX-20 (Experimental)		
Sub-total	2348	7340
Aircraft Tu-95		
Mya-4		
Tu-22M		
TOTAL:	2698	8040

destructiveness rather than mere yield, and is thus relevant to weapons with a capability against area targets (cities, industrial complexes etc); and CMP takes into account destructiveness allied with accuracy, and thus is relevant to weapons with a capability against point targets (command centres, missile bases etc).

Estimated Equivalent Megatonnage USA table 2

System	Total warheads		Total EMT	
ICBM Minuteman II	▲▲▲▲▲ ▲▲▲▲▲			
Minuteman III	▲▲▲▲▲▲▲▲▲▲▲▲ ▲▲▲▲▲▲			
Titan	▲▲▲▲			
SLBM Poseidon C-3	▲▲▲▲▲▲▲▲▲▲▲ ▲▲▲ ▲▲▲			
Trident C-4	▲▲▲▲▲▲▲▲▲▲▲			
Sub-total	7679		2161	
Aircraft B-52G	▲▲▲▲▲▲▲▲▲▲▲▲			
B-52H	▲▲▲▲▲▲▲▲			
FB-111A	▲▲			
TOTAL:	9719		3727	

Key for USA and USSR

▲ 2000 warheads ▲ 100 warheads ▴ 10 warheads  1000 EMT 100 EMT   10 EMT

EMT takes into account the fact that destructiveness does not increase arithmetically with warhead yield, but rather the two-thirds power of its yield. This approximation provides assessments such as an EMT of 0.34 for a 200-kiloton warhead. One of the difficulties with such an assessment is that the practical utility of very large warheads is exaggerated, for their area of destructiveness is likely to exceed the area to be destroyed.

The destruction of point targets (which depends on the ratio of blast overpressure to the target's degree of hardness) is more dependent on accuracy than mere warhead yield. By this estimation method the CMP (counter military potential) of any warhead is therefore reckoned by dividing its EMT yield by the square of its CEP (Circular Error Probable). Accuracy thus becomes of paramount importance against hard targets, relatively small differences of only a few metres in CEP making all the difference between whether a warhead is estimated to be effective or not.

EMT and CMP are approximate assessment methods which help to clarify the different military value that can be given to a weapon system if its intended target is known. But weapons are targeted in a mix of ways, and at best EMT and CMP analysis can only point to trends. It is safe, however, to conclude that while the USA and USSR enjoy an approximate parity in ICBM and SLBM warheads (about 7,500 each) the numerical

Estimated Equivalent Megatonnage USSR table 2

System	Total warheads	Total EMT
ICBM SS-11		
SS-13		
SS-17 Mod 1 / Mod 2		
SS-18 Mod 1 / Mod 2 / Mod 3 / Mod 4		
SS-19 Mod 2 / Mod 3		
SLBM SS-N-5		
SS-N-6 Mod 1 / Mod 2 / Mod 3		
SS-N-8 Mod 1 / Mod 2 / Mod 3		
SS-NX-17		
SS-N-18 Mod 2 / Mod 3		
SS-NX-20 (Experimental)		Experimental
Sub-total	7340	5805
Aircraft Tu-95		
Mya-4		
Tu-22M		
TOTAL:	8040	6505

balance swings in favour of the USA (about 9,7000) rather than the USSR (8,000) if bomber-delivered warheads are taken into account. But using the yardstick of EMT, we must come to another conclusion, namely that the USSR has an advantage of the USA of about 2.65:1 in ICBMs and SLBMs, or of about 1.6:1 if aircraft-delivered warheads are included.

The trend is also moving in the direction of the USSR, which has generally had a superiority in launchers, and is continuing to close the gap in terms of terminal accuracy.

For all their technical sophistication, nuclear weapons are still no more than pieces of hardware which can and do, go wrong. It would be foolish, therefore, to rely upon any weapon system as being 100 per cent reliable. In the design of such weapon systems, care is taken to provide the highest possible reliability by quality control and double or triple redundancy — a provision of one or two back-up items of equipment crucial to a successful flight. But this can lead to enormously expensive weapons so allowance must be made for an 'overkill' factor. Here many more weapons than would otherwise be assumed necessary for the purpose in hand must be built to allow for technical failures, operational failures, and unforeseen climatic or geographical conditions.

Despite breathtaking electronic wizardry, the guidance system, the fusing, the initial calculation of trajectory and several other factors in the missile's flight cannot be guaranteed 100 per cent reliability or accuracy. Assuming that any one feature is 95 per cent reliable or accurate, and that there are six such factors to be taken into account, the final probability of success will be 0.95 x 0.95 x 0.95 x 0.95 x 0.95 x 0.95, which emerges as just under 74 per cent. If the number of factors is increased to 10, the probability then drops to just under 60 per cent. Thus with the best design and manufacture in the world, the chances of a missile detonating on its target are no better than three in five if 10 major factors are taken into the reckoning.

But of these three out of five missiles which could detonate accurately, none is at full readiness for launch all the time. Missiles (particularly the older types) demand intensive and regular maintenance, so that at any given moment a large proportion of any missile force is likely to be unserviceable as there may be a man probing them with a circuit-tester, or replacing an electronic element, or cleaning a mechanical feature such as a valve. In addition, it is likely that only two-thirds of the world's submarine-launched missile force is operational at any one time because missiles carried in such submarines are operational only when the submarine is actually on patrol. It is the usual practice for the missiles to be made safe before the submarine enters its home port at the end of a routine patrol, and for the missiles to be removed for maintenance and storage after the submarine moors. At any given moment, therefore, a considerable portion of the world's SLBM force is not available for service even though the general rule is to have two full crews for each boat, an alternation of these crews ensuring that each boat spends as little time inactive as possible.

Even if the missile is launched and then operates perfectly, climate over the target can have effects unforeseeable (and in any event uncontrollable) by the firer. Although the firer may opt for a particular kilotonnage of warhead to produce the damage required, long experience both with atmospheric nuclear testing and conventional explosives has shown that a high cloud base can cause a blast wave to 'skip' harmlessly over an intermediate zone but nonetheless damage an outer zone, so that there is the possibility in certain weather conditions of inflicting damage in the wrong place. Conversely, a low cloud base can reflect the blast wave back to the ground and thus expand the theoretical damage radius by a considerable degree. Again, rain in the atmosphere can become radioactive from a nuclear burst and then drift to fall upon some area not targeted by the firer.

Terrain features also affect the explosion. A detonation at the head of even a shallow valley can be channelled down the valley to have damaging effects at distances well in excess of the theoretical damage radius, while places outside the valley, though still inside the theoretical radius, may well escape entirely. This factor played a considerable part in the reduction of damage and casualties in the atomic bomb attack on Nagasaki compared with that on Hiroshima three days earlier on 9 August 1945.

An additional consideration is the availability of older and newer missiles in the weapons mix. The newer weapons are more accurate and more reliable, but military planners are loath to take out of service the older types until the new type is fully operational, and political authorities also see the remaining older types as useful bargaining chips in arms limitation talks. So the older weapons sometimes remain in limited service, adding to the nuclear stockpile though their military utility is perhaps below the required standard.

Considerations such as these combine with others to give a little validity to the oft-asserted proposition that perhaps only a small fraction of missiles fired will actually survive all the anomalous factors to reach their appointed targets, burst at the right heights with the anticipated accuracy, and so have the desired effects. Thus if the planners reckon that 250 warheads are necessary to have the intended strategic and/or tactical effect, some 2,500 might be maintained to be sure of being able

Right: Overkill is a concept used to explain why more weapons than seem necessary are retained in nuclear arsenals. Frequently apparently excessive numbers of weapons are needed to cater for the probability of failure among items of equipment as complicated as ICBMs. The diagram shows some of the many factors affecting a missile's ability to reach its target and thus help explain the considerations that are taken into account when sizing a nuclear force. The probability of these factors occurring is stated as low, extremely low, or unpredicted.

	target reached
	warhead malfunctions and so fails to detonate EXTREMELY LOW
	warhead misses target as a result of errors in the targeting programme VERY LOW
	anomalous conditions destroy warhead during re-entry UNPREDICTED
	damage to warhead from close-in nuclear explosion causes burn-up during re-entry UNPREDICTED
	failure in warhead dispensing sequencer VERY LOW
	failure in warhead bus control rockets VERY LOW
	failure in upper-stage rocket VERY LOW
	failure in inertial navigation system EXTREMELY LOW
	missile encounters storm and is heavily damaged UNPREDICTED
	failure to stage correctly VERY LOW
	failure in launch sequence VERY LOW
	silo door fails to open EXTREMELY LOW

US Titan II

to effect such a plan. But political and economic constraints prevent this simple ten-fold increase. Instead a reasonable compromise is made based on test flights of the missiles which show good overall reliability. The extra number is required to **insure against accidental failure, and against** anomalies. This, therefore, is overkill, in which important targets can in theory be killed two or three times over. The reasoning behind it is a complex mixture of military, technical, political and economic factors.

One of the main pressures for the modernisation of strategic weapon systems rests on the ability to introduce significant improvements in weapons reliability and performance. This has the effect of reducing the number of weapons required to accomplish missions previously needing a larger number of systems. Consideration of the overkill factor should not be taken to mean that a large number of nuclear weapons will not work. Rather, a use of many of these weapons in complex strike plans such as pre-emptive attacks against ICBM silos (no matter how accurate a missile is estimated to be) will always have a high degree of uncertainty, due to unpredicted factors.

It would be fair to point out also, that the military are usually resistant to parting with any weapon they have and are familiar with for one which is novel and may require them to think old problems out afresh. Thus the conservatism of the military, and the opposition of the anti-nuclear movement to technological innovation serves to perpetuate an overkill factor in the sizing of strategic nuclear forces.

The problems inherent in maintaining older missile systems in a strategic arsenal are exemplified by the story of the Titan II ICBM the oldest and largest of the United States inter-continental ballistic missiles. The Titan has been a launch vehicle of exceptional reliability and in modified form has been used both as a satellite launch vehicle and for the Gemini series of manned spaceflights. The reliability for satellite and manned space launches was obtained by comparable methods to those applied to military ballistic missiles, except that in the case of manned spaceflights special additional precautions were undertaken by introducing additional redundancy in vital systems.

As a result of the general confidence built up in the Titan a series of measures deemed necessary to keep it in the military inventory at an acceptable level of reliability were clearly identified. Consequently the missile itself was not flight tested after the mid-70's for reasons of expense and shortage of missiles (since these had long ceased production). The main arguments for the continued maintenance of the missile in the US arsenal were that it was the largest US ICBM and that it had the greatest throw-weight of any US ballistic missile. The 54 then deployed Titans accounted for more than half the ICBM deliverable megatonnage of the United States. Moreover the missile was primarily seen as a bargaining chip in the strategic arms limitation negotiations between the United States and the Soviet Union.

In theory the Titan II retained a high level of reliability and the only problem for its continued maintenance in the arsenal was the cost associated with the continued maintenance of a missile for which all major spares and components had ceased production. Major system changes were made to improve the accuracy of the system by upgrading the guidance system (tested on other launch vehicles). But the biggest failure was a lack of attention to the increasing cost of routine maintenance of the missile system. This neglect resulted in two serious accidents involving the missiles while they were being serviced.

By comparison the Soviet Union conducts a much higher level of operational testing and maintains large numbers of older systems in its nuclear arsenal. For example, the Soviet Union currently maintains a significant number of SS-4 and SS-5 IRBM for which the SS-20 is considered a replacement. However, the older missiles have not been withdrawn at the same pace as SS-20 deployment. This may be comparable to the American reluctance to part with Titan without some comparable reduction by the Soviet Union. In cases where the Soviet Union has considered it worthwhile to withdraw a missile system it is usually because the missile has been unsuccessful in development or early deployment evaluation and testing. This was the case for the SS-14 though in such cases it is often thought that bureaucratic and institutional pressures are such that there is some incentive to continue to maintain the system even in low numbers rather than admit its development failure directly.

Merely partial success in testing some Soviet weapons leads only to modifications in existing weapons, incorporating a component or subsystem of the new system which would improve the older systems. A dramatic case of a major weapon system being derived from an unsuccessful development is the case of the SS-20 which was derived from the upper two stages of the SS-16, a missile that was generally unsuccessful in testing and was subsequently abandoned. The patterns of development, deployment, and operational testing are so significantly different for the United States and the Soviet Union that the manner by which the two Superpowers arrive at decisions over the necessary levels of forces based on these considerations alone results in quite large and asymmetric force compositions. It is recognised by many western analysts that the pattern of Soviet research development and deployment leads to rather higher numbers than follows from the kind of process employed by the United States. However, the American process is more conducive to innovation and results in a much higher degree of technological sophistication.

SS-14 Scapegoat

Unlike the USA, which has vast expanses of ocean to her east and west, a completely friendly and allied power to the north, and militarily weak countries to her south, the USSR is exposed to a number of hostile neighbours across her vast borders. So while the USA remains the principal ideological adversary, the Soviet Union perceives other supplementary threats to her security.

The supplementary threats are those presented by the problems in Eastern Europe which require Soviet military presence to contain, and the confrontation with NATO. To the West these 'threats' may seem to be unrealistic but problems such as those in Poland serve to reinforce the Soviet view that the West seeks to undermine the Soviet hegemony of Eastern Europe. To the east China, for all her resources of manpower, could not hope to make much impression on the whole of the USSR, but from the Soviet point of view, European nations (Germany in particular) have displayed hostility towards Russia and invaded twice in her recent history. China is ideologically split from the Soviet version of communist doctrine, and also has serious territorial disputes with the Soviet Union. To the south Afghanistan and Iran represent unstable areas which must be contained. Simplistic though this summary may be, it summarises threats that undoubtedly seem real to the Soviets.

These fears are reflected in the disposition of Soviet forces tasked with a response to any realisation of these broad threats to her security. The only possible response to an American strategic attack would be the unleashing of a wave of ICBMs, and these are in general deployed in a belt running east/west across central Russia facing north towards the polar route to the USA; further ICBMs are located in western Russia. The European threat is met by the theatre forces of the USSR's western military districts, which control some 64 divisions, more than 3,600 tactical aircraft and some 480 IRBMs to supplement the 30 Russian divisions in eastern Europe against a threat perceived mainly as conventional with nuclear possibilities. The Chinese threat is seen as being mainly conventional, and the theatre forces in the eastern USSR comprise 52 divisions backed by a mere 1,700 tactical aircraft and about 95 IRBMs, these two latter forces being deemed sufficient to counter Chinese air and nuclear power. Mobility, and speed are thus essential characteristics of Soviet forces to cover the variety of threats perceived across their enormous landmass.

Right: The map illustrates the geostrategic features which dominate the security of the Soviet Union. Immediately apparent is the extremely long frontier. There is only constrained access to the open sea from ice-free ports. The strongest deployment of forces is perhaps derived from historical precedent: all major invasions of Russia have been made from that Western approach.

USA SLBMs

USA SLBMs

Pacif
Total
Naval

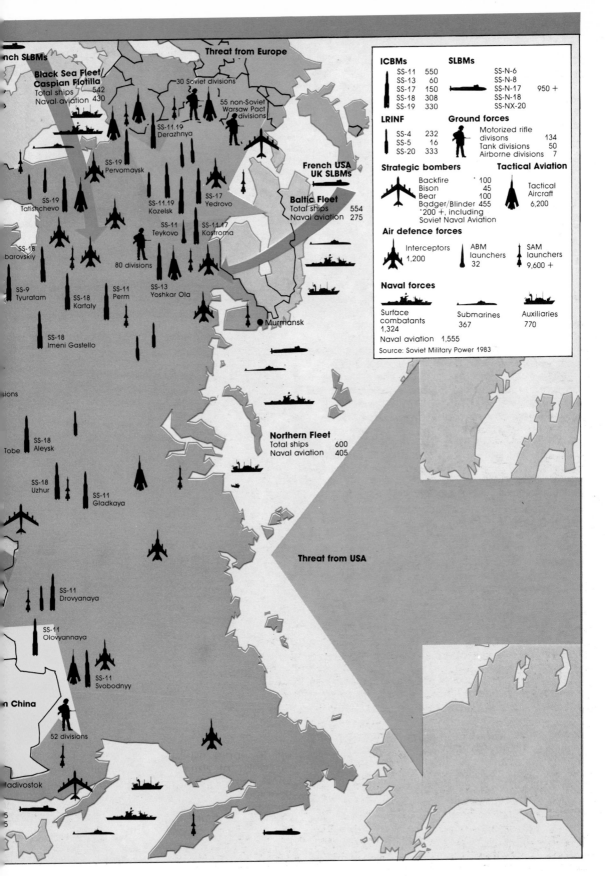

China's Defence

China possesses the world's largest conventional army: some 3,150,000 men with about 10,500 tanks and 11,800 pieces of artillery. But this force would find it difficult to offer an effective defence against the only major opponent conceivable, the USSR. With Russia, China has ideological differences complementing the traditional border disputes inherited by the USSR from Tsarist Russia: the Pamirs allocated to Russia by a secret protocol with the UK in 1896; the Great North-West Area ceded to Russia in 1864; Inner Mongolia absorbed into the USSR in 1944, and the Great North-East Area ceded to Russia in portions during 1858 and 1860.

It is understandable then that China should develop nuclear weapons as an effective means of striking deep into the territory of the Soviet Union. A nuclear development was launched in the 1950s, and the first atomic weapon was detonated on 16 October 1964. An air-dropped atomic weapon dropped on 14 May 1965 had been preceded five days earlier by the successful drop of a more powerful hybrid weapon with some thermonuclear material. The first successful missile-delivered fission-based warhead was exploded on 27 October 1965, and the first successful aircraft-delivered fusion (thermonuclear) device followed on 17 June 1967. By the early 1970s China could be reckoned among the world's 'operational' nuclear powers but although the country has warheads, even into the mid-1980s it still expected to have no truly effective means of delivering them. China does have a number of different missile types, but in test firings these have shown an alarming failure rate, and the obsolescence of the types combines with small numbers to provide China with a largely symbolic missile-delivered deterrent. In the aircraft-delivered category, the B-6 bomber is merely a copy of the elderly Soviet Tupolev Tu-16 medium bomber, and lacks the electronic countermeasures capability to penetrate deep into Soviet airspace.

China does present something of a nuclear threat to the USSR, however, as the Soviets acknowledge by deployment of considerable nuclear forces in eastern Russia, targetted (specifically) on Chinese installations and cities. With the development of newer Chinese missiles, located perhaps in a submarine class that has been under development for many years, the threat to the USSR is increasing towards a credible Chinese deterrent.

Right: The geo-strategic factors affecting Chinese security problems are illustrated in this map. Treaties of friendship including some military base facilities, exist with the Soviet Union, India, North Korea and Vietnam.

The Soviet occupation of Afghanistan may concern China because of movement of guerrilla forces into its territory. Also the conflict in Kampuchea is a source of concern because of the involvement of Vietnam with whom China has been in direct conflict in recent times.

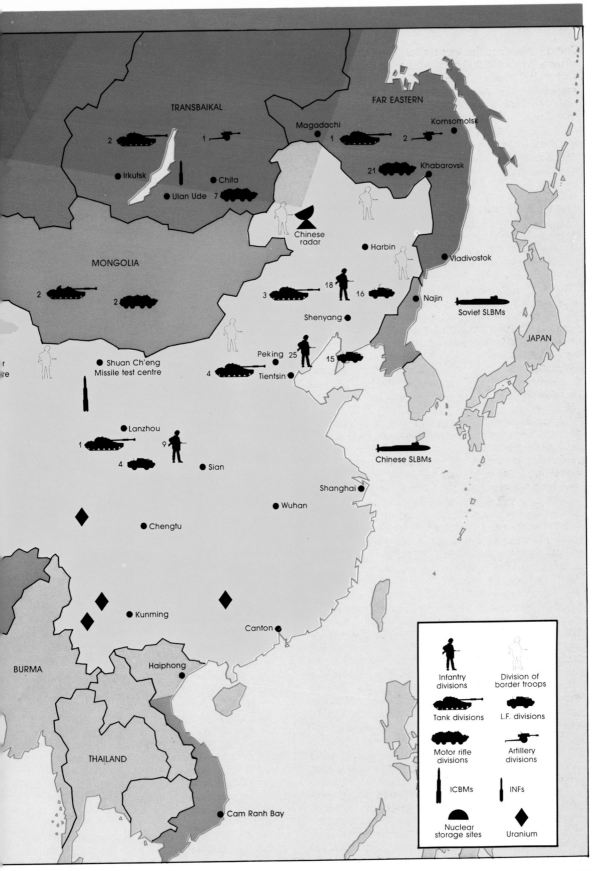

TRANSBAIKAL

FAR EASTERN

2 ● Irkutsk

Magadachi

1

Komsomolsk

2

21 Khabarovsk

● Chita

● Ulan Ude 7

Chinese radar

Harbin

Vladivostok

MONGOLIA

2

2

3

18

16

Najin

Shenyang

Soviet SLBMs

JAPAN

● Shuan Ch'eng Missile test centre

Peking 25

15

4 Tientsin

Chinese SLBMs

1 ● Lanzhou 9

4 ● Sian

Shanghai

● Wuhan

◆ Chengtu

◆

● Kunming

◆

◆

● Canton

BURMA

● Haiphong

THAILAND

● Cam Ranh Bay

Infantry divisions

Division of border troops

Tank divisions

L.F. divisions

Motor rifle divisions

Artillery divisions

ICBMs

INFs

Nuclear storage sites

Uranium

France and the UK: Independent Deterrent Powers?

Despite strenuous Soviet attempts in the early 1980s to persuade NATO and the world in general that the British and French nuclear arsenals should be regarded merely as an extension of the American deterrent, both the UK and France have refused to be drawn into accepting that they are not independent nuclear powers. Only such a stance, and the possession of the weapons to make such a stance credible, it is argued, enables each of these countries to ensure that its interests are taken into account in Soviet foreign policy design and strategic thinking.

Both the UK and France have regarded the United States as a staunch ally but, equally, they have recognised that complete identity of interests between sovereign states cannot be assumed at all times, especially when national survival may be at stake.

But are the British and French nuclear deterrents credible, in the sense that the use of the British and French nuclear arsenals could inflict so much damage on the USSR that it would not be worth while for the Soviets to launch an attack on either of the countries? Priority would be given to targets in western Soviet Union, and, as the accompanying map indicates, the successful use of all the weapons deployed by the UK and France could cause huge physical damage to the USSR's industrial regions. Reference to the Overkill section will show some of the uncertainties associated with the flight of the missiles. There are others involved in executing an attack, but the Soviets must work on the assumption that a significant proportion of the weapons would work, as indeed may happen. In these terms, the British and French deterrents may be considered to be of real deterrent value, for each country has the numerical and technical strength in its nuclear arsenal to cripple much of the USSR, given the political will to use such weapons under extreme pressure from Soviet aggression.

However, there are problems with the maintenance of a truly independent weapons capability for medium powers such as Britain and France. The main requirement for independent capability is to face the prospect that some situation could arise where the Soviet Union felt able to threaten Britain or France in isolation, and without fearing any involvement of the United States. But under such circumstances small deterrent forces, particularly based on a few SSBNs, could be made vulnerable to Soviet attack submarines at some time in the future.

These considerations of vulnerability and survivability of the force, and the limited political utility of the nuclear options available from the force, have reduced the emphasis on the purely independent aspects of the deterrent. Both Britain and France have sought options within a broader context of conceivable confrontation between the superpowers. Britain has always committed its nuclear forces to NATO and allowed the weapons

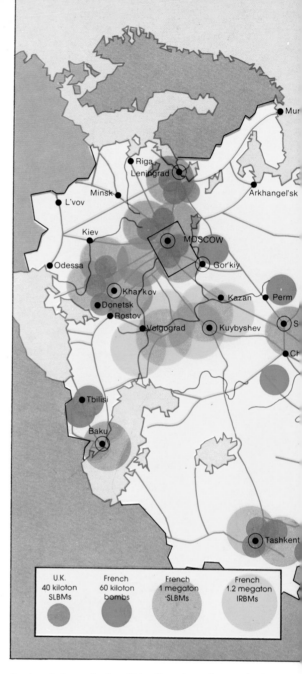

U.K. 40 kiloton SLBMs	French 60 kiloton bombs	French 1 megaton SLBMs	French 1.2 megaton IRBMs

to be integrated within the American strategic nuclear war-plan called SIOP (Single Integrated Operations Plan). As a result the co-ordination of British and American targeting for nuclear war is made more effective. France, though, left the military structure of the NATO Alliance in 1966 partly because she thought it necessary to maintain her capability for national deterrence independent of American strategy.

Both the UK and France are currently planning major modernisation of their strategic nuclear forces. The UK plans to replace its current fleet of 4

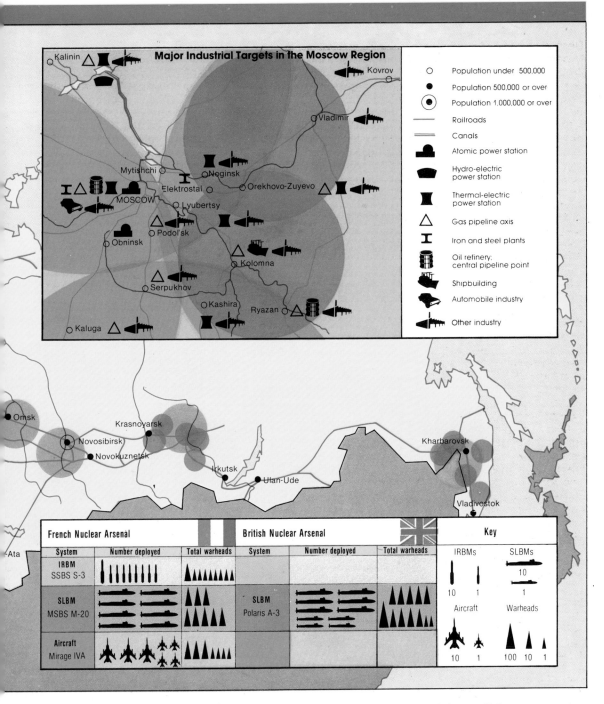

Major Industrial Targets in the Moscow Region

Polaris submarines with a comparable number of Trident submarines of its own design. These will carry 16 Trident SLBMs each but each missile will have the potential to be armed with up to ten MIRV thus providing a significant increase in the number of warheads available on station. This feature is extremely important for small deterrent forces because the operational characteristics of a small submarine force are such that at any time only one or two submarines may be available for patrol, the others being in refit or routine servicing.

In its planned modernisation France anticipates maintaining a role for intermediate range nuclear capable aircraft including those based on aircraft carriers. Increased importance is to be given to the nuclear submarines while the land based IRBMs will be phased-out of service largely due to their increased vulnerability to pre-emptive attack either from aircraft or missiles. France also places a priority on the development of shorter range nuclear forces with air deliverable weapons and much improved short range battlefield missile systems such as Pluton.

No military or political command structure can function effectively in times of crisis without its supreme head. Naturally enough, all such structures make provision for alternate commanders, but in nuclear warfare the switch involves delay and the allocation of responsibility to a vice-commander who previously may have been denied full access to relevant decisions. Therefore, it is of paramount importance to the USA, (which has a very different politico-military command structure from the USSR), to preserve the life of the President and his senior political and military aides who comprise the National Command Authority. The essential factor is that the NCA be kept up to date with events, and in a position to issue meaningful orders, so the NCA must be kept both safe and in touch with the evolving pattern of the conflict.

The key to such a situation is the Advanced Airborne National Command Post (AABNCP), which achieves on the national scale what the various marks of EC-135 command aircraft achieve at the operational level for the Strategic Air Command. Operated for the NCA by SAC's 1st Airborne Command and Control Squadron (home-based at Offutt AFB in Nebraska but also operating from Andrews AFB in Virginia) with a complement in 1983 of four Boeing E-4 aircraft (three E-4As and one E-4B, with the E-4As under progressive modification to E-4B standard). The force will be completed by another two new-built E-4Bs, providing the USA with six highly survivable aerial command posts for the NCA. Each aircraft has inflight-refuelling capability, enabling missions

Boeing E-4B advanced airborne command post

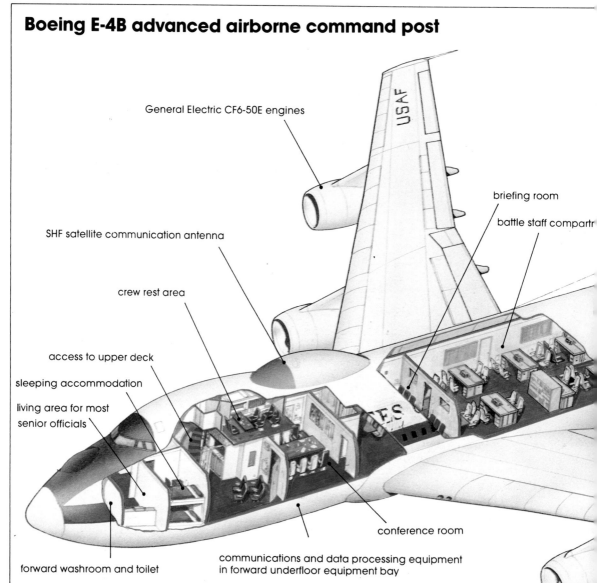

General Electric CF6-50E engines

USAF

briefing room

battle staff compartr

SHF satellite communication antenna

crew rest area

access to upper deck

sleeping accommodation

living area for most senior officials

forward washroom and toilet

conference room

communications and data processing equipment in forward underfloor equipment bay of up to 72 hours to be considered, two complete flight crews being provided for the purpose. The entire upper deck of the E-4B is reserved for the flight crews, with a rest area and bunks.

The President would be of little use if he were out of touch with the US strategic retaliatory forces. Thus most of the 4,620 sq ft/429 m² available floor area of this Model 747 derivative is occupied by highly specialised communications equipment, with 13 separate radio systems spread as far through the electromagnetic spectrum as possible to defeat jamming and the disruptive effects of nuclear explosions. Operating on the highest frequency is the satellite communications system, with its steerable dish antenna for SHF (super high frequency) satellite links in a blister fairing above the upper deck. Some 11 other systems operate on the UHF (ultra high frequency), VHF (very high frequency), HF (high frequency) and LF (low frequency) wavebands. There is also a VLF (very low frequency) system for communications with submerged submarines, which uses a 5 mile/8 km copper wire trailed from the tail of the aircraft in an arc some 4,000 ft/1,220 m deep. Security is provided by the AUTODIN system, and penetration by very high transmitter powers.

Some 25 onboard telephones can be patched into the communications system, and 12 of these have encryption facility for secure voice transmission to other aircraft and ground stations. Under the main deck floor are the communication systems themselves, plus the sophisticated power-control management system for the high electrical demands of the whole E-4B system.

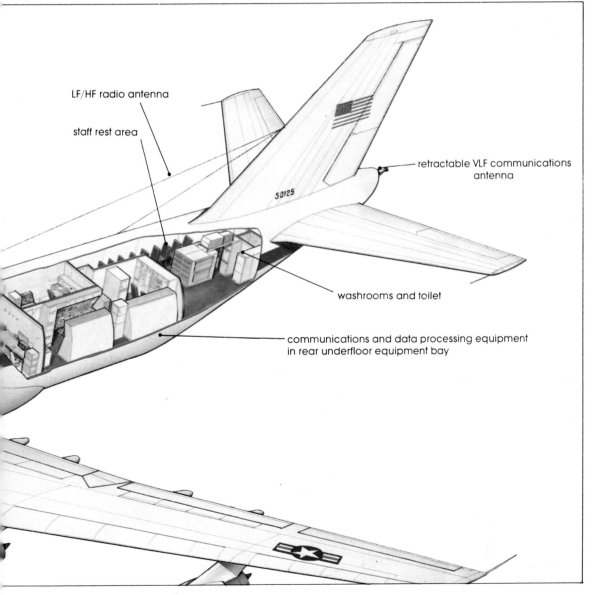

LF/HF radio antenna

staff rest area

retractable VLF communications antenna

washrooms and toilet

communications and data processing equipment in rear underfloor equipment bay

Systems as complex and vital as the defence networks of the USA and USSR can survive as workable entities only through the unimpaired working of command, control and communication (C^3) facilities, which must therefore have sufficient redundancy to maintain links despite the sabotage or destruction of certain elements, the incapacitation of others through the effects of electro-magnetic pulse (EMP) phenomena associated with nuclear explosions, and simple systems failure in other sections. Only if unimpeded or alternative channels are maintained can the leadership control the nation's war effort. Little is known of the Soviet C^3 apparatus, though key features must be the hardening of underground command bunkers against blast, radiation, EMP, seismic shock and sabotage, and the provision of hardened channels of communication (landline and radio) to hardened command centres for the various command levels.

More is known of the US effort, the C^3 structure of the Department of Defense being the agency through which the President and Secretary of Defense (as the key National Command Authorities) control the armed might of the USA. This system is very expensive and highly redundant (there are 43 channels of communication to the strategic nuclear forces, for example), but has come under increasing suspicion of inadequacy. This inadequacy is centred not so much on the physical components of the system (though these need a wide degree of hardening against EMP) but on the authorities' inability or unwillingness to undertake the realistic training to hone factors such as the President's escape from Washington to an acceptably short time.

Closely allied with C^3, and in some respects inseparable from it, is C^3I (command, control, communication and intelligence), which provides the means of assessing the enemy's intentions and actions, and so of using the C^3 network to maximum effect. The American C^3I system is thus based on satellites (warning, surveillance, communications and meteorology); undersea and ground warning systems; worldwide automatic data-link networks; automatic data-processing equipment; worldwide voice, telephone and teletype links; and a number of land, sea and air command posts.

At the centre of the C^3 web are the National Command Authorities, who normally work through the agency of the Joint Chiefs of Staff but have a Minimum Essential Emergency Communications Network link directly to the Strategic Integrated Operations Plan Forces (the US nuclear offensive forces). The Joint Chiefs of Staff work with the National Military Command System, whose three main props are the National Military Command Center in the Pentagon, the Alternate National Military Command Center near Washington, DC, and the National Emergency Airborne Command Post (or Advanced Airborne National Command Post, the presidential Boeing E-4B aircraft) linked by special communications and the Automated Data-Processing System. The entire system at this level is designed to provide the personnel and equipment for the reception, evaluation and display of information needed for executive decisions relevant to the direction of strategic forces.

Further down the command ladder, but interlinked with the National Military Command System, is the Defense Communications System, a worldwide network linking US embassies, unified commands, specified components, Department of Defense agencies, and service headquarters (land, sea and air) through three main subsystems: the Automatic Voice Network (with some 17,000 terminals), the Automatic Digital Network (with some 1,500 terminals for the secure transmission of data and messages) and the Automatic Secure Voice Network. These are all part of a fixed worldwide net operated, like the National Military Command System's communications, by the Defense Communications Agency. It provides for routine traffic in peace, but in war would operate a pre-emptive subsystem to give precedence to high-level C^3 messages. The system is heavily interlinked with that for the fixed, alternate and mobile headquarters of the National Command Authorities and National Military Command System.

Last come the mobile or transportable communications assets organic to field forces (land, sea and air), and the fixed communications of bases within and outside the continental USA. But through the Worldwide Military Command and Control System, elements of these tactical/operational formations are linked to the Unified and Specified Commands. Such units are the Ballistic Missile Early Warning System stations, warning satellites, the Pave Paws net and theatre nuclear forces, all of which need highly survivable communications comparable to those of the Minimum Essential Emergency Communications Network, which is connected with the Worldwide Military Command and Control System.

The whole C^3 network is under constant improvement (being allocated some 7 per cent of the US defence budget for 1984), and the accompanying chart indicates how the basics of the system will work towards the end of the 1980s, after the introduction of MILSTAR two-way communications satellites, which offer the possibility of unjammable communications, and the ELF communications system for superior links with submerged submarines, one of the major problems of today's system.

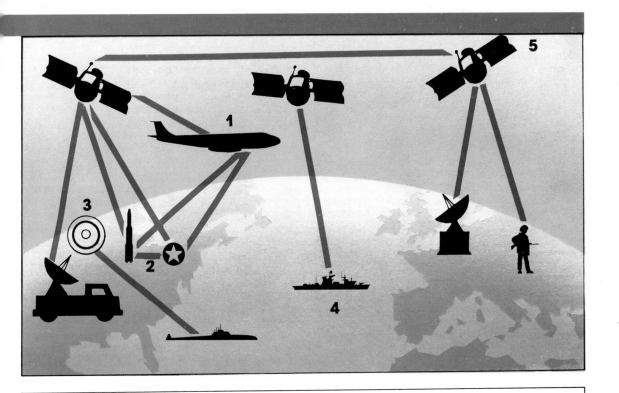

1. The President is provided with all radio communications wavelengths in the Boeing E-4B airborne command post aircraft, ensuring that he can communicate with the Pentagon, submarines, Strategic Air Command and a number of fixed and mobile receiving stations despite weather problems. The most important of these radio systems in the mid-1980s are for use in conjunction with the Defense Satellite Communications Systems II and III series satellites (called 'Discus I' and 'Discus II'), which will in the later 1980s be supplanted by the Milstar series, designed to provide both tactical and strategic communications for all the US services and their command authorities.

2. 'Hardened' land lines provide good channels of communication between ICBM sites in the USA and command authorities such as SAC and the Pentagon. These lines are resistant to electro-magnetic pulse effects, while multiple redundancy and alternative routeing provide optimum suvivability against physical attack.

3. Communications with missile-launching submarines are the most difficult of those associated with the strategic triad, and rely on the VLF/ELF (very low and, extremely low-frequency) transmissions from land bases. Further communication access to submerged submarines is provided by Lockheed C-130 Hercules with special equipment, though these are to be replaced by more versatile Boeing E-6A aircraft ordered in 1983.

4. Navstar is the satellite component of the Global Positioning System, using a planned total of eight satellites in three types of high orbit to provide world coverage sufficient for an operator with the lightweight receiver to determine his position to within 15 m/16.4 yards. This is a great asset to weapon-delivery accuracy, and plans are in hand for the installation of GPS receivers on the next generation of cruise missile and other weapons.

5. Milstar will provide the US forces and command authorities with instant global communication highly resistant to enemy jamming, while the small size and thus mobility of the receiver will permit the equipment to be issued down to the level of field commands and units operating nuclear weapons such as the BGM-109A ground launched cruise missile and Pershing II ballistic missile.

The President and the NCA leave Washington, DC in one of the E-4B AABNCP communications aircraft.

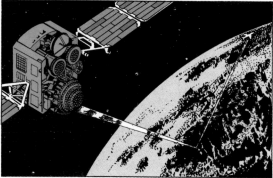

NORAD headquarters under Cheyenne Mountain monitors the Soviet attack.

NORAD, The President and other command authorities are kept fully in touch by satellite.

Aboard the E-4B incoming data is processed, and evaluated and executive orders issued.

Command Under Fire

Strategic nuclear options under a policy of Mutual Assured Destruction require the destruction of a very large proportion of the civilian population and industrial capacity. Because any decision to initiate the use of nuclear weapons carries the prospect of escalation to this level of destruction considerable emphasis has been continually placed on improving the means of control of nuclear forces. A crucial aspect of strategic command and control is to provide for the survival of the National Command Authority comprising the political and military leadership, and the means by which this authority can communicate its decisions to the nuclear forces. While there is only scant information about this aspect of Soviet nuclear forces it is generally believed that it shares the same principles as for the United States.

The United States has developed a complex arrangement of parallel systems with sequential features to ensure that a chain of command can continue even if partially destroyed. This is achieved by multiple redundant computer-controlled communication systems which increase the number of targets that must be attacked to significantly disable the system.

The American system begins with the President and that element of the National Command Authority that is required to be immediately available to him in crisis. If a nuclear alert reaches an advanced state the President and his NCA staff board a Boeing E-4B advanced airborne national command post aircraft at Andrews Air Force Base outside Washington D.C. This aircraft is a highly modified Boeing 747 airliner, packed with special communications systems, work areas for the NCA, and rest and sleep areas. All these facilities are necessary for the effective performance of the NCA in an aerial mission that may last three or more days with the aid of inflight-refuelling.

The concept of the aircraft is to provide for the President and his NCA staff a highly survivable war headquarters. The E-4B is fitted with protective thermal shielding to minimise the effects of heat from nuclear explosions. Equally, all the electronics are hardened so far as is possible, against the effects of electromagnetic phenomena associated with nuclear weapons. The fleet of six E-4 aircraft is operated by the Strategic Air Command for the NCA. The gamut of communications available on board includes super high frequency radio, and low and very low frequency radio which requires an antenna more than 5 miles/8 km. long to be trailed from the aircraft in flight. The low and very low frequencies are essential for direct communication with submerged submarines. Satellite communications links are maintained utilising equipment housed in a bulged fairing above the upper deck of the aircraft behind the flight deck.

In spite of the extensive communications facilities it remains possibile that the NCA may lose contact with other authorities during nuclear exchanges. To deal with this, the organisation of the chain of command permits the authorised military commands (principally the Strategic Air Command and the U.S. Navy) to continue operations already sanctioned by the President. SAC headquarters are in Omaha, Nebraska, but alternate headquarters capability is provided by a number of Boeing EC-135 command aircraft kept permanently airborne on a rotational basis.

Improvement in the accuracy of Soviet ICBMs has meant that there is an increased probability of success for any attack directed at the land based command centres, either as the result of direct hits or by the seismic shock resulting from a large nuclear explosion in the close vicinity of an underground command centre. In the event of the loss of land based command centres immediate control of SAC operations would be assumed by the senior general aboard one of the airborne EC-135 aircraft, with ultimate control being maintained by the NCA — assuming that these communications can be established and kept in a nuclear environment. The U.S. Navy has a land based command centre for control of the ballistic missile submarine force called the Alternate Space Defence Centre, located in Florida. Instantaneous or 'real-time' communications with submerged submarines is difficult, so the Navy also keeps aircraft with very low frequency radio on routine patrol at all times to help establish early contact with submarines when necessary. These TACAMO (TAke Command And Move Out) aircraft are currently versions of the Lockheed C-130 Hercules, with long endurance and the ability to carry the sizeable communications equipment and long trailing antennae. But these aircraft are soon to be replaced by the Boeing E-6, a modified version of the model 707 airliner. Even with these measures communication with submerged ballistic missile submarines remains a difficult task, because of the absence of effective real-time communication.

If the President cannot be brought back into the command sytem, the status of highest command authority is transferred to the Vice-President. But the E-4B has been designed to provide the maximum safety and the widest feasible spectrum of communications facilities to enable the President to maintain control of a possible nuclear conflict with minimum interruptions.

Since the E-4B can be refuelled in flight it is anticipated that it could remain airborne for a few days at a time. If a conflict can be relatively quickly terminated on mutually acceptable terms, the E-4B may still be able to land on a remote airfield which would then become the location for the first evaluations of the horrifying consequences of a nuclear conflict and the size of the task for post-nuclear recovery.

SS-19 ICBMs destroy the Cheyenne Mountain headquarters.

In ground-located headquarters, attacks by US missile submarines are ordered and controlled.

The Presidential E-4B is kept airborne by inflight-refuelling.

If the conflict ends after a limited exchange the E-4B can be landed at a remote airfield.

In the event of a war between the Superpowers, Europe is likely to be the principal strategic concern, whether or not the sources of the conflict originate there. In the event of a conventional attack by the forces of the Warsaw Pact on Western Europe, all the possibilities of escalation into a full-scale nuclear conflict through the use of first tactical and then intermediate nuclear weapons exist. It is considered that Europe would inevitably be drawn into a war between the Superpowers because of the Soviet Union's fears for a vulnerable eastern Europe, and the strategic importance of the continent for both Superpowers. The nuclear threat posed in Europe by the nuclear weapons deployed, or rapidly deployable by the UK, France, and the, USA, either separately (in the case of France) or in conjunction with the NATO powers, as seems more likely, represents an unacceptable threat to the Soviet Union.

The existence of nuclear weapons already located in Europe, or ready to be brought into the continent by air in the time of crisis makes it very likely that any nuclear war would involve Europe. Strong political, economic, and cultural ties link the USA with the western European countries, and this relationship has been naturally extended into the military field in two ways: the USA's European partners in NATO hope the American 'nuclear umbrella' will reach across the Atlantic to protect them against Soviet aggression, while the Americans see the European NATO countries as being the free world's first line of defence against Soviet aggression, which the United States is heavily committed to avert.

Such a situation calls for immense trust between the USA and the European NATO countries, especially those in which American-controlled nuclear weapons are deployed, or marked for future deployment. The USA must have complete faith in the European nations' ability and willingness to combat Soviet aggression with all the means at their disposal, and the European countries must believe that the Americans are willing to risk their own country (through the threat of total nuclear war), as part of the overall defence of Europe. In its most immediate form, this trust is most tangible to the Europeans in the 'dual key' control of nuclear weapons deployed for tactical and theatre use in Europe. Currently these weapons include nuclear artillery projectiles, battlefield missiles, free-fall weapons for use on tactical aircraft and, at the upper end of the scale, nuclear theatre missiles such as the Pershing I operated by the West German air force. The dual-key system ensures that in war complete consultation will take place between allies before the authorisation to use these weapons is given. At the same time, the dual-key system places great strain on intra-alliance trust, and raises the spectre of unacceptable delay in operational deployment at times of intense crisis.As an example, consider the importance of the Pershing I missiles stationed in West Germany. If Soviet forces were threatening major cities such as Frankfurt and pressing close to the Rhine in the west, the West German authorities might well wish for the release of the Pershing as a means of strangling the Soviet advance. Only in such a way, the West Germans might argue, could the Western alliance prevent the destruction of West Germany. The Americans, on the other hand, could decline to permit the use of the missiles on the grounds that the possible loss of Frankfurt must be balanced against the hope of confining the war to a non-nuclear conflict in which it might be better to trade some losses in Europe for a reduced chance of the war escalating further.

The problem is made more immediate by the prospect of the new American intermediate weapons (the BGM-109H Tomahawk cruise missile and the Pershing II ballistic missile) being deployed in Europe without dual-key control, based, like existing weapons in solely American possession, on agreement to consultation on use, rather than on any physical control. In these circumstances, the host countries must assure themselves of the Americans' real intention of using these weapons for the security of the alliance as a whole rather than for purely American purposes. The latter would leave Europe exposed to the terrible possibility of paying the price for American strategic objectives, and this consideration has therefore played an important part in the debate over installing such weapons in European countries. Nevertheless, without the presence of intermediate American nuclear systems capable of reaching Soviet territory Europe might be exposed to Soviet nuclear threats in crisis against which Europe might not be able to call on the US strategic nuclear forces for its own protection.

A parallel communication network provides NATO links to all involved allied authorities and major NATO Commanders.

Right: The communications links for the command and control of US GLCMs in Britain are shown above. Direct satellite communication is maintained between the US NCA and EUCOM, the headquarters of US forces in Europe. EUCOM maintains direct links to SHAPE (Mons) and upon authorisation orders for dispersal are forwarded to the GLCM base in a number of possible ways. This authorisation will always follow consultation between the American President and the head of state in the country where the GLCMs are based (in this case the Prime Minister). Orders can be transmitted directly from the USA, either from command centres or the airborne command post via satellite to the GLCM base; or authorisation can be sent from EUCOM through the US base at Ramstein and concurrently from SHAPE through the SACEUR (Supreme Allied Commander Europe).

Because of the redundancy of communications systems and alternative centres of command the system is considered highly survivable.

The missiles are armed in a similar manner to other American nuclear weapons utilising what are termed Permissive Action Links (PALs). The PAL is a six digit code which has a specific and changing sequence. Attempts to enter an incorrect sequence can result in the permanent disarming of the warhead. At high levels of alert the launch crews are sealed-off in their cabins with air supplies filtered to protect against Chemical and Biological Warfare (CBW). Equipment is carried to detect the presence of chemical or biological agents in the atmosphere and once detected all exposed personnel would be required to suit-up in protective clothing.

The preparations for launch of the missiles following an alert require assigning each missile designated target coordinates and flight data for its guidance system. A launch window is given, that is a time period when the missiles would be launched should the final authorisation be given. The arming of the warheads is authorised at the appropriate time in advance of entering the launch window, after which the crew conduct a launch countdown sequence. This sequence involves preparing the TEL which elevates the missile compartment to an angle of 45 degrees, and the missile launch tubes open exhaust gas vents at the rear of the tubes. Upon the final authorisation to launch at a specified time within the launch window the launch crews commence the final countdown and fire the missiles.

On ignition a solid propellant booster blasts the missile from the launch tube and within fifteen seconds the cruise missile's wings have unfolded and its own jet engine ignited as the booster rocket falls away. The missile has already been set on the appropriate course but the missile's guidance system is set to update several times during its flight to target to correct for errors due to changes in wind direction and deviation in its own inertial navigation system.

During its flight to target the nuclear warhead of a cruise missile like all nuclear warheads is protected against accidental detonation by its own Arming Fusing and Firing system, and this is only activated in the case of cruise if some two dozen events throughout the flight have taken place in correct sequence and been recorded as having been accomplished by the missile's computer. Since the flight of the missile may take it over neutral or friendly territory at low altitude it is hardly surprising that such care is taken to insure against an accidental detonation of a thermonuclear warhead with an explosive yield in the range of 150-200 kilotons — which is ten times the explosive force of the atomic bomb that destroyed Hiroshima.

The deployment of cruise missiles is organised into flights comprised of 16 weapons. A cruise missile

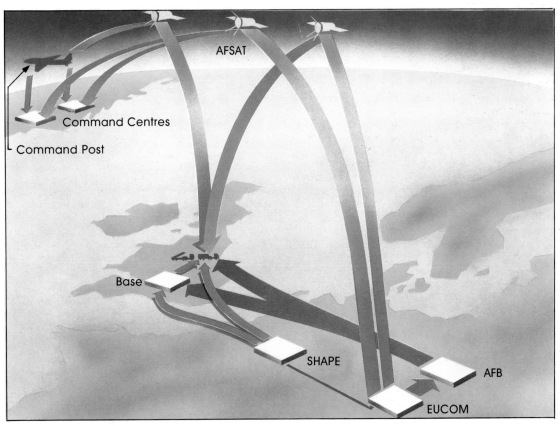

flight consists of four vehicles carrying four missiles each and called Transporter Erector Launchers (TELs), and two Launch Control Centres (LCCs). These main components of the flight are supported by a number of other vehicles necessary for logistic support and security of the flight during its journey from the Main Operating Base to operational deployment areas. In peacetime each cruise missile flight will be located on a Main Operating Base such as Greenham Common and the TELs and LCCs housed in specially constructed protective bunkers that would be resistant to surprise attack by conventional munitions delivered by aircraft or missiles. The bunkers are themselves partly concealed by earth which provides additional blast protection. A typical Main Operating Base might maintain three or four cruise missile flights, one or two of which would always be kept on Quick Reaction Alert (QRA).

In the transit from base to deployment area each cruise missile flight will travel as a convoy comprising some 22 vehicles and 69 people: the flight commander, four launch officers, 19 maintenance personnel, a medical attendant, and a security guard of 44 soldiers. This convoy remains in direct communication with the Main Operating Base at all times. But should this link be broken for any reason the LCC can communicate directly with other command centres through a satellite link code-named Flaming Arrow. The satellite communication system itself is designed to minimise the effects of jamming a single satellite or even the destruction of a few by ASATS.

Below: A cruise missile launch control centre is equipped with communications facilities for maintaining contact with its command authorities and with the targetting data necessary to pre-program cruise missiles against targets designated by the National Command Authority. The vehicles are towed by eight wheel drive tractors and can cross rough country or ford rivers more than a metre (three feet) deep.

Right: The illustration shows the deployment of a cruise missile flight prior to camouflage net and other concealment measures which make aerial detection very difficult. Also shown are the power cables and electrical links for control of the missile programming and launch control centres and the transporter erector launchers of the cruise missiles. Other vehicles are those associated with the logistic support of the launch and control tasks and for the security of the cruise missiles and launch crews.

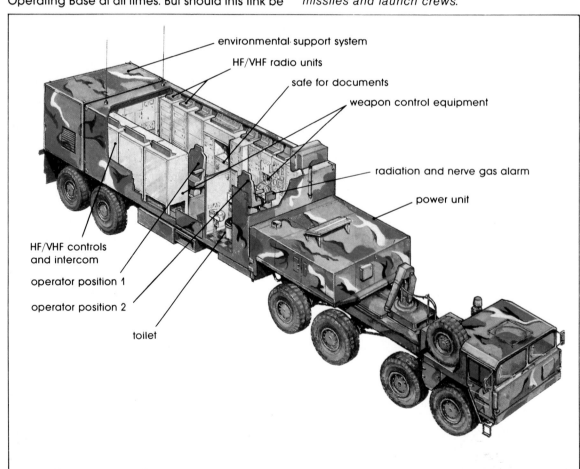

environmental support system

HF/VHF radio units

safe for documents

weapon control equipment

radiation and nerve gas alarm

power unit

HF/VHF controls and intercom

operator position 1

operator position 2

toilet

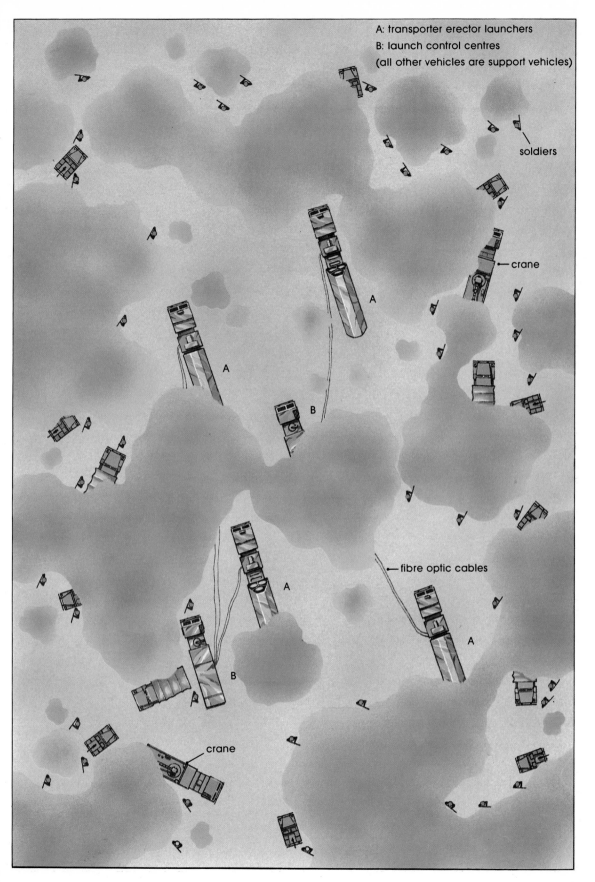

A: transporter erector launchers
B: launch control centres
(all other vehicles are support vehicles)

soldiers

crane

B

A

A

fibre optic cables

A

B

A

crane

Conventional balance

Comparison of NATO and Warsaw Pact manpower and equipment — WARSAW PACT

Manpower Total ground forces in place in Europe	
Divisions	
Ground force equipment Main battle tanks	
Arty, MRL	
Guided anti-tank weapons	
Naval units Submarines: attack	
Ships	
Aircraft	
Helicopters	

Over the past 20 years the balance in conventional forces has favoured the Warsaw Pact. For many years NATO forces took some comfort from the fact that while their Warsaw Pact opponents might be numerically stronger, they were at the same time qualitatively weaker. With emphasis more on numbers of primary weapons: main battle tanks, towed and self-propelled artillery, surface-to-surface missile launcher systems, and aircraft, the Warsaw Pact forces could thus be balanced by NATO forces with more effective weapons systems qualitatively capable of meeting the unfavourable odds in numbers. NATO has had a superiority in numbers among the manpower deployed along the iron curtain, but of these a much larger proportion than in the Warsaw Pact armies are of 'tail' personnel needed for NATO's complex logistic requirements, the consequence of collectively

defending a very large and geographically dislocated area equally. Additionally, the Soviets have enjoyed a superior ratio of fighting manpower to logistic support (referred to as a 'teeth to tail' ratio). This logistic planning provides for large-scale offensive operations along typically austere Soviet lines, assisted in part by the high level of standardisation of weapons equipment within the Warsaw Pact armies.

Within the ground forces, it is notable that the Warsaw Pact enjoys a considerable superiority in armoured divisions and in the numbers of MBTs available. The force ratio of Warsaw Pact to NATO tanks is three to one. The overall divisional strength is somewhat better than appears on the table for NATO, because Warsaw Pact divisions are smaller than NATO's. The disparity in aircraft (as in some other areas) could be compensated for by an

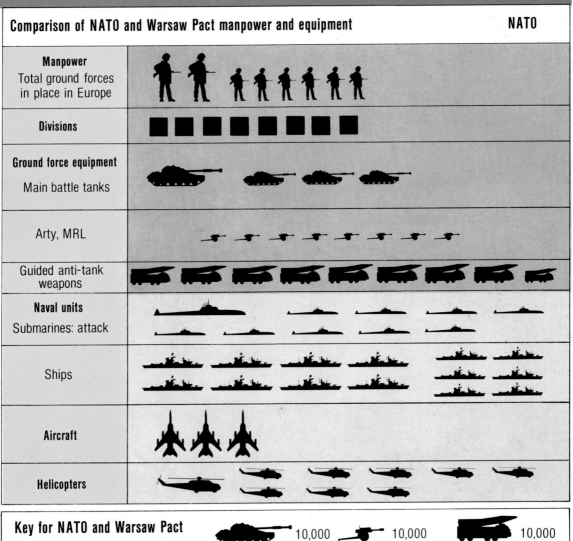

Comparison of NATO and Warsaw Pact manpower and equipment   NATO

Manpower Total ground forces in place in Europe	
Divisions	
Ground force equipment Main battle tanks	
Arty, MRL	
Guided anti-tank weapons	
Naval units Submarines: attack	
Ships	
Aircraft	
Helicopters	

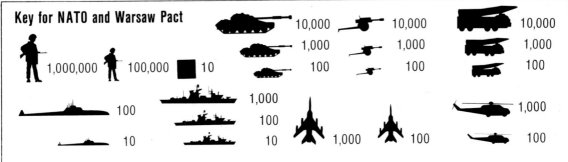

Key for NATO and Warsaw Pact

	10,000	10,000	10,000
1,000,000 100,000 ■ 10	1,000	1,000	1,000
	100	100	100
100	1,000		
	100	1,000	1,000
10	10	1,000 100	100

early decision in crisis to fly in additional numbers from the U.S. but it is feared that in a crisis such a response might appear too provocative and be resisted by political decision makers.

NATO places its faith not only in the quality of its personnel and equipment but in the necessary political decisions that must be made at the appropriate time during a crisis to allow re-inforcement to begin which would give NATO forces a much more favourable force balance than can be depicted in the static comparison of in-place forces shown here. But the uncertainties associated with the type of crisis anticipated and the time NATO may take to reach a decision are such that it is wise to reflect at first on the balance of in-place forces in Europe. For if NATO readily agreed to reinforce for any crisis it is likely that Soviet planners would exhaust NATO with false alarms. By the time the Warsaw Pact really planned to initiate conflict, NATO military staff might find it even more difficult to persuade NATO politicians that the situation being observed seemed like the 'real' invasion this time!

Long- and Medium-range Nuclear Systems for the European Theatre — WARSAW PACT

System	Inventory	Warheads available
IRBM SS-20		
SS-5 Skean		
MRBM SS-4 Sandal		
SRBM SS-12 Scaleboard		
Scud A/B		
Scud B/C		
SS-22 (SS-12 replacement)		
SS-23 (Scud replacement)		
SLBM SS-N-5 Serb		
Sub-total	1436	2066
Nuclear-capable tactical aircraft		
TOTAL:	4124	6041

Any attempt at assessing theatre nuclear forces in Europe is made particularly difficult by the fact that apart from dedicated theatre weapons (SS-20 and Pershing I, for example), many ICBMs and SLBMs could easily be retargeted. Another imponderable is the number of bomber and fighter-bomber aircraft that would be tasked with nuclear-weapons roles in time of war. In the accompanying table it has been assumed for comparative (and therefore somewhat artificial) purposes that all would carry nuclear weapons, and that these weapons would have about the same yield for all aircraft types.

The Soviet Union have an overall superiority of about seven-to-two in arriving warheads. In large part this is attributable to the fact that there are many more Soviet nuclear capable aircraft than NATO ones (without reinforcement from the US).

Long- and Medium-range Nuclear Systems for the European Theatre   NATO

System	Inventory	Warheads available
IRBM SSBS S-3		
SRBM Pershing IA		
SLBM Polaris A-3		
MSBS M-20		
Sub-total	**342**	**342**
Nuclear-capable tactical aircraft		
TOTAL: (ex. US SLBMs)	**1643**	**1883**
MRBM Pershing II		
GLCM BGM-109H Tomahawk (Yet to be deployed)		

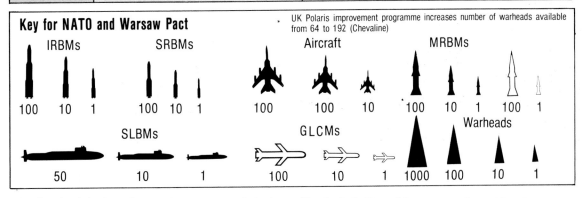

Key for NATO and Warsaw Pact

* UK Polaris improvement programme increases number of warheads available from 64 to 192 (Chevaline)

IRBMs	SRBMs	Aircraft	MRBMs
100 10 1	100 10 1	100 100 10	100 10 1 100 1

SLBMs	GLCMs	Warheads
50 10 1	100 10 1	1000 100 10 1

Also the Soviet aircraft are of more recent design than their NATO counterparts although newer NATO aircraft are now being introduced. Even so, the overall superiority of the missile-delivered warheads is striking, and although the balance drops to just under two-to-one in favour of the Soviets when the U.S. SLBMs allocated to NATO are included, there is no doubt that the Soviets have a marked superiority in theatre nuclear weapons.

The installation at European sites of the Pershing II and BGM-109H ballistic and cruise missiles will redress the balance somewhat in terms of numbers and capabilities, but it is unlikely that their deployment will be complete before 1990, and by that time the Soviets may have increased the numbers of SS-20 missiles or have introduced large numbers of newer weapons such as the SS-22 and SS-23.

Balance of Power: Nuclear 2

Estimated Equivalent Megatonnage   **WARSAW PACT**

System	Total warheads	Total EMT
IRBM SS-20	(pictograph)	(pictograph)
SS-5 Skean	(pictograph)	(pictograph)
MRBM SS-4 Sandal	(pictograph)	(pictograph)
SRBM SS-12 Scaleboard	(pictograph)	(pictograph)
Scud A/B	(pictograph)	(pictograph)
Scud B/C	(pictograph)	
SS-22 (SS-12 replacment)	(pictograph)	(pictograph)
SS-23 (Scud replacement)	(pictograph)	Dual capable yield not available
SLBM SS-N-5 Serb	(pictograph)	(pictograph)
Sub-total	2,066	Not available
Nuclear-capable tactical aircraft	(pictograph)	Varies with weapon load
TOTAL.	6,041	Not available

In conventional forces the Warsaw Pact has a certain measure of superiority over its opposite numbers on the NATO side of the iron curtain. This numerical superiority is most marked in those parts of the Warsaw Pact forces relevant to offensive warfare. The tendency is considerably more marked in the nuclear superiority of the Soviet forces over the NATO forces: the gross details of this superiority are shown on the preceding pages, and are given more useful interpretation in the chart above.

It is worth noting that the Soviet SS-4 and SS-5 missiles are both obsolescent, and that for comparative purposes it is assumed that each nuclear-capable tactical aircraft carries one 20-kiloton bomb. Even so, the salient feature that emerges most strongly is the importance, in terms of numbers and EMT, of the Soviet SS-20 and SS-22 missiles, and the strength of the USSR's force of nuclear-capable tactical aircraft. The latter include such advanced types as the Mikoyan-Gurevich MiG-23 and MiG-27, the Sukhoi Su-20

Estimated Equivalent Megatonnage — NATO

System	Total warheads	Total EMT
IRBM SSBS S-3	(chart)	(chart)
SRBM Pershing 1A	(chart)	(chart)
SLBM Polaris A-3	(chart)	(chart)
MSBS M-20	(chart)	(chart)
Sub-total	342	122
Nuclear-capable tactical aircraft	(chart)	Varies with weapon load
TOTAL: ex. US/SLBM	1883	Not available
MRBM Pershing II	(chart)	(chart)
GLCM BGM-109H Tomahawk (Yet to be deployed)	(chart)	Yield not available

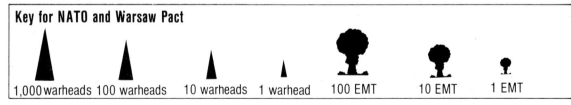

Key for NATO and Warsaw Pact

1,000 warheads | 100 warheads | 10 warheads | 1 warhead | 100 EMT | 10 EMT | 1 EMT

series and the exceptionally formidable Su-24 Interdictor, all available in large numbers to give the Soviet tactical nuclear forces at least aerial parity with their NATO counterparts, many of whose aircraft are presently quite elderly although being replaced quite rapidly.

In land-based systems the Soviet lead is very pronounced, being countered only partially by the numerical and technical superiority of the British and French SLBM forces, which could, in time of war, be bolstered by about 10 American missile submarines. The British, French and American SLBMs are all superior to the Soviet SS-N-5 type.

It is clear, therefore, that the NATO decision to deploy Pershing II and BGM-II and BGM-109H ground-launched cruise missiles in Europe is a prudent decision in purely military terms. The cruise missiles offer a considerable increase in available 'firepower', and the Pershing IIs are so accurate that their relatively small EMT is more than countered by the potential destructiveness especially against hard targets. Even so, it must be emphasized that the deployment of these two new weapons in the European theatre affects the margin of overall Soviet superiority, but not its very nature: the Soviets will still have significant advantages in intermediate nuclear forces due to the numbers and powerful warheads of their SS-20s and SS-22s.

While NATO would concede that the standard threat upon which it bases the planning of its forces contains known artificialities, it is considered prudent to plan for a situation that would highlight the principal defence problems for the alliance. Thus the scenario depicted here is not one that is necessarily anticipated to occur, but it represents an option available to Soviet planners where they might expect to gain advantage in a conflict with NATO.

Central Europe, and Germany in particular, are foremost in Soviet strategic priorities in Europe. For this reason it is anticipated that if a conflict were to begin, it would start here, for if the Warsaw Pact were to strike at either of NATO's flanks first they would have shown their intentions and would provide NATO the time to reinforce central Europe, thus considerably reducing the chances of Soviet success there.

The scenario shows the main possible axes of advance for Warsaw Pact forces through Germany: the North German Plain, the Fulda Gap and Hof Corridor. Reinforcements for NATO forces are assumed to be arriving by air and sea from the United States. In the northern region the Warsaw Pact have attempted to seal off the Baltic approaches by amphibious assault, and to gain control of northern Norway to reduce harrassment of its navy moving out towards the Atlantic. In the south the Warsaw Pact has invaded northern Italy to gain control of the important industrial areas and to secure naval bases on the Mediterranean. The Warsaw Pact invasion of Greece and Turkey across Thrace has been to secure access to the Mediterranean for the Soviet Black Sea fleet. All these objectives would meet the defence forces of NATO. While this scenario is not necessarily anticipated to occur, it permits planning and exercising to take place and under circumstances where classified anticipations of actual Soviet military operations can be evaluated.

It is upon scenarios such as these that the size and operational characteristics of NATO forces are determined. Force capability assessments must anticipate future developments in Soviet weapons and gauge the numbers of weapons systems deployed. The performance of NATO forces against this anticipated threat can then be evaluated by a number of complex analytical methods, often utilising computer simulation of hypothetical NATO vs Warsaw Pact engagements to highlight the strengths and weaknesses in the relative force capabilities. The ratios compared by numbers of weapon types do not reflect the asymmetry of forces resulting from differences in either operational doctrine, or in the qualitative performance of the weapon systems. Thus while force ratios are useful for general illustrative purposes they do not adequately represent the nature of the force balance for which other more sophisticated methods would be used.

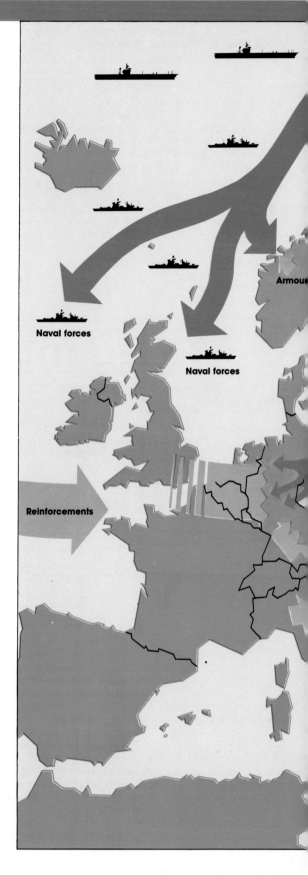

Naval forces

Naval forces

Armour

Reinforcements

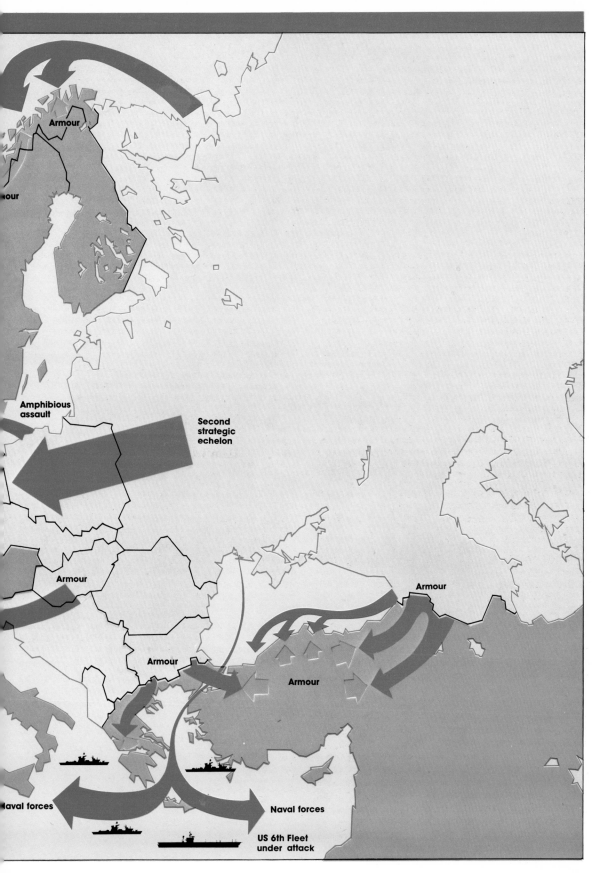

Armour

our

Amphibious
assault

Second
strategic
echelon

Armour

Armour

Armour

Armour

Naval forces

Naval forces

US 6th Fleet
under attack

Only the richest and technologically most advanced nations can undertake an entirely indigenous nuclear industry for either civil or military needs. Given the world wide need for nuclear power for the generation of electricity, therefore, it is hardly surprising that there should be an extensive and lucrative trade in the elements of nuclear power generation technology and equipment.

This wide international market is characterised by three important factors: firstly, its sub-division into several very strongly defined sub-markets; secondly, its high level of concentration; and thirdly, its growing interdependence technologically and thus financially. The very nature of this market structure has important corollaries in the political sectors, for the dominant supplier nations can delay (and perhaps prevent) nuclear-weapon proliferation.

Moves in this direction began during the 1950s, when the USA began to alter their nuclear bi-lateral agreements to include a stipulation that any country receiving American nuclear material, equipment and technical knowledge would use them only for peaceful purposes, with the recipient country agreeing to American safeguards. Matters were taken a step further with the Nuclear Non-Proliferation Treaty, whose signatories agreed to accept safeguards formulated by the International Atomic Energy Agency, for all their atomic facilities. The flaws in the NNPT were its lack of real powers, its failure to prevent the transfer of technology, and its failure to compel a member selling to a non-member to impose the full scope of the safeguard clauses on the recipient.

In 1975 the seven main sellers of nuclear technology and equipment (the USA, the USSR, the UK, Canada, France, West Germany and Japan) formed the so-called 'London Club' to tighten the provisions of the NNPT. The club was later expanded by the accession of Belgium, Czechoslovakia, East Germany, Italy, the Netherlands, Poland, Sweden and Switzerland, and it was decided that sensitive technologies (enrichment, reprocessing and heavy-water plants, the last of which had not featured at all in the NNPT) would be subject to a moratorium, while buyers would have to provide more stringent safeguards against the seizure of nuclear equipment and technology by criminals or terrorists.

Counter to the ideals of nuclear non-proliferation, the activities of the 'London Club' may backfire as third-world countries, notably Argentina, may decide to develop an indigenous industry for their own purposes and also for export wholly outside the framework of the NNPT and the 'London Club'. Should this occur, the ideals of the NNPT will clearly have failed, and evidence of this tendency is provided by the rapidly increasing number of nuclear agreements between third-world countries.

Should there be any doubt about the inter-relationship of civil and military nuclear power, it is necessary to remember only that civil nuclear power gives its operator access to military nuclear power in four key areas: direct access to weapon-grade fissile materials, production facilities for weapon-grade fissile materials, the establishment of a corps of trained personnel, and so-called peaceful nuclear explosives.

An indication of the nature of the international market is given by the listing of nuclear co-operation agreement partners in the third world, which puts the USSR, the UK, Canada, France and West Germany well up the list. The USSR is particularly jealous of her nuclear position, and though capable of exporting every aspect of the nuclear market, does not do so in three significant fields. This tendency is also notable to a lesser extent among other technological leaders (see Table), it being in the area of sensitive technologies that no exports are permitted under the rules of the 'London Club'.

The table lists the main exporters of nuclear technology and identifies the principle areas of trade. The sale of nuclear power reactors is the least sensitive in terms of potential for nuclear weapons proliferation concerns, whereas reprocessing facilities and the transfer of enriched uranium are possibly the greatest source of worry. Since considerable international attention is drawn to the direct sale of complete facilities there has been an increasing tendency for the near nuclear nations to purchase nuclear technology in subunits or component parts, frequently through a third party supplier in order not to raise objection by the governments concerned with proliferation who are also willing to impose embargoes on specific nuclear technology transfers that could be utilised towards weapons applications. It can be seen from the table for example, that the majority of nations producing nuclear technology are prepared to sell components and these are difficult to immediately identify as being potentially utilised for weapons applications unless the recipient country is directly identified. Thus components sold to South Africa but prohibited to Israel could find their way to the latter especially as nuclear cooperation exchanges are known to have taken place between the two countries and Taiwan. Similarly, Pakistan was discovered to have obtained nuclear reprocessing component technology from the Netherlands, Switzerland and other sources before the full scope of her purchases were identified as an embargo —breaking activity.

Country	Nuclear steam generators	Other components	Uranium ore processing	Conversion	Fuel element production	Reprocessing	Uranium enrichment
Argentina			✓		✓		
Australia			✓				
Belgium		✓			✓		
Canada	✓	✓	✓	✓	✓		
France	✓	✓	✓	✓	✓	✓	✓
Great Britain	✓	✓		✓	✓	✓	✓
India		✓	✓				
Italy	✓	✓			✓		
Japan	✓	✓			✓		
Netherlands		✓			✓		✓
Portugal			✓				
South Africa			✓				
Spain		✓	✓		✓		
Sweden	✓	✓	✓		✓		
Switzerland		✓					
USA	✓	✓	✓	✓	✓		✓
USSR	✓	✓			✓		✓
W. Germany	✓	✓	✓		✓		✓

Potential Members of the Nuclear Club

	Non-Proliferation Treaty status	nuclear co-operation agreements	uranium reserves	research reactors
Argentina	non-member	Bolivia, Canada, Colombia, Ecuador, India, Italy, Paraguay, Peru, USA	23,000 tons assured & 39,000 more tons estimated	five in operation
Brazil	non-member	Iraq, Italy, USA, Venezuela, West Germany	62,000 tons assured & 58,000 more tons estimated	three in operation
Egypt	signed on 1st July 1968, but did not ratify	USA, Egypt	none	one in operation
India	non-member	Argentina, Bangladesh, Belgium, Czechoslovakia, Denmark, East Germany, France, Hungary, Iraq, Philippines, Romania, Spain, USA, USSR, West Germany	30,000 tons assured & 23,000 more tons estimated	four in operation & three under construction or planned
Iraq	member since 29th October 1969	Brazil, France, India, USSR	not known	one in operation & one under construction was destroyed in Israel air attack
Israel	non-member	USA, South Africa	small	two in operation
Libya	members since 26th May 1975	Argentina, Pakistan, USSR	not known	one planned
Pakistan	non-member	France, Libya, UK	uncertain	one in operation
South Africa	non-member	France, USA, Israel	462,000 tons assured & 74,000 more tons estimated	two in operation
South Korea	member since 23rd April 1975	Canada, France, USA	3,000 tons assured	two in operation
Taiwan	member since 27th Jan 1970 expelled from I A E A in 1972	USA	none	five in operation

power-generation reactors	sensitive technologies			trained personnel	minimum time to build a bomb
	enrichment	reprocessing	heavy-water plants		
one in operation & one under construction, plus four more planned	none	demonstration plant planned	experimental plant operation & production plant to be supplied in 1983 by Switzerland	very good	3 years
none in operation & three under construction, plus six more planned	demonstration plant to be supplied in 1983 by West Germany	demonstration plant to be built in 1984 by West Germany	none	moderate	5-6 years
one planned	none	laboratory facility	none	poor	7-10 years
three in operation & five under construction, plus two more planned	research plant	two plants in operation and a third planned	five in operation and three more planned	excellent	has tested nuclear device
none	none	none	none	poor	6-10 years
none	research (isotope separation by laser)	one plant	one plant	excellent	assumed none
one planned	none	none	none	none	10 years
one in operation and several planned	pilot model in operation and demonstration model under construction	one in operation and one under construction	none	excellent	few months-1 year
two under construction	pilot model in operation, one under construction and another planned	assumed to be under development	none	excellent	under 1 year
one in operation and two under construction, plus six more planned	none	none	none	excellent	4-6 years
two in operation and four under construction, plus several planned	research (isotope separation by laser)	dismantled laboratory facility	none	excellent	2-3 years

Link Between War and Peace

To understand why uranium is vital for nuclear weapons and nuclear power it is helpful to know a little of the physics involved.

Atoms are the 'building blocks' of matter. Though their presence and behaviour can be observed with special experimental apparatus they are too small to be visible. An atom is comprised of a nucleus and electrons which orbit the nucleus. The nucleus of an atom is composed of protons and neutrons and different atoms are distinguishable by the size and composition of the nucleus and the number of electrons that surround it. The uranium atom is the heaviest atom occurring in nature and as such it is potentially unstable. The term 'heavy' refers to the number of protons in the nucleus. The potential instability of the uranium atom would cause an enormous release of energy when its atom is split. There are two forms: uranium 235 (92 protons + 143 neutrons) and uranium 238 (92 protons + 146 neutrons). The majority of uranium occurring in nature is U238 with a much smaller fraction of U235 which is less stable because it has fewer neutrons.

A piece of uranium containing tens of billions of atoms is unstable in that some of the atoms are splitting spontaneously all the time. The process does not result in a chain reaction and releases comparatively little energy. However, if the concentration of uranium atoms in a piece of refined ore were to reach a critical mass then a chain reaction would occur – the uranium undergoing spontaneous fission would explode, releasing enormous energy. Thus for nuclear weapons two pieces of mass are kept separate, but then explosively forced together to undergo spontaneous fission as the critical mass is achieved by their being fused together.

In nuclear power stations the use of nuclear material is required only to generate heat so that the level of enrichment can be much less than for nuclear weapons. Since it is also vital to avoid reaching a critical mass several precautions are taken to keep the chain reaction under control.

Uranium is a metal found in the ground as uranium ore and mined in several countries. The main producers at present are led by the United States, Canada, the USSR, South Africa and Namibia, and France; there is also thought to be substantial production in China, East Germany and Czechoslovakia. In its natural state uranium is unsuitable either for warheads or for use in most nuclear power stations. The ore must be refined and the uranium "enriched" to increase its content of the potentially explosive isotope uranium 235. Enrichment requires expensive technology, and is therefore limited to comparatively few industrial countries; the USA, the USSR, the UK, France, the Netherlands, West Germany, China, Japan and South Africa — although a few others are working to develop nuclear fuel enrichment facilities.

Plutonium does not occur in nature but is created by the neutron bombardment of uranium 238. It may be used as a reactor fuel but its main use is as fissile material for nuclear weapons. It is prepared in a "reprocessing" plant — and the only countries known to possess such plant are the USA, the UK, France, the USSR, China, India and Japan. Israel is also thought to have one; and Pakistan, Italy, Belgium, Spain, West Germany and Argentina are working to develop the facility. So despite the wide spread of countries with uranium reserves, and the comparatively large number of countries with nuclear power stations, the crucial link between the two — and the crucial link between

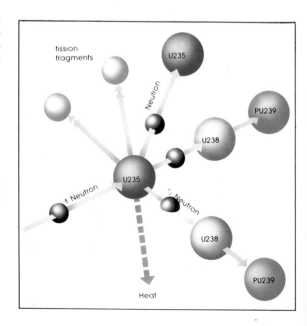

Right: A chain reaction occurs when a mass of fissile material in the form of enriched uranium or plutonium is brought together so that spontaneous fission takes place. The amount of fissile material required for this is termed the critical mass. In the illustration the neutron bombardment of the uranium isotope U235 causes the spliting of the atom and the reaction releases energy, fission fragments, and neutrons; these in turn bombard other atoms causing a chain reaction to take place. In reactors the chain reaction is controlled by careful calculation of the degree to which the fissile material in the reactor is fissioning. For the purposes of a nuclear weapon a calculated critical mass is explosively forced together to ensure that the explosive reaction will take place.

The diagram also shows that the chain reaction creates the plutonium isotope Pu239 which is particularly suitable for weapons applications. Thus any nuclear reactor may be used to make this fissile material for nuclear weapons.

nuclear fuel production facilities and nuclear warheads — lies at the moment in the hands of relatively few nations.

Uranium ore must be processed through a number of stages before it can be used in nuclear technology. Its route to the warhead is via the nuclear reactor, where it is also used as fuel to generate electricity. Most reactors exist only to produce electricity,but any country with nuclear reactors is closer to the materials necessary to make a nuclear weapon than one without.

Firstly, the uranium has to be mined. The rocks containing uranium are dynamited, crushed to powder and mixed with water. The resulting mud goes through a series of chemical treatments, leaving a bright yellow powder of uranium oxide known as 'yellowcake'. This is the form in which uranium ore is usually transported and traded.

The next stage is the difficult and expensive process of enrichment. Uranium ore consists of two forms of isotope: U238 and U235; the latter, being less stable, is most unstable as fissile material. The uranium ore is refined to increase the proportion of U235, as uranium contains only 0.7% uranium 235 (less than one part in 100): for use in nuclear power stations, the proportion is usually increased to between 1.5 and 3%. For warheads, a higher level of enrichment is necessary; in advanced weapons the level may be as high as 90%, but for a simple nuclear device it can be much lower.

After enrichment, the uranium is made into pellets, which are packed together to make fuel rods. It is then ready for use as nuclear fuel.

Nuclear reactors, which produce electricity from uranium, work like conventional power plants: water is boiled to make steam and this is used, to drive turbines which generate electricity. The difference is that in nuclear reactors the heat used to boil the water comes from the atom-splitting chain reaction, whereas other plants burn oil or coal. There are three main types of uranium-fuel reactor, and they are named after materials which they use: the light-water reactor, the heavy-water reactor, and the gas-cooled reactor.

In the light-water reactor (LWR), which is the most commonly used worldwide, water is used to keep the uranium fuel from overheating and as a 'moderator' — a material which slows down and absorbs some of the neutrons produced by the chain reaction and thus helps keep the reaction under control. The light-water reactor comes in two kinds. One is the boiling water reactor (BWE, made mainly by the American company General Electric) in which the nuclear fuel boils water that is circulating around the fuel rods, and the steam is used to drive the turbine.

The other kind of LWR is the pressurised water reactor (PWR, many of which are made by the American company Westinghouse). The PWR has two water loops: in the first loop, water is circulated around the fuel at very high pressure which

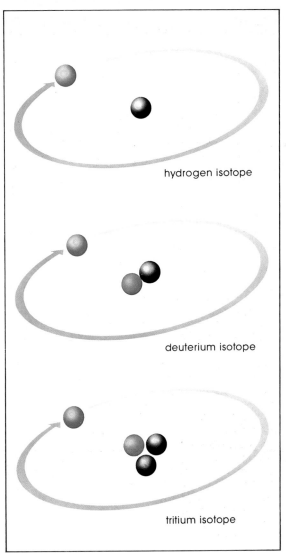

Above: *Many elements exist in more than one form, each with the same number of protons but a different number of neutrons. Hydrogen has three "versions", or isotopes: hydrogen, deuterium, and tritium. Deuterium and tritium are important isotopes for thermonuclear weapons design in which they are used as fuels for the thermonuclear reaction — hence the term Hydrogen Bomb.*

prevents the water from boiling even though it reaches 600°F. This very hot water goes into thousands of narrow tubes to heat a second, separate loop of water, which boils and drives the turbine with its steam.

The best-known type of heavy-water reactor (HWR) is the Canadian CANDU, which uses as coolant a substance called heavy water, different from ordinary (or 'light') water because it contains an hydrogen Isotope called deuterium. CANDU functions on uranium with low levels of enrichment and its name stands for Canadian Deuterium Uranium Reactor.

The gas-cooled reactor (GCR) uses gas rather

than water to take the heat from the fuel. The advanced gas-cooled reactor (AGR) is a British invention, called 'advanced' because its fuel is highly enriched uranium rather than natural uranium, which was used in Britain's first gas-cooled reactors.

All these uranium-fuel reactors are known as 'thermal' reactors because the neutrons in them — after they have been slowed down by the moderator — are in 'thermal equilibrium' with their surroundings — that is, they have the same temperature.

There is a fourth main type of reactor, only just beginning to come into commercial operation in a few countries now. This is the fast breeder reactor (FBR). It uses plutonium, rather than uranium, as its fuel.

In a fast breeder reactor, the neutrons are not slowed down by a moderator (hence the word 'fast'). Much more heat is created than in a thermal reactor, so the coolant used is a liquid metal, usually sodium, in two separate locks. The word 'breeder' comes into the name because the plutonium fuel is surrounded by uranium 238 which, under the bombardment of the neutrons from the plutonium, turns into — or 'breeds' — more plutonium. This can later be fed back into the reactor as more fuel, or diverted to make nuclear weapons.

When a uranium fuel rod is taken out of the thermal reactor after use, a small part of the uranium has turned into other elements, one of which is plutonium. Some of these elements are highly radioactive. Most of the radioactivity (over 90%) will disappear within three years — but some could still cause harm to humans after thousands of years. So the disposal of nuclear waste is a big problem.

One alternative is 'reprocessing'. This means extracting the plutonium and some of the uranium for use in fast breeder reactors. In Britain, a big reprocessing plant is due to be completed at Windscale in Cumbria in the late 1980s, with half its capacity intended for reprocessing used fuel from overseas. While some argue that reprocessing is the best thing to do with waste, because it keeps plutonium within the nuclear industry, there are others who fear that transporting and storing it increases the risk of accident.

One reason why the fast breeder reactor is attractive to many in the nuclear industry and in governments is that it 'breeds' fuel, thus helping to reduce the costs associated with the generation of electricity.

An additional problem is associated with the costs, and health hazards associated with mining uranium and its availability on the world market as demand increases. A report in 1980 by the International Atomic Energy Agency and the Organisation for Economic Co-operation and Development has said that uranium demand would overtake supply in the 1990s unless breeder reactors were introduced. But a recent report for the US

Department of Energy suggested that enough uranium will be available for 100 years of nuclear power without the breeder.

What worries many people is that reprocessing and breeders will be likely to contribute to the spread of nuclear weapons. In 1974, India carried out a nuclear explosion using plutonium which had been reprocessed from one of its CANDU reactors. Stringent safeguards had been placed on enriched uranium sold to India for other reactors to prevent its being used for nuclear weapons though no-one had been able to stop India reprocessing waste from the CANDU, which used India's own unenriched uranium. India had built a reprocessing plant back in 1964, to extract plutonium in accordance with longterm plans for breeder reactors.

Pakistan, has not yet exploded a nuclear device but in the 1970s, it signed a contract to buy a reprocessing plant from France. At the time Pakistan had only one nuclear power reactor, a CANDU. The reprocessing plant would have been able to handle fuel from 11 reactors. Pakistan said it planned to build 24 nuclear plants by the year 2000, including breeder reactors, and it wanted the

Right: A schematic diagram of a water-cooled reactor core shows the steel pressure vessel inside a containment chamber of concrete. Inside the pressure vessel is a graphite core in which the fuel rods and control rods are inserted from above under computer control to maintain the chain reaction. Water is pumped through the pressure vessel to a heat exchanger (not shown) to generate steam to drive turbines which generate electricity.

The pressurised water reactor is the most popular design of reactor and versions of it also form the reactor units of nuclear submarines and aircraft carriers. But PWRs are sold only under IAEA safeguards so it is difficult to use such reactors to make fissile material and divert it for weapons applications without being detected. At least part of the reason for this is that the process would be slow if PWRs were utilised in this way and the activity would be easily detected by those tasked with monitoring compliance with the safeguards. Therefore most proliferation concerns surround different nuclear facilities especially those associated with uranium enrichment, and fissile material reprocessing. The main problem of proliferation arises from the fact that countries wishing to pursue civil nuclear power programmes also seek to reduce their dependence on foreign suppliers over time and thus always plan nuclear programmes that include the acquisition of reprocessing facilities and research reactors which are also the ideal means by which they may pursue nuclear weapons development if this were their intention.

Nuclear reactor

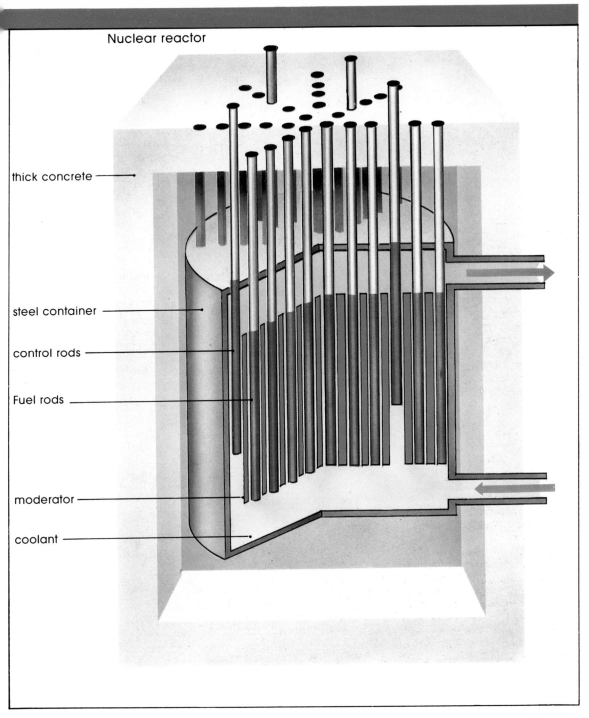

thick concrete

steel container

control rods

Fuel rods

moderator

coolant

reprocessing plant to supply plutonium for the breeders well in advance. After pressure from the United States, the contract was eventually dropped.

A few years later Pakistan set out to build a uranium enrichment plant — for which experts considered it has no need in its civil nuclear power programme. Since embargoes on sensitive technology transfer were in force Pakistan used industrial espionage in Europe to find suppliers for all the key components. Some of the Pakistani

purchases were discovered and stopped, but it is suspected that most of the equipment they required has been obtained. Pakistan is still proceeding with its enrichment project by obtaining additional technology and material through Middle Eastern countries which have bought them and then sold them on to Pakistan. It has also been buying components for its reprocessing plant, which though incomplete for its stated purpose may well soon fulfil the requirement of providing nuclear material to build a bomb.

Russian forces from Afghanistan cross into Pakistan to attack Afghan guerrilla camps.

Disputes in Kashmir break into wide-scale rioting requiring Indian military intervention.

Kashmiri refugees/rebels begin to cross frontier into Pakistan pursued by Indian forces.

Indian troops attempt to close the Kashmiri frontier with Pakistan. Clashes occur between forces.

Indo-Pakistan Scenario

It is widely accepted that there are a number of countries on the threshold of developing a nuclear weapons capability. Some of these states are already suspected of having clandestinely developed small stockpiles of fission-based nuclear weapons as bombs deliverable by aircraft. India has actually conducted a nuclear test but has subsequently claimed that it does not intend to develop nuclear weapons, and that the purpose of the test was to evaluate the uses of nuclear explosives for peaceful purposes. By contrast Israel and South Africa are often suspected in press reports of having already developed a nuclear weapons capability either without conducting a test or by having successfully accomplished this without being detected. This prospect is very remote because of the extensive seismic and satellite detection systems deployed by the United States and Soviet Union.

Many of the near nuclear states are in regions of endemic political instability: Israel, Egypt, and Iraq, in the Middle East; Brazil and Argentina in South America; Taiwan and South Korea in East Asia; Libya and South Africa; and lastly India and Pakistan. In each of these areas there are clearly identifiable and persistent sources of domestic instability and inter-state conflict. This does not necessarily mean that the possession of nuclear weapons would result in irresponsible behaviour by one of these states. But it is reasonable to assume that the possession of nuclear weapons between states that have a recent history of conflict and domestic instability adds considerable risks.

The scenario illustrated contains most of the characteristics discussed above. There is absolutely no reason to believe that this scenario is an especially likely one, or that India and Pakistan are amongst the most likely states to use nuclear weapons against each other. However, we may develop a scenario drawing on factual material to give some realism to our identified concern.

India and Pakistan have disputed the sovereignty of Kashmir since their independence, and have fought wars arising from disagreements originating from this issue. India has already tested a nuclear 'device' and Pakistan is thought capable of developing one in short order. Both countries have complex domestic problems that frequently erupt in riots, wide scale strikes, and civil disorder and which require the use of military forces to bring them under control. But now Pakistan faces an additional difficulty in that it is providing refuge and support for Afghan freedom fighters who move from camps in the north west frontier province into Afghanistan to engage in guerrilla war against the Soviet occupying forces. India maintains a Treaty of Friendship with the Soviet Union and is a major recipient of Russian advanced weapons.

Although Pakistan has found support from the United States for the purchase of essential military equipment and obtained certain bi-lateral committments for U.S. support against the consequences that could follow from Pakistani provision of operating camps for Afghan freedom fighters, it has been unable to convince the President of the threat it feels from India. Equally, India has failed to impress upon Pakistan the ambiguous nature of its relationship with the Soviet Union, and failed to convince the United States of its fears that modern American weapons supplied to Pakistan will strain good relations between the two countries.

We must now speculate that due to some extraordinary successes in their guerrilla campaigns in Afghanistan the Mujadeen freedom fighters are posing an unprecedented threat to the occupying Soviet forces. As a result a decision is taken in the Kremlin to undertake air attacks against the guerrilla encampments in Pakistan. Unconnected with these events the domestic political situation in Kashmir has rapidly deteriorated in sporadic rioting with some factions calling for unification with Pakistan.

Before the full dimensions of the crisis are apparent in Moscow the authorised attacks have been conducted. The Indian Prime Minister conspicously fails to condemn these attacks, while asserting that the trouble in Kashmir is being given covert support by Pakistan. Before international mediation can be brought to bear on the problem both nations have put their forces on alert.

Domestic pressure builds in Pakistan to provide support for Kashmiri rebels who begin to cross into Pakistan to escape from Indian forces. Indian troops attempt to close the frontier but a number of hot pursuit incidents result in clashes between Indian and Pakistani forces.

India, confident that Pakistan has supported the Kashmiri rebellion, launches a conventional armoured offensive against Pakistani armed forces in the region of Lahore. Both sides begin airstrikes against bases considered to support nuclear capable aircraft.

As the intensity of the conflict increases and the overwhelming weight of Indian firepower is brought to bear, the Pakistani high command deliberates the prospect of a nuclear strike against a major Indian city. Time is running out, many airbases have already been struck. However, careful countermeasures using decoy aircraft and ground equipment have so far ensured that the Pakistani aircraft and its nuclear weapon remains available for use. Weighing in the minds of the Pakistani high command is the concern that the Indian nuclear response will be assured and inevitable; it has been withheld because the Indian conventional forces were steadily overwhelming the Pakistani forces.

Indian armour, with infantry and artillery support, thrusts into Pakistan.

The conflict escalates and Indian numerical superiority takes its toll on Pakistani forces.

A crisis meeting of the Pakistani high command deliberates over the prospect of nuclear use.

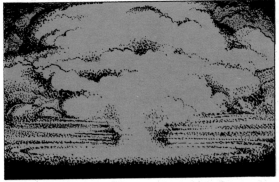

Pakistan might see a nuclear pre-emptive strike as the only course open to them.

Italian terrorist faction decides to hijack a train-load of radioactive waste.

The train is ambushed and the guards over-powered.

The train is moved by the terrorists onto a bridge over a major river.

The terrorists radio their demands for the revision of government policies etc.

Terrorist Blackmail

Though nuclear warfare offers the most serious threat to the continued existence of the world order, there are lesser, but nonetheless very considerable, dangers associated with the nuclear industry as a whole. These fall into two basic categories: firstly, faults in the design, construction or operation of nuclear power plants, which under extraordinary circumstances might lead to a melt-down and escape of nuclear fuel from the reactor vessel, or some other release of radioactive material or gas: secondly, the exploitation of fissionable material (or its associated waste products) which are considered by some to be inadequately guarded, by politically motivated groups.

Perhaps the most vulnerable of all radioactive materials are the wastes from processing facilities and power plants. These waste products are normally removed as radioactive slurry for disposal in deep underground tanks or, sealed in corrosion-resistant containers for dumping at sea. Such waste might be seized by political factions to whom the most destructive policies seem the most effective.

In Italy, for example, terrorist groups such as the Red Brigade, comparatively "successful" in the 1970s, have in recent years suffered notable defeats, with many of their leading lights arrested, tried and imprisoned, or killed in gunfights with security forces. In a desperate situation it might seem attractive to such a group to gamble all on a decisive stroke, taking advantage of some weakness in the security measures for the transportation of radioactive waste. Italy has four operating nuclear power stations, with another four under construction, and there is considerable movement of nuclear raw materials and waste products through the countryside.

Suppose that a terrorist group planned to hijack a trainload of nuclear waste being transported from a power plant to the coast, where it would be transferred to a specially prepared ship for dumping in the Atlantic. A little inside information, careful planning, and perhaps some bank robberies to finance the operation, would be sufficient for the group to launch a coup which they might think to be a powerful weapon for blackmail.

The heavy train, with the waste sealed in special tanker cars, protected by a handful of guards, makes a slow night passage towards the coast across the mountains. The terrorists have an opportunity to ambush the train in a defile close to a major river crossing. The train is already moving slowly because of its load and the gradient, so a small rock slide is sufficient to bring it to a halt. Here the terrorists can seize the train with its potentially deadly load, and overcome the crew and guards. With the improvised rock slide quickly cleared, they would move the train up the line to the central span of the bridge across the river.

With the hostages under guard, a reinforcement group in waiting removes the track on either side, and weakens the outer spans of the bridge's structure, while supplies of food, water, clothing and ammunition are brought up to the train. The leader of the group radios the Italian authorities to inform them of the situation. He tells the government that unless 'political prisoners' are freed from Italian jails and the social, political and economic balance shifted towards the terrorists' preferred polarity, the train will be toppled into the river below, spreading contamination to the farming and urban areas through which it flows. A deadline for meeting the demands is set.

The Italian authorities gather for a crisis meeting; the terrorists prepare charges to split the waste trucks and drop the central span of the bridge into the river.

Urgency would be injected into the situation if the terrorists' deadline passed, and some of the hostages were shot to indicate their captors' resolve. 'Political prisoners' might then be freed, but the government would protest that social moves would be impossible within the time limits imposed. Meanwhile the authorities would call for ideas or aid from other Western nations and the United Nations would be asked for support. But a second deadline is approaching, and the terrorists prepare to tip the train into the swiftly running river. Downstream, areas have been evacuated, reservoirs closed off from the river, and decontamination crews placed at strategic points.

Such a scenario is entirely hypothetical, but the prospect is frightening, for while security of nuclear materials is carefully considered and can be improved further, there is virtually no means by which every possibility can be accounted for in security measures. While there is no need for complacency it is perhaps reassuring to note the effectiveness of special forces for situations such as the one described.

While concern for the hijacking of nuclear material is of the highest priority all conceivable precautionary measures have been considered to prevent such an incident taking place. These measures can be divided into three categories: the first is in the design of transportation containers and in the operational procedures followed for transportation; the second is in precautionary observation of likely terrorist groups or other organisations that might consider undertaking the hijacking of nuclear material; and lastly in the specialised training of military personnel in anti-terrorist operations. It is of course, hoped that the first two categories have been covered with sufficient effectiveness to deter consideration of nuclear hijacks by terrorist groups. Even so they are under constant re-evaluation and improvement, but as a last resort the use of special forces can be made and has been shown to be remarkably effective given the political will to allow the necessary conduct of operations which are violent but conclusive.

Crisis meeting of Italian cabinet orders deployment of specialist anti-terrorist unit.

Terrorists shoot some hostages as an indication of their determination & set time limit.

Italians call for world help as the terrorists' time-limit approaches.

Terrorists prepare to blow up bridge as time limit expires.

There are a number of ways of delivering a nuclear weapon to its target. The explosive can be carried within missiles, artillery, mines and torpedoes, or bombs, which in turn are air, sea or land launched.

Missiles: Generally rockets, though some types are propelled by jet engines and resemble pilotless aircraft. The principal missile types are:

ICBM — Intercontinental Ballistic Missile. 'Intercontinental' for obvious reasons; 'ballistic' because the flight path is affected by the earth's gravity after the velocity achieved by the rocket motors. Range is over 3,975 miles/6,400 km.

IRBM — Intermediate Range Ballistic Missile. Intermediate between an intercontinental

SLCM — Submarine-launched cruise missile similar to other cruise missiles but configured for underwater launch from submarine torpedo tubes.

Once at target the warhead is detonated. A simple warhead is a single cylinder with the nuclear explosive, and this is detonated by a fuse system which operates according to the effect desired, exploding the warhead on contact with the target, or above it. If the missile's path takes it out of the earth's atmosphere, the warhead becomes part of a re-entry vehicle which is resistant to the thermal effects of re-entering the atmosphere. A multiple re-entry vehicle (MRV) contains a number of warheads. Once in the atmosphere it opens and allows the warheads to fall free so that they disperse around the target area. A multiple independently-targeted re-entry

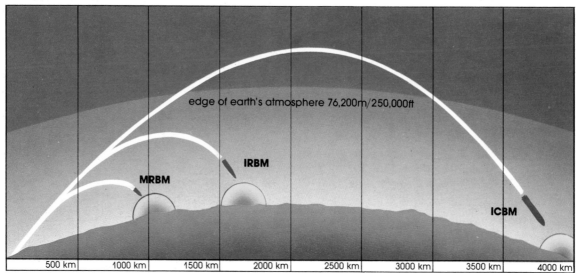

and a medium range missile, and thus between 1,490 miles/2,400 km and 3,975 miles/6,400 km.

MRBM — Medium Range Ballistic Missile. Having a range of between 500 miles/800 km and 1,490 miles/2,400 km.

SRBM — Short Range Ballistic Missile. Having a range up to 500 miles/800 km.

ALCM — Air-Launched Cruise Missile. A winged bomb, usually jet-propelled, launched by being dropped from an aircraft so that its jet engine gets (literally) a flying start.

GLCM — Ground-Launched Cruise Missile. Similar to an ALCM but rocket-boosted off a ground launcher so that it builds up sufficient speed for the jet motor to take over and sustain it in flight.

SLBM — Submarine-Launched Ballistic Missile. Fired from a submerged submarine, this is ejected through the water by gas pressure and its rocket ignites when it reaches the surface.

Above: *Medium-range, intermediate-range and intercontinental ballistic missiles are all capable of strategic roles, and differ most significantly from each other in terms of range. However, the IRBM and ICBM are generally fitted with more advanced penetration aids (penaids) and multiple warheads.*
Right: *The ICBM has taken the science of missile design to extreme refinement. Most of the system is a 'brute force' propulsion package designed to elevate the payload into a long-range ballistic trajectory controlled by an onboard computer integrating data from an inertial guidance platform and, quite frequently, a very sensitive star tracker.*

vehicle (MIRV) also contains a number of warheads but these are mounted on a "bus" with small rockets and with a flight computer programmed for specific targets, so that when the warheads are dispensed from the MIRV bus, they each fly off to their own target. A manoeuvrable re-entry vehicle is one which is capable of manoeuvring off a ballistic course to make

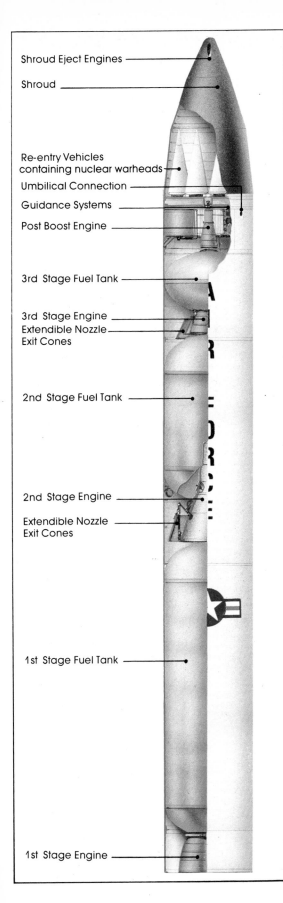

Shroud Eject Engines

Shroud

Re-entry Vehicles
containing nuclear warheads

Umbilical Connection

Guidance Systems

Post Boost Engine

3rd Stage Fuel Tank

3rd Stage Engine
Extendible Nozzle
Exit Cones

2nd Stage Fuel Tank

2nd Stage Engine

Extendible Nozzle
Exit Cones

1st Stage Fuel Tank

1st Stage Engine

interception more difficult.

Missiles normally travel at supersonic speeds which reduce the time in which their approach can be detected. A battlefield missile firing at 22 miles/35 km range and low altitude takes just under one minute to reach its target. An ICBM firing at 7,500 miles/12,000 km range, and with a trajectory which takes it out of the earth's atmosphere, would take about thirty minutes to reach its target. In both cases since the missile is supersonic, the victim would have no audible warning of its approach; but the ionisation around the path of the re-entry vehicle leaves a visible trail in the atmosphere.

Artillery: Some artillery weapons are provided with nuclear shells. They are in every respect conventional cannon, and they fire conventional shells for most of the time. Due to the demands of the nuclear device it is not yet possible to make a nuclear projectile below about 6 in/152 mm diameter, and most current nuclear artillery is in the region of 205 mm calibre (8 inch howitzers, for example). The range of the weapon is usually slightly less than the maximum range of the cannon, since the nuclear shell is heavier than a conventional one. The accuracy is to normal artillery standards. Fusing is very complex to prevent any premature functioning and also to make quite sure that it functions properly at the target. Conventional artillery usually fires a few ranging shots before settling down to fire for effect, but this is obviously impossible with a nuclear shell and special ranging shells are provided; these have the same ballistic flight but burst with a cloud of orange smoke so as to mark the point of burst for observers who can then make corrections before firing the nuclear shell.

Mines and Torpedoes: Nuclear sea and land mines are possible. They operate in the same way as their explosive counterparts but are far more wide-ranging in their effect. They are ideally placed in some confined area over which an enemy must pass en route to his objective. There are also nuclear torpedoes, for use by submarines and surface ships. They are principally intended for the attack of missile-carrying submarines so as to ensure complete destruction.

Bombs: Bombs dropped by aircraft are perhaps the most commonly-visualised nuclear weapon, since it was free-fall bombs which were used at Nagasaki and Hiroshima. Bombs are still held in national armouries but are relatively less important today. The drawback is not the bomb but the vulnerability of the aircraft carrying it. For this reason missiles, both ballistic and cruise, have assumed greater importance than bombs. Today's 'bomb' is more likely to be an air-launched 'stand-off' or 'cruise' missile which the aircraft carries partway to the target then launches before it arrives in the danger zone.

The short-term warning systems of the two major powers cover most of the vulnerable missile/aircraft routes to each nation, but are centred on the shortest trans-polar flight paths. The nerve centre of the American warning system is NORAD in Cheyenne Mountain, Colorado. Available to NORAD are inputs from all the early warning satellites providing surveillance and warning, and controlled from Guam in the Pacific, Pine Gap in the USA and Nurrungar in Australia; and BMEWS, facing northern Russia from the three stations of the USAF's 474L system at Clear in Alaska, Thule in Greenland and Fylingdales Moor in the UK. The BMEWS' 12 radars can pick up and track satellites, ICBMs and IRBMs, but are ineffective against MIRVs. These are tracked by a number of other specialised US radars. The maximum range of the BMEWS system is 3,000 miles/4,830 km.

Also in Cheyenne Mountain is SPADATS, controlled by SPADOC for the identification of all man-made objects in space, and the dissemination of this information with command and control decisions to all relevant bodies. There are two main input sources for SPADATS: the 'Cobra Dane' phased-array radar installation at Shemya in the Aleutian Islands, and the USAF's 496L 'Spacetrack' system with detection and tracking radars at Irinclik in Turkey, and with optical trackers in New

Mexico, California, New Brunswick, South Korea, Italy, New Zealand and Hawaii. Two associated systems are the US NAVSPASUR with three transmitting and six receiving locations in the south-east USA; and the US Air Force's PARCS at Grand Forks, North Dakota. PARCS is a phased-array radar with a range of 1,725 miles/2,775 km, with a coverage arc of 130° facing north, for the identification of individual RVs moving from the Arctic Ocean towards the central USA. There are a number of other complementary radar installations, and the USA has under intensive development a GEODSS, with three out of five sites built, (South Korea, Hawaii and New Mexico) and PACBAR

These are intended for the detection of incoming ICBMs and SLBMS, but there are also two systems intended specifically for the detection of SLBMs. The more important of these is the 'Pave Paws' net, currently made up of two phased-array radars, on the US east and west coasts, which will be complemented by another two radars in the south-east and south-west of the USA. Each of these radars has a range of 3,400 miles/5,470 km. At the Alternate Space Defense Center in Florida there are two other radars effective against SLBMs launched from the Atlantic or Caribbean. This system is linked to NORAD headquarters, 'Spacetrack' and SPASUR, and has the useful

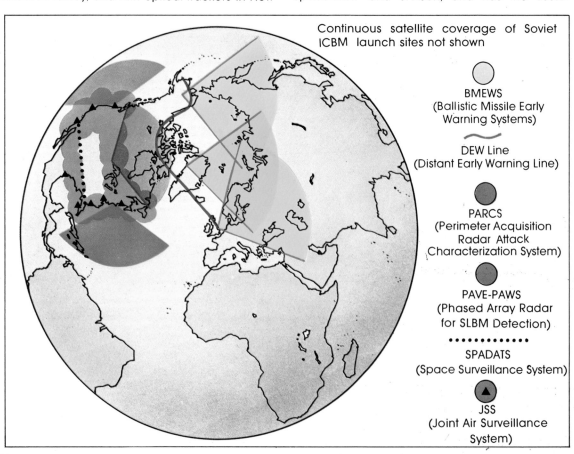

Continuous satellite coverage of Soviet ICBM launch sites not shown

BMEWS
(Ballistic Missile Early Warning Systems)

DEW Line
(Distant Early Warning Line)

PARCS
(Perimeter Acquisition Radar Attack Characterization System)

PAVE-PAWS
(Phased Array Radar for SLBM Detection)

SPADATS
(Space Surveillance System)

JSS
(Joint Air Surveillance System)

secondary ability to track fractional-orbital bombardment system (FOBS) vehicles.

For aircraft there are three main systems available to NORAD: the 414L system, the DEW Line, and the CADIN/Pinetree Line. The 414L system currently comprises two 'over-the-horizon' backscatter radars in Maine, with a range of 2,400 miles/ 3,860 km, while a third is to be built in Washington state and a fourth is planned for the southern USA. The DEW Line comprises 31 radars of conventional type located roughly along the 70°N parallel from Point Lay in western Alaska through 21 stations in Canada to Greenland, with another two stations in Iceland. These stations can pick up aircraft and cruise missiles at a range of 200 miles/320 km and at up to 40,000 ft/12,200 m. The CADIN/Pinetree Line comprises 24 back-up radar stations in southern Canada. Further south any intruding aircraft are picked up by the JSS, operated by the US Air Force and Federal Aviation Administration with 84 radars reporting to 7 Regional Operations Control Centers.

The whole system is backed up by photographic-reconnaissance satellites such as the CIA's KH-11 series with a life of some 50 to 80 days in orbit.

The comparable system for the Soviet Union is operated by the Troops of Air Defence. This force controls the Russian ABM, SAM and interceptor force, and relies on extensive radar warning systems for information of any threat. It is believed that the Troops of Air Defence number some 630,000 personnel, and have some 7,000 radars and satellites. Two satellites in elliptical semi-synchronous orbits provide the USSR with information of American missile deployment and hence on launches of ICBMs. These satellites are backed up by an ICBM warning system of at least five long-range radars of the 'Hen' series, with ranges in the order of 3,730 miles/6,000 km located to cover the west, north-east, south-east and south approaches to the USSR. This now elderly system is being supplemented by a new phased-array radar complex, each of the 10 probable sites being able to 'see' to 1,240 miles/2,000 km. For the defence of Moscow, and associated with the 'Galosh' ABM system, there are 'Cat House' and 'Dog House' intermediate-range radars with ranges of about 1,865 miles/3,000 km. It is reported that these are to be supplemented by a phased-array radar in the near future. These systems provide the USSR's main radar warning against missile attack.

Against aircraft incursion there are three 'over-the-horizon' backscatter radar complexes, located at Minsk in western Russia, Nikolayev in the Caucasus and in the Far East; a fourth complex may also exist. These important radars are aimed mainly at the USA and arctic regions. There is also a massive system of intermediate-range aircraft-detection and tracking radars of the 'Tall King' series, with a range of 370 miles/600 km and capability up to high altitudes, and very substantial numbers of radars associated with SAMs and AA guns.

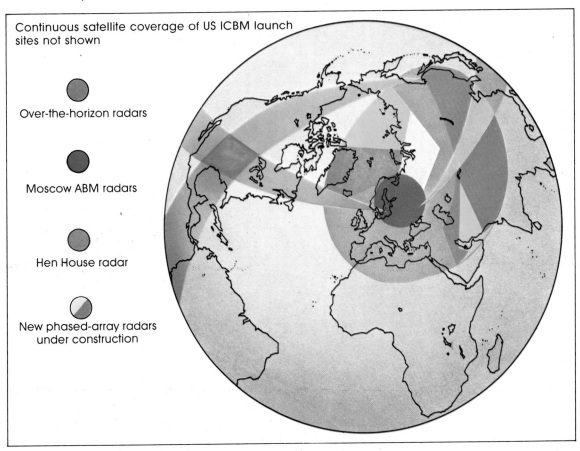

Continuous satellite coverage of US ICBM launch sites not shown

Over-the-horizon radars

Moscow ABM radars

Hen House radar

New phased-array radars under construction

Strategic Missiles

Strategic missiles fall into three groups:
(1) Ballistic missiles, land-launched
(2) Ballistic missiles, submarine launched
(3) Cruise missiles, land, air or sea launched

The strategic nuclear armoury has revolutionised warfare. The long range strategic weapons were developed initially as land-based systems which had no more than moderate accuracy but are now likely to obtain a probable direct hit on targets as small as a missile silo or military bases on the opposite side of the world.

Land-based weapons, which can cover distances of up to 9,500 miles/15,000 km were followed by the development of sea-based weapons. These are carried in submarines and launched whilst the vessel is submerged. Vast research into underwater detection and techniques for anti-submarine warfare has so far failed to reveal exactly where a submarine is at any one moment, thus its nuclear missiles remain immune from attack.

The third system is to use what amounts to a small, fast, unmanned aeroplane with an advanced guidance system which can be programmed to fly very close to the ground, to avoid radar detection.

These cruise missiles can be launched either from land bases (such as mobile launchers) or from submarines or warships or from aircraft in flight. In every case, the mobility of the launch vehicle is a factor which militates against detection and a pre-emptive strike, while the flight profile of the missile enhances its chances of arriving on target.

Intercontinental ballistic missiles, the strategic arsenal otherwise known as ICBMs, are launched into space, from where the warhead following a ballistic trajectory re-enters the earth's atmosphere above the target. The ICBMs originally carried a single, usually massive warhead but most modern ICBMs are capable of carrying more than one re-entry vehicle each containing a nuclear warhead. In some cases, each re-entry vehicle is independently manoeuvrable and can be directed to its own target, a considerable distance from the targets of the other warheads, so that a single missile can engage as many as 10 targets hundreds of miles apart. The 'bus' carrying the re-entry vehicles also carries decoys and other 'penetration aids' intended to deceive detecting radars and ABMs and permit the warheads to reach their targets unopposed.

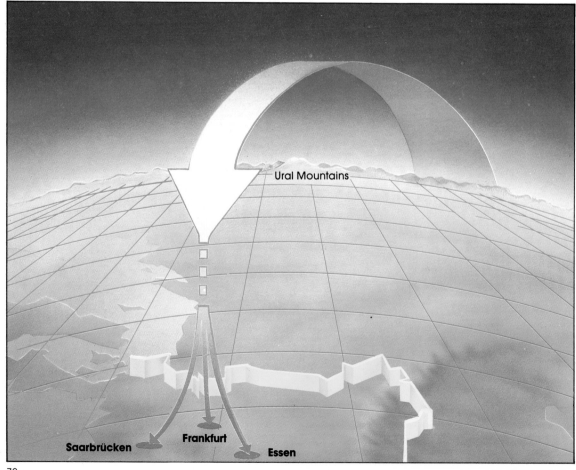

Ural Mountains

Saarbrücken Frankfurt Essen

Theatre Weapons

Medium range missiles are best described as theatre missiles. They are for use at ranges beyond the immediate battlefield but at targets which, nonetheless, have some bearing upon what is happening there, such as railway junctions into which troops and supplies are being delivered, rear-area repair facilities, headquarters, and communications complexes. The activities of these are all of vital importance to the progress of a battle or to the stabilisation of a defensive front. The battlefield commander can be assisted by attack against the enemy's centres of command and control and logistic supply for the disruptive effect this will have on forces at the front.

The line between tactical and strategic missiles is hard to draw. The same missile can frequently be used in either role by simply changing the programming of its guidance system. It can also depend upon the ownership of the missile and its location whether it is regarded as strategic or tactical. For example, an American cruise missile with 600 miles/1,000 km range deployed on bombers in the United States could only be strategic but a Soviet missile with the same range deployed in East Germany could have tactical applications.

Below left: Strategic nuclear weapons are very long-ranged systems, designed to deter war by threatening unacceptable destruction upon any nuclear attacker. To this end they are fitted with warheads of great destructiveness (or of lesser destructiveness delivered with greater accuracy) and provided with all manner of decoy and evasion systems. Thus each superpower seeks to persuade its opponent that it can (and has the will to) destroy area targets of population or industrial value, or point targets of political or military significance.

Below: Theatre nuclear weapons resemble strategic weapons in basic capability, but are designed to eliminate, over shorter ranges, such targets as will have a significance in a particular theatre of war.

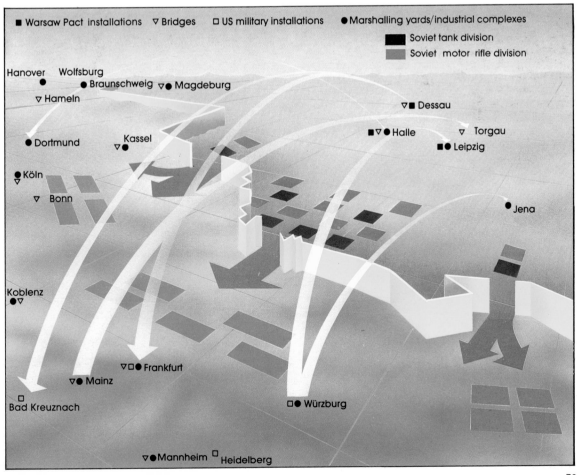

■ Warsaw Pact installations ▽ Bridges ☐ US military installations ● Marshalling yards/industrial complexes

■ Soviet tank division
▨ Soviet motor rifle division

Hanover
●
Wolfsburg
● Braunschweig ▽● Magdeburg
▽ Hameln

▽■ Dessau

● Dortmund
Kassel
▽●
■▽● Halle
▽ Torgau
■● Leipzig

●Köln

▽ Bonn
● Jena

Koblenz
●▽

▽☐● Frankfurt
▽● Mainz
☐
Bad Kreuznach
☐● Würzburg

▽●Mannheim ☐ Heidelberg

These are theatre nuclear weapons for use by the divisional corps or army commander. They are used within the corps sector in order to have immediate effect upon the conduct of the battle. Since the weapons are nuclear, political authorisation is needed before they can be used, but the military commanders are entirely responsible for target selection.

This category of weapons once contained the smallest nuclear weapon ever devised, the American 'Davy Crockett'. These were readily portable recoilless guns, and fired a small nuclear projectile over a range of 2,500 yards/2,000 metres. The yield of the warheads was never made public. The system was disliked by many military commanders and they were withdrawn before 1970.

More representative of this group of weapons are the artillery projectiles, covering ranges up to about 16-19 miles/25-30 km; the free-flight rockets such as the now-obsolete Honest John, with a range of about 22 miles/35 km; and such guided missiles as the US Corporal, Sergeant, Lacrosse (all now obsolete), Pershing and Lance, and the Soviet FROG/SS-21 rockets.

It is within this group of weapons that the crossover point between conventional and nuclear war is thought to fall. All are capable of being used with conventional warheads and artillery certainly would be so used in the conventional phase of combat.

The knowledge that changing from conventional to nuclear is not technically difficult is always present in a commander's mind, and the point at which the desire to 'go nuclear' arises must be a reflection of the commander's ability to perceive the future course of the battle. The commander who can see several conventional alternatives to a given tactical problem will be less likely to demand permission to use nuclear weapons. Much the same applies to the higher level of command: without firm resolve and good tactical sense, the higher commander could be convinced by the lower that the situation was beyond salvaging by conventional means and be persuaded to begin

the process for nuclear permission which would take at a minimum, many hours of political consultation.

Artillery and Mines

Artillery
Nuclear artillery is considered to be an extension of conventional artillery insofar as the weapons involved are conventional weapons with unconventional ammunition for use when the need arises. There are only a handful of artillery weapons which are able to fire nuclear projectiles:

US 8 inch Self-Propelled Howitzer M110
The same weapon as the M114 towed howitzer but mounted on a tracked chassis to improve mobility, it has the same range, fires the same shell, but requires only 5 men to operate. It has recently been improved by adopting a new barrel and ammunition, and is now called the M110 A1 or M110 A2 depending upon the degree of improvement incorporated. The M110-A2 can fire the nuclear shell to a maximum range of 22,200 yards/ 21,300 m. Like the M114, the M110 and its variants are widely distributed throughout armies of the world, but only the US Army has the nuclear projectile, though it would be made available to certain NATO artillery units should the need arise in time of war.

US 8 inch Howitzer M115
An elderly design of towed howitzer developed by the USA in the late 1930s and currently in wide use throughout the world in its conventional role. It is provided with the Nuclear Projectile M422, which is believed to have a 2kt yield. The howitzer has a maximum range of 18,400 yards/16,800 m, can keep up a sustained rate of fire of one shot per minute for conventional ordnance and requires a

M110 8in SP Howitzer

detachment of 14 men. It is towed by a heavy truck-tractor which also carries some ammunition.

US **155mm Self-Propelled Howitzer M109 A1**

This equipment is provided with a nuclear shell which ranges to 20,000 yards/18,100 m, but, as with the 8 inch howitzer, the nuclear ammunition is available only to the US or NATO units in time of war. In wide use throughout NATO and other armies.

USSR **152mm Self-Propelled Gun-Howitzer M1973**

The same ordnance as the D-20 towed equipment, mounted on a tracked chassis. Although no specific statement about nuclear projectiles for this weapon has been made, it is a logical assumption that if a nuclear shell is available for

USSR **152mm Gun-Howitzer D-20**

A conventional towed gun with a maximum range of 19,600 yards/17,400 m. It is understood to be provided with a 2 kt nuclear shell.

Mines

Nuclear land mines are defensive weapons and would need to be placed on the territory of a host nation. Yet these small but immensely destructive mines would destroy substantial areas of friendly territory along with those of the enemy. As a consequence their potential use has always been doubtful and it is conceivable that they will be withdrawn either through arms control, negotiation or unilaterally by NATO.

155 mm FH 77B

the towed gun, then the same shell should be available for the same gun in the self-propelled role.

Few other artillery pieces have been provided with nuclear projectiles. Weapons of smaller calibre than 5.9 inches/15 cm will not be equipped because of the technical problems of miniaturising a nuclear device.

USSR **180mm Gun S-23**

The largest artillery piece in the Soviet arsenal, a conventional towed gun with a range of 33,000 yards/30,400 m. It is reputed to have a nuclear projectile of 2 kt yield.

Above: Nuclear shell or Artillery Fired Atomic Projectiles AFAPs have been made by the United States for 155mm and 203mm towed and self-propelled artillery. It is widely considered that many 155mm and 203mm pieces would be capable of firing AFAPs but only a few systems are specifically designated for nuclear roles. This may have as much to do with the number of crews trained in nuclear roles as with conceivable technical limitations of the non-designated systems. The artillery piece above is assumed to be nuclear-capable and would also be able to fire binary chemical warfare shells.

The Neutron Weapon

The enhanced-radiation warhead, popularly called the neutron bomb (though no application of this weapon so far envisaged has anything to do with bombs) is essentially a scaled-down hydrogen fusion device with a yield in the 1-10 kt range. It takes its title from the increased radiation effect due, in particular, to the greater proportion of neutrons it produces. Under ideal conditions, some 80% of the energy of reaction is released in the form of very fast neutrons; in a purely fission device only a very small portion of the yield is given out as fast neutron and gamma radiation.

So far as most military analysts are concerned, the neutron weapon has one task, the neutralisation of large forces of tanks. It is the only weapon guaranteed to kill and disable the crews of armoured vehicles in a given area, no matter how many of them there may be. The fast neutrons emitted will pass through all types of armour, and they will do this at ranges up to 10 times the radius of the heat and blast effects which damage the tank. The design of the neutron warhead reduces the actual physical effects of heat, so that blast and fallout are reduced to minimum levels.

For example, a 1-kt neutron warhead detonated 3,200 ft/1,000 m above the ground will instantly disable the crews of every tank within a 1,000 ft/300 m radius of Ground Zero; the crews would die within 48 hours. Crews within a 2,300 ft/700 m radius will be disabled within five minutes and die within six days. Crews at 2,300-4,300 ft/700-1,000 m from Ground Zero will be disabled within a few hours and die within a few weeks. At greater distances there will be casualties but these may probably recover after hospitalisation.

In spite of its ability to pass through armour, the neutron can be stopped by a suitable thickness of earth. Defenders in the vicinity of the burst will be safe if they have 5 ft/1.5 m of earth above them.

The neutron warhead is essentially a defensive weapon. The targets are personnel in the open and the crews of armoured vehicles. In any battle involving prepared positions, these people can only be the attackers, since the defenders are dug in with ample overhead cover. There would be no conceivable benefit in using a neutron warhead to attack a prepared position, since the defenders would be resistant to its effects. The civil defence task is easier in that protection against exposure to radiation becomes the primary problem.

The NATO armies, notably the US, British, and possibly the French, see the neutron warhead, fired from field artillery and battlefield rocket launchers, as the principal counter to Soviet armoured strength. The Soviet battle plan for an invasion of the West would be to concentrate their armour on several axes in order to make a high-speed offensive which, by weight, speed and surprise would break through the Western defences at one or more points. The neutron weapon is the perfect answer to this, since it would permit the NATO forces to stop an advance dead in its tracks for the minimum expenditure in lives.

From the purely military point of view, the neutron weapon is a useful option for any defender, whilst it has much less value for an attacker. It is a formidable defensive weapon for the West but one with perhaps fewer attractions to the Russians.

The use of neutron warheads for artillery projectiles and Lance battlefield missiles was first put forward in 1977-78 in the USA. There was immediate and vociferous objection from the Soviet Union and public concern in Western Europe, particularly in Germany. Later President Carter slowed the programme. It was revived by President Reagan in July 1981 with his order to prepare about 1,180 warheads for 380 Lance rockets and about 800 8-inch artillery shells. These are initially to be stored in the USA, but since their theatre of possible employment is most likely to be Central Europe, there has since been much political discussion about the implications of their deployment, though without any firm conclusions so far.

Right: NATO defences are positioned largely on specially selected 'killing grounds' in areas that the Warsaw Pact forces must cross. The focus of Soviet armour in such areas is a likely target for neutron weapons.
Below right: Combat engineer vehicles can quickly build the earth-covered extemporised shelters to protect friendly troops, providing adequate warning is given.
Below far right: The standard infantry NBC suit provides no protection against radiation but offers useful protection against fallout and chemical or biological agent contamination.
Below: The neutron and standard fission detonations compared.

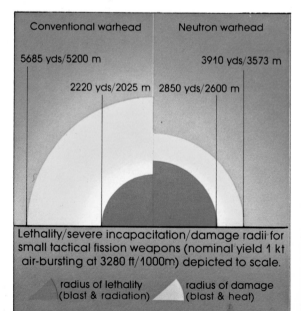

Conventional warhead	Neutron warhead
5685 yds/5200 m	3910 yds/3573 m
2220 yds/2025 m	2850 yds/2600 m

Lethality/severe incapacitation/damage radii for small tactical fission weapons (nominal yield 1 kt air-bursting at 3280 ft/1000m) depicted to scale.

radius of lethality (blast & radiation) radius of damage (blast & heat)

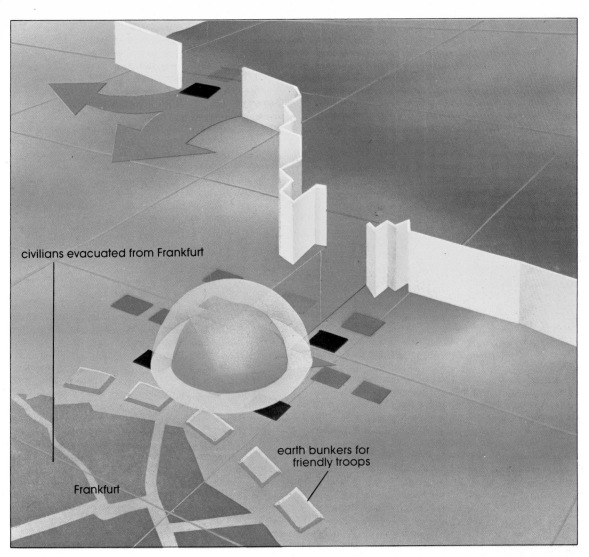

civilians evacuated from Frankfurt

earth bunkers for friendly troops

Frankfurt

The amount of guidance required by a missile depends upon the degree of accuracy demanded from it. An artillery shell, with no independent guidance and following a ballistic trajectory, can be expected to land within 165 ft/ 50 m of the aim point and for most purposes this is quite satisfactory. With a nuclear projectile the area of the burst will be greater than the amount of error, so the mission may be accomplished. Similar considerations apply to spin-stabilised free-flight rockets; fin-stabilised rockets tend to be less accurate but still manage to closely follow a true ballistic trajectory.

Accuracy begins to recede with the longer-range weapons, and integral guidance becomes necessary. Any projectile or missile passing through the air is acted upon by a variety of forces: humidity, air pressure, air temperature, wind speed, and direction, and the rotation of the earth itself, all act to deform the planned trajectory. In short range fire – up to, say, 12-19 miles/20-30 km – it is possible to take meteorological observations and deduce corrections to apply to the firing data in order to compensate for the various abnormal conditions. The simplest example of this is to consider the effect of a crosswind blowing from the firer's left: if he aims directly at the target, the winds blow the missile off to the right. He therefore alters his aim to another point to the left of the target so that the missile is blown until its course strikes the target.

Once the range is in excess of 19 miles/30 km, there can be no way of obtaining the necessary trajectory correction data for longer ranges, and the process of attempting to calculate corrections across a course of, say, 1,500 miles/2,500 km, with trajectory conditions varying considerably from place to place, is a major task which requires inertial guidance systems comprised of gyroscopes and accellerometers.

The simplest form of guidance is to radio instructions to the missile, basing the directions upon radar observations of its position. These instructions are converted into mechanical operations – moving fins or steerable nozzles in the rocket motor, switching rockets on or off, extending

Below: *Once the MX missile (now designated MGM-118A Peacekeeper) has left the atmosphere and discarded its nose cone, the MIRV bus is manoeuvred into exactly the optimum trajectory by its guidance and control system. The bus is then aligned with the first target and at the right moment a warhead is released into the atmosphere together with decoy(s) if necessary. The process is repeated until all the warheads have been deployed.*

Above: *The terrain-comparison (Tercom) guidance of the US cruise missile series is designed to update the inertial navigation system. At predetermined times during the flight, the Tercom is turned on to gain a digitally processed image of a presurveyed major landmark, and this is compared with a stored image so that the onboard computer can assess the inertial platform's deviation and issue course corrections. The process is repeated several times to keep the deviation error from the planned trajectory to a minimum and so give the missile excellent terminal accuracy.*

air brakes and so on, all of which modify the flight path to bring it to the trajectory calculated to end at the target.

Unfortunately this simple system is open to electronic countermeasures (ECM). It is simple to jam the radio signal or distort it; if the sender resorts to coded instructions to his missile it is possible to decode them, and send false information to steer the missile to some other area.

Another command system is to place a TV unit in the missile and have the operator, on the ground, view the received picture. The operator can then compare the picture with maps of the target area, pick out the target visually, and then steer the missile to impact. The system is highly accurate, and also highly vulnerable to ECM measures. A way round this limitation was sought by giving the

missile a memory of stored maps with which to compare pictures of the ground, but the technical difficulties proved too great to permit success in the 1950s. However, in the late 1960s Tercom (terrain-comparison) guidance was finally evolved for the new generation of cruise missiles planned for US service. This system uses radar images of key waypoints (derived from satellite reconnaissance and stored as digital matrices) which the onboard computer compares with actual radar images to produce steering commands that successively reduce to near-zero the missile's deviation from its planned route. A sophisticated version of the same principle (DSMAC, or Digital Scene-Matching Area Correlation) provides extreme accuracy in the terminal stage of the flight.

Ballistic missiles use inertial guidance, a system which gives the missile total independence from the ground and from jamming once fired. In effect, the launch officer informs the missile of its launch position and the position of the target relative to this starting point, plus the ballistic trajectory linking the two points. Once launched, the computer inside the missile measures any deviation from this trajectory (using an inertial platform based on mechanical or laser gyroscopes) and issues steering corrections. Thus the effects of wind or other atmospheric conditions are countered by computer instructions to the control units, which move control surfaces or vector the thrust of the engine to bring the actual and planned trajectories into congruence.

Submarine-launched ballistic missiles (SLBMs) are the world's optimum delivery system for nuclear warheads: their launch platforms are highly mobile nuclear-powered submarines able to operate for protracted periods in the vast ocean areas from which they can launch their missiles into any part of a potential enemy's land mass. They are accurate, can carry many small but devastating warheads, and their launch platforms are potentially reusable once the missiles have been fired, while attacks on ballistic missiles (SSBNs) at sea would cause much less collateral damage compared with a missile strike against ICBMs in fixed silos.

The countering of a possible enemy's SLBM force is one of the major tasks faced by the navy of each superpower, and it is also of crucial importance to the navies of the USA's NATO partners, who are also threatened by the SLBMs of Soviet submarines and who perceive a threat to their maritime lifelines from Soviet nuclear-powered attack submarines.

In order to transit from their operational bases into the Atlantic, Soviet submarines must pass a barrier of NATO detection systems forming an arc called the Greenland-Iceland -UK (GIUK) gap. There are, other operational areas but Soviet SSBNs deploy primarily in the Northern Pacific and Atlantic Ocean. The Soviet Navy's Northern Fleet, with its headquarters at Severomorsk and bases at Archangelsk, Motovskij Gulf, Polyarny and Severodvinsk, has on average a complement of 16 SSBNs, and a number of these must pass through the GIUK gap to operational deployment areas in the Atlantic.

NATO use satellite observation of the Soviet bases, with optical, infra-red and radar sensors to detect the movement of submarines in and out of harbour. The SSBNs may then be tracked through part of the outward trip to provide tactical units (aircraft, ships and submarines) with a head-start. The first definite detection threat faced by Soviet SSBNs is the Sound Surveillance System (SOSUS) and aircraft patrols in the gap between Spitsbergen and northern Norway. Farther to the south, the Soviet submarines run into the routine operational areas of NATO attack submarines (with highly sensitive active and passive detection systems); the patrol areas of additional anti-submarine aircraft (both shore- and carrier-based, with sensors that include sonar buoys, radar and magnetic-anomaly detection); and tactical submarine-hunter groups with specialist surface vessels such as destroyers and frigates with anti-submarine helicopters.

Still farther to the south is another SOSUS barrier, the gap between Greenland and Iceland being additionally protected by an Anti-submarine Captor minefield, in which the individual acoustic homing torpedoes can be released by remote control in time of war. Finally, as the Soviet SSBNs enter the north eastern Atlantic Ocean there operate a number of submarine hunter-killer task groups to follow up leads from air and surface forces farther north.

It is an impressive and elaborate detection system. Necessarily so, given the seriousness of the threat. But it is a detection system of great cost and complexity, and could develop weaknesses under crisis or wartime conditions. The system allows observation of the number of Soviet SSBNs that transit to and from their operational deployment areas off the eastern coast of the United States. Any abnormal SSBN activity is therefore a possible crisis indicator, but once in their operational areas SSBNs will be difficult to locate and destroy. Lastly, it is worth noting that the detection task is made somewhat easier by two major limitations of Soviet submarines: they are larger than their NATO counterparts, and they are also considerably noisier; both these factors make detection less difficult than it would otherwise be.

Right: The map illustrates the vital importance of mutual cooperation between the forces of the NATO nations if effective monitoring of Soviet submarine activity is to be undertaken. Any weaknesses in the links between the different services and countries could if identified, be exploited by Soviet submarines to ease their transit towards the eastern Atlantic.

The most obvious recognition of abnormal activity is identified by changes in the numbers of Soviet SSBNs on routine patrol. Others would be the extension of patrol duty beyond the normal period, or the appearance of additional SSBNs not usually deployed in that area. Other features are the pattern of the patrol itself. For example, certain transit routes are known to be favoured over others in peacetime, and deviations from this pattern may have significance for those involved with the analysis and assessment of Soviet SSBN activity.

Two factors influence the value of monitoring Soviet SSBN movements in this way. As the effective range of Soviet SLBMs increases there is less reason for a crisis deployment of SSBNs to distant operational areas which would require transit across the GIUK gap. Secondly, over a period of time it is possible to gradually increase the level of 'normal' deployment so that it is difficult to determine whether or not submarines on patrol are being called to an alert level that could be associated with increasing tension or crisis — unless of course, this was a specific intention of a Soviet commander for the purposes of deception.

In the future priority will not only be attached to observing the transit of Soviet submarines to their operational patrol areas but to the tracking of their movements on patrol. To a limited extent this is already possible but is constrained by inadequate technical means and the advantages that accrue from the acoustic unpredictability of the ocean environment for sonar surveillance systems.

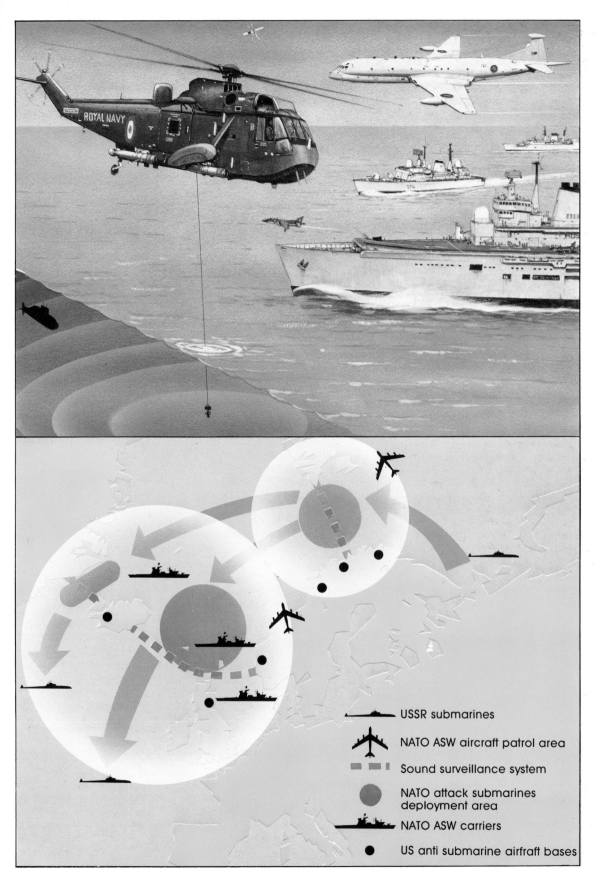

USSR submarines

NATO ASW aircraft patrol area

Sound surveillance system

NATO attack submarines
deployment area

NATO ASW carriers

US anti submarine airfraft bases

The ways in which nuclear and thermonuclear warheads can be delivered are extremely diverse. They range from static weapons such as mines (land and sea); free-fall weapons (delivered by platforms as different as small tactical aircraft, huge strategic aircraft and warships, the last delivering nuclear depth-charges), to ballistic weapons ranging in size and capability from the nuclear torpedo and artillery-fired shell to an enormous assortment of missiles launched from the land, sea and air. Currently, well to the fore, there are various types of cruise missile.

It is impossible to deal with all the current weapons within the confines of a relatively small technical section, so emphasis has been placed on showing typical examples of the various types of delivery system, both tactical and strategic, so as to provide an overall picture of the types of weapon currently available to the nuclear powers.

STRATEGIC SURFACE-TO-SURFACE MISSILES

These are considered to be the ultimate arbiters of nuclear power, for they have the range, payload and accuracy to deliver crushing strategic blows. In historical terms the tendency has been to increase size for greater payload and range, and then a return to smaller weights as guidance systems, miniature warheads and improved propellants (with solid propellants generally replacing storable liquid propellants) came to the fore from the 1960s onwards. There are of course exceptions, such as the monstrous Soviet SS-9 and SS-18, while even the SS-11, SS-17 and SS-19 are considerably heavier than the US Minuteman series. American technological superiority has ensured that the Minuteman and its successor, the Peacekeeper (ex-MX) are valued in treaty terms according to their weight as ICBMs. Older weapons such as the US Titan II and Soviet SS-13 are still in service in small numbers, and other strategic contenders are the small Chinese and French missile forces. China's missiles are technically inferior to those of other nuclear powers, but still offer a significant capability, while France's geographical position in relation to the USSR means that she can rely on an IRBM rather than ICBM force.

STRATEGIC AIR-TO-SURFACE MISSILES

Despite a strident campaign of propaganda directed against the air-launched cruise missile, the USSR has been the main possessor of this type of weapon since the 1950s, and it still deploys substantial numbers of the nuclear-tipped AS-3 Kangaroo, AS-4 Kitchen, AS-5 Kelt and AS-6 Kingfish missiles, generally considered to be 'brute force' weapons with useful capabilities against ships and land targets, but of short range and limited capability in the face of electronic counter-measures. The decisive (or possibly decisive) weapon of the 1980s in this category is the AGM-86B cruise missile, whose procurement has been curtailed pending the development of a new generation of such weapons using stealth technology and superior aerodynamics to mitigate the chances of detection and to provide higher performance over comparable long ranges.

STRATEGIC MANNED BOMBERS

Realistically the manned bomber can no longer be used as a delivery platform for free-fall bombs against a determined and technically advanced opponent. Instead, the current generation of weapons such as the nuclear-tipped Short-Range Attack Missile (AGM-69A) is being replaced by air-launched cruise missiles. To this extent, therefore, the bomber has begun a process of change from a deep penetrator of enemy airspace with a small but potent payload, to a higher-performance shallow penetrator with a large number of cruise missiles for the actual attack. Thus aircraft such as the US B-52 and Soviet Tu-95 Bear are in the process of replacement by platforms such as the US Rockwell B-1B and Soviet Tu-26 Backfire, and the new Blackjack, which can hug the ground at transonic speeds to break though the enemy's radar defences before releasing either cruise missiles or bombs.

STRATEGIC SURFACE-TO-SURFACE, NAVAL

Complementary to the ICBM force as the world's most powerful weapons, the submarine-launched ballistic missile is usually much smaller and lighter than its land-based counterpart as it need not have the same range requirement. Virtually undetectable, submarines offer the capacity of relatively shorter-range launches against important targets. SLBMs have always made full use of miniaturisation techniques, and have developed in recent generations as highly effective delivery systems for MIRVs and MaRVs.

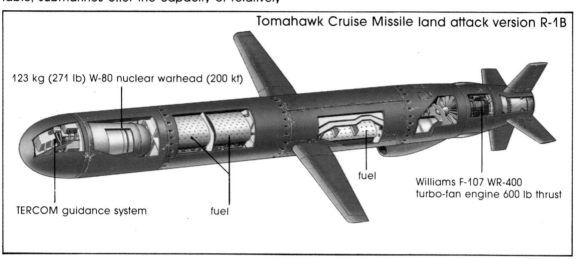

Tomahawk Cruise Missile land attack version R-1B

123 kg (271 lb) W-80 nuclear warhead (200 kt)

TERCOM guidance system   fuel

fuel

Williams F-107 WR-400 turbo-fan engine 600 lb thrust

ANTI-BALLISTIC MISSILE

The USA has shelved its anti-ballistic missiles (Spartan and Sprint), leaving the Soviet ABM-1B Galosh as the world's only operational anti-ballistic missile. This exo-atmospheric nuclear-tipped giant is designed to deal with missiles targeted on Moscow; its further deployment or that of a new system is prohibited by treaty.

THEATRE SURFACE-TO-SURFACE MISSILES

This category of weapons plays a decisive part in the history of the 1980s, with NATO fears of the USSR's great numerical and potential superiority having prompted the development of the ground-launched cruise missile (BGM-109H) and Pershing 2 as a counter primarily to the long-range SS-20. Also available to the Soviets are large numbers of older systems such as the SS-4, SS-5, and SS-12. Newer, highly capable Soviet missiles are entering service in the 1980s to replace both these and shorter range types such as the Pluton.

TACTICAL NAVAL WEAPONS

Naval warfare offers perhaps the greatest possibilities for nuclear confrontation without inevitable escalation. Both the superpowers control large nuclear arsenals, and while the USA concentrates on weapons intended mainly for the destruction of Soviet submarines (ASROC, SUBROC and other nuclear systems such as depth charges and torpedoes), the Soviets place greater emphasis on the destruction of American surface and submarine forces, both of which could deal devastating blows against the USSR. Such weapons are the SS-N-3 Shaddock, the SS-N-7 Siren, the SS-N-9, the SS-N-11 and the SS-N-14. Very little is known about these Soviet weapons.

USA **MINUTEMAN**

Description: Three-stage solid-propellant rocket carrying nuclear multiple warhead. Launched from underground silo, though air-launched and mobile types have been evaluated.

Targets: Strategic: defence complexes, missile sites, command centres, manufacturing areas, other political or economic value targets.

Strengths: Deployed in 'hardened' silos and relatively proof against counter-strikes. Multiple warhead allows one missile to strike up to three different targets. Latest circuitry permits re-targeting during flight from airborne command post. Guidance system resistant to jamming.

Weaknesses: Launch silos detectable by satellite photography and considered vulnerable to a pre-emptive attack by accurate ICBMs.

History: Studies began in 1956; development in 1958; first tethered firing 1959; first free flight 1961; in service December 1962. Minuteman II: longer and heavier, more range and better accuracy, introduced 1966 and replaced Minuteman I. Minuteman III: improved propulsion and control, new multiple warheads, 1977. Complete replacement of II prevented by lack of funds and force now consists of a mixture of II and III.

Dimensions:

Length	59.7 ft/18.2 m
Diameter	6.0 ft/1.82 m
Weight	76,000 lbs/34,500 kg
Accuracy	Circular Probable Error 400 to 240 yds/365 to 220 m
Range	8,080 miles/13,000 km
Payload	(Minuteman II) Avco Mk 11B/C re-entry vehicle with one 1-2 Mt nuclear warhead. (Minuteman III) General Electric Mk 12A re-entry vehicle with three 335 Kt nuclear warheads, or Mk 12 re-entry vehicle with three 170 Kt nuclear warheads.

Guidance: Inertial, with three pre-programmed, selectable targets for the independent warhead units. Target can be changed in-flight, using information stored in the missile computer memory.

Deployment: Approximately 1,250 missiles have been built and 1,000 are distributed as follows:

341 Strategic Missile Wing (SMW) Malmstrom, Montana	200
44 SMW, Ellsworth, South Dakota	150
91 SMW, Minot, North Dakota	150
251 SMW, Whiteman, Missouri	150
90 SMW, Warren, Wyoming	200
321 SMW, Grand Forks, Nebraska	150

These locations represent the Wing HQ; the missiles are widely distributed around the surrounding area, located in buried silos. Those of 341 SMW are said to be spread through an area of over 84,000 square miles/217,560 km^2, and those of the other wings will be similarly dispersed.

Countermeasures: Pre-emptive strike against silos; use of anti-missile missiles.

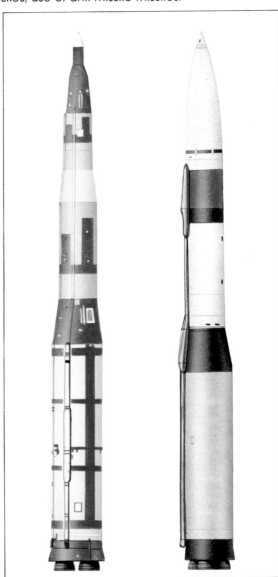

Right: Minuteman II
Far right: Minuteman III

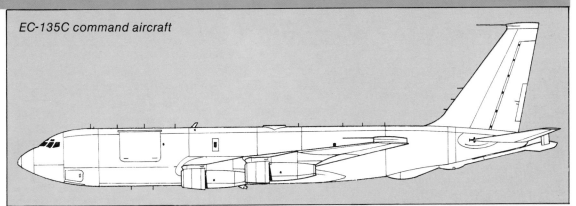

EC-135C command aircraft

No deterrent system can remain credible if its potential opponent believes, rightly or wrongly, that there is a possibility that the system may be rendered unworkable in time of war. So, as one of the three legs of the US strategic triad, the force of Minuteman ICBMs must be (and must be seen to be) operable under the worst possible circumstances. Part of this credibility rests upon the assumption that a significant part of the missile force can survive a pre-emptive first strike by accurate Soviet ICBMs such as the SS-18. No less important is an adequate system of command and control: primary command responsibility is exercised by Strategic Air Command headquarters and then by the subordinate 8th and 15th Air Forces through the relevant air division and missile wing structure. However, it is wholly conceivable that any of these command formations (and/or its radio and landline communications) could be knocked out by sabotage or a first strike, so provision is made for overall command from the air by means of Boeing C-135 flying command posts such as the EC-135B illustrated above. There are 14 such aircraft operational with SAC, operating from Offutt and Ellsworth Air Force bases. These aircraft have low vulnerability to enemy attack once airborne, and at least two are kept in the air, complete with a commanding general and his battle staff, on a permanent basis as a back-up in the event of the destruction or incapacitation of other command echelons.

Below: *Deployment of Minuteman missiles dispersed throughout six U.S. states*

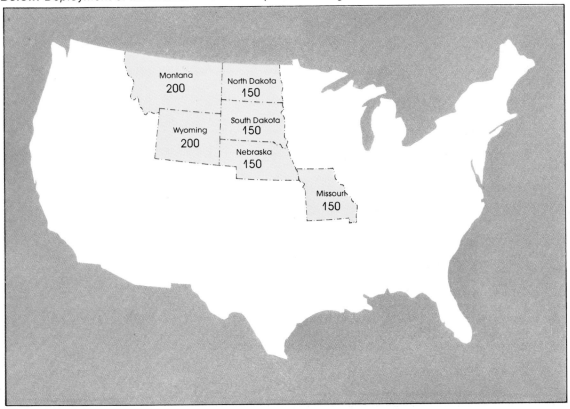

Montana 200
North Dakota 150
Wyoming 200
South Dakota 150
Nebraska 150
Missouri 150

USA **MX (MGM-118A Peacekeeper)**

Description: Three-stage solid-propellant missile carrying about 10 nuclear warheads.

Targets: Strategic: defence complexes, missile sites, command centres, manufacturing areas, other military targets.

Strengths: Advanced inertial guidance greatly improves accuracy. A manoeuvring warhead bus makes interception difficult, and renders assessment of likely targets almost impossible.

Weaknesses: Expense, and the fact that environmental and political pressures have dictated an interim basing system, comparable to the type most vulnerable to a first strike by the Soviet Strategic Rocket Forces.

History: Project began in 1974 with realisation that new Soviet ICBMs posed a serious threat to Minuteman missiles in their silos, and that some Minuteman technology was 20 years old. Development of the MX has progressed steadily and the first development missile was scheduled for test-flight in 1983. The selection of the basing mode for the missile was resolved in the same year, MX is slated for service in 1986, after the launch of 20 test rounds, with full deployment by 1989.

Dimensions:

Length	70,85 ft/21.6 m
Diameter	7.65 ft/2.33 m
Weight	190,475 lbs/86,400 kg
Accuracy	CEP 165 yds/150 m
Range	8,100 miles/13,000 km or more
Payload	Advanced Ballistic Re-Entry Vehicle (ABRV) containing 10 W-78 350 kt warheads, plus decoys.

Guidance: Advanced Inertial Reference System (AIRS) capable of being oriented during manufacture; it retains its heading during transport, so needs no re-alignment when installed in the firing site, and is resistant to nuclear weapons effects.

Deployment: This has been the subject of intense political and environmental pressures, and the decision has been made to use revamped Minuteman silos with additional hardening (physical and electronic).

Countermeasures: As a result of the decision to locate the planned 100 units in Minuteman silos, the Peacekeeper ICBM may now be regarded as having comparable vulnerabilities to Minuteman ICBMs. These vulnerabilities to Soviet pre-emptive ICBM attack may be redressed by a launch-under attack policy, or missile site defence by endo-atmospheric ABM. Countermeasures are very limited if the missiles are successfully launched.

Below: two methods under consideration for the defence of the MX. Top: cutaway of the shelter over the underground "racetrack" system. Middle: a plan of the closed loop "racetrack". Bottom: the tunnel system, showing a break in the trench from which the missile can be launched.

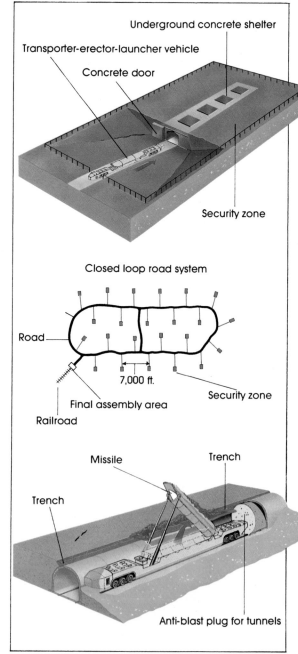

Underground concrete shelter

Transporter-erector-launcher vehicle

Concrete door

Security zone

Closed loop road system

Road

7,000 ft.

Security zone

Final assembly area

Railroad

Missile

Trench

Trench

Anti-blast plug for tunnels

Description: The SS-13 is a three-stage solid-propellant rocket, probably the first solid fuelled missile to enter Soviet service, and carries a thermonuclear warhead. Soviet development of solid propellant missiles has been comparatively unsuccessful, and this is reflected in the low numbers deployed.

Targets: Strategic: defined in Soviet doctrine as enemy nuclear forces and their command and control systems as a first priority, with other military targets as the second priority.

Strengths: The usual strengths associated with solid propellant ICBMs, such as high system availability and good reliability probably do not apply. The system has shown generally poor performance characteristics.

Weaknesses: Since the deployment of the SS-13 was relatively small and no improved models have ever been developed, it appears likely that there were irresolvable technical weaknesses in the design. Thus the main weaknesses of the system will be due to its predicted reliability which is assumed to be poor. But the Soviet Union is known to maintain a number of weapon systems of uncertain reliability and questionable military utility for reasons which are difficult for western analysts to interpret.

History: SS-13 was first seen in public in 1965; it entered service in 1968 and thereafter some 60 were deployed in silos, but by 1970 manufacture and deployment had ceased.

Dimensions:
SS-13
Length	65.5 ft/20 m
Diameter	5.5 ft/1.7 m
Weight	77,000 lbs/35,000 kg
Range	6,250 miles/10,000 km
Accuracy	CEP 2,185 yds/2,000 m
Payload	Nuclear, 750 kt

Guidance: Inertial.

Deployment: The United States Department of Defence considers a single deployment area, Yoshkar Ola for the SS-13. Some 60 missiles are estimated to be installed in underground silos.

Countermeasures: Usual methods of direct strike and anti-missile systems against Ss-13; there is no other counter than pre-emptive strike, early warning anti-missile systems, but launch preparations may not be difficult to detect in this case.

There remains considerable incentive for the Soviet Union to develop solid propellant ICBMs/SLBMs comparable to the Minuteman/Poseidon of the United States. The solid propellant missiles in general offer a much higher degree of system reliability, lower service and operational maintenance costs, and much faster response times to alerts than liquid propellant ballistic missiles. To date, the Soviet Union's difficulties in developing solid propellant rocket motors with the necessary performance characteristics to carry nuclear warheads to intercontinental ranges

Below: SS-13 fired from silo

appear to have been insurmountable. These difficulties have not been observed for short, medium, and intermediate range missiles. Even so, the development of missiles such as the intermediate range SS-20 have been derived from attempts to develop a land mobile successor to the SS-13. The designation given to this system was SS-16. During its flight tests the first stage of the missile consistently failed to meet the required performance specifications, possibly because the Soviet chemical industry is not yet able to produce solid propellant rocket motors of the size required for the first stage of an ICBM.

USSR **SS-17 and SS-19**

Description: These rockets were developed in competition with one another as a replacement for the SS-11, and are therefore considered together.

SS-17 is a two-stage rocket using storable liquid propellant. It is the first Soviet rocket in service to use the 'cold launch' technique, in which the missile is ejected from its underground silo by gas pressure, after which the rocket motor is ignited. This means that the rocket efflux does not damage the structure during launch.

SS-19 was developed at the same time as SS-17, probably as an insurance and also to act as a spur to the design teams, and uses the conventional 'hot launch' system in which the rocket motor is ignited in the silo. According to some agencies it is less technically advanced than the SS-17 but it seems to achieve the same results. In spite of the competitive development, both missiles have been taken into active service.

Targets: Strategic: defined in Soviet doctrine as enemy nuclear forces and their command and control systems as priority with military stockpiles, other military targets as secondary.

Strengths: Both missiles are reputed to be extremely accurate and both carry multiple independently-targeted warheads.

Weaknesses: Comparable with other land-based ICBMs.

History: Development must have begun in the late 1960s, since the first flight test of the SS-17 known to the West took place in 1972. SS-19 was the first to be deployed, in 1975, with SS-17 following in 1977, a delay doubtless due to the need to modify existing silos to operate the 'cold launch' technique.

Dimensions
SS-17
Length	80 ft/24.5 m
Diameter	8.25 ft/2.5 m
Weight	143,300 lbs/65,000 kg
Range	6,200 miles/10,000 km
Accuracy	CEP 490 yds/450 m for both models
Payload	(Mod 1) MIRV, 4 x 750 Kt
	(Mod 2) Single, 1 x 6 Mt

SS-19
Length	88 ft/27 m
Diameter	8.25 ft/2.5 m
Weight	172,000 lbs/78,000 kg
Range	6,200 miles/10,000 km
Accuracy	(Mod 1) CEP 454 yds/500 m
	(Mod 2) CEP 330 yds/300 m
	(Mod 3) CEP 330 yds/300 m
Payload	(Mod 1) MIRV, 6 x 550 kt
	(Mod 2) Single, 5 Mt
	(Mod 3) MIRV, 6 x 550 kt

Guidance: SS-17: inertial, with on-board computer which controls the manoeuvres of the MIRV-bus. SS-19: inertial, with on-board computer which can detect deviations from the pre-programmed course and issue control commands to correct small errors in the flight path.

Deployment: SS-17: about 150 are reported to have been installed in underground silos converted from SS-11 use. SS-19: about 300 have been installed, also in former SS-11 silos. The current indications are that the SS-19 has proved satisfactory, cheaper, and easier to make than the SS-17 and the greater part of the ICBM force will use the SS-19.

Countermeasures: Pre-emptive or deployment of early warning systems and anti-missile forces.

Below left: SS-17   *Right:* SS-19

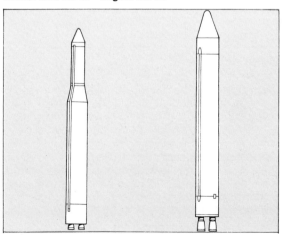

USSR **SS-18**

Description: SS-18 is the largest ICBM in the world and the weapon which demolished the West's deterrent credibility. It is a two-stage rocket using storable liquid propellant with a post-separation boost unit for the re-entry vehicle. The warhead may be single or multiple, but is of immense power.

Targets: Whilst this is presumably to be classed with all other strategic missiles so far as target options are concerned, its range, accuracy and enormous payload suggest that it would primarily be directed at Western nuclear missile installations and secondly at other military targets.

Strengths: Accurate, multiple warheads.

Weaknesses: Comparable with other ICBMs.

History: Development began in late 1960s and first missiles were deployed operationally in 1974. Silos built for the SS-9 were converted to the 'cold launch' technique used by this missile, at a rate of about 50 a year until the end of the 1970s.

Below: The use of a cold-launch system (with compressed gas rather than exhaust driving the missile out) means that the SS-18 silo can be reused and the missile can carry a slightly heavier payload.

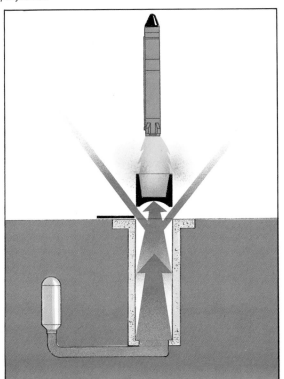

Dimensions:

Length	121.3 ft/37 m
Diameter	10.5 ft/3.2 m
Weight	485,000 lbs/220,000 kg
Range	7,500 miles/12,000 km
Accuracy	(Mod 1) CEP 490 yds/450 m
	(Mod 2) CEP 490 yds/450 m
	(Mod 3) CEP 380 yds/350 m
	(Mod 4) CEP 380 yds/350 m
Payload	(Mod 1) Single, 50 Mt
	(Mod 2) MIRV, 8 x 900 Mt
	(Mod 3) Single, 30 Mt
	(Mod 4) MIRV, 10 x 500 Kt
	(Mod 5) MIRV, 10 x 750 Kt

Guidance: Inertial. Computer controlled MIRV-bus with motor control which can distribute individual warheads to pre-set pattern.

Deployment: The USSR maintains 308 of these missiles.

Countermeasures: Early warning and anti-missile systems, though these would have to be extremely complex and numerous to cope with the MIRV warhead.

Below: MIRVed SS-18s are capable of destroying several targets with their independent re-entry vehicles, each carrying up to 10 warheads.

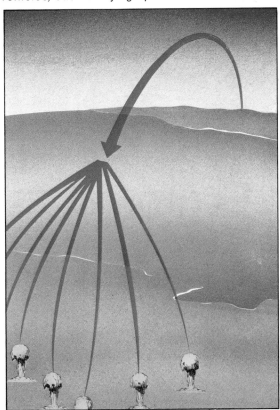

FRANCE **SSBS S-3**

Description: SSBS (Sol-Sol-Ballistique-Stratégique) is a medium range two-stage solid-propellant rocket with nuclear warhead, stored in and launched from an underground silo.

Targets: Strategic: cities, industrial areas, weapons complexes.

Strengths: Forms third leg of French nuclear forces 'TRIAD'.

Weaknesses: Vulnerable to pre-emptive attack. As a purely national programme it has proved extremely expensive and insufficiently credible.

History: Development began in 1959; first experimental launches in 1965; became operational in 1971. The S-3, an improved model, was begun in 1973 and entered service in 1980.

Dimensions:

S-3
Length	45 ft/13.7 m
Diameter	59 in/1.50 m
Weight	56,879 lbs/25,800 kg
Range	2,175 miles/3,500 km
Accuracy	Not disclosed
Payload	Thermonuclear, 1Mt

Guidance: Inertial, incorporating technology licensed from the USA.

Deployment: Two squadrons each with nine S-3 missiles are dispersed on the Plateau d'Albion in central France. Each group is commanded by a Central Fire Control Room and both are linked to Strategic Nuclear Force HQ. The first of these squadrons, equipped with S-2 missiles, became operational in 1971, the second in 1972. A plan to construct a third group was cancelled, for economic reasons, late in 1974.

The S-3 version has replaced the S-2 in the same silos, though the silo installations have been extensively modernised.

Counterforce: A pre-emptive strike would be feasible, since it should be assumed that the location of the silos has been detected by satellites.

Right: Chinese ballistic missiles, from left to right the CSS-1, CSS-2, CSS-3 and CSS-4.
Far right: Test-launch of the CSS-4, which has also orbited Chinese satellites.

Below: Section through a typical SSBS silo

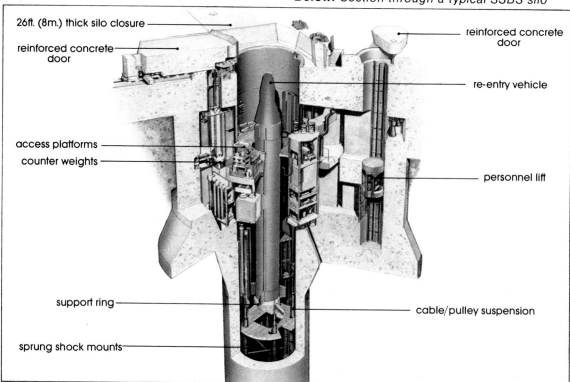

26ft. (8m.) thick silo closure

reinforced concrete door

reinforced concrete door

re-entry vehicle

access platforms

counter weights

personnel lift

support ring

cable/pulley suspension

sprung shock mounts

China, People's Republic: CSS-1, CSS-2, CSS-3, CSS-4

Description: Information on Chinese missiles is not readily available, and so the four operational missiles are treated together.

The first missile to become known in the West was the CSS-1 (Chinese designation T-1), which went into service in 1972 as a liquid-propellant single-stage MRBM based on the Soviet SS-3 and SS-4. Launch is from a concrete pad, and range with a 20-kiloton warhead is about 800 miles/1,100 km. Some 50 are thought to have been deployed in northern China.

The CSS-2 (T-2) is a single-stage IRBM using storable liquid propellants, and estimates as to warhead and range differ widely, from 300 kilotons to 1 megaton for the former, and from 1,555 miles/ 2,500 km to 2,485 miles/4,000 km for the latter. Some 50 are located at fixed sites. The type entered service in about 1971.

The CSS-3 (T-3) may be an IRBM, but is possibly a limited-range ICBM: estimates of the range of this storable liquid-propellant two-stage missile vary from 2,800 miles/4,500 km to 4,350 miles/7,000 km. The CSS-3 is silo-launched, and the small number (about 10) each carry a thermonuclear warhead of about 2-3 megatons.

China's only genuine ICBM is the CSS-4 (T-5), a small number of which (about four) are operational in silos in central China. The missile is a two-stage weapon with liquid propellants, and a 5-megaton thermonuclear warhead can be carried over a range of about 8,080 miles/13,000 km. It is worth noting that the first successful Chinese SLBM was fired in 1982, and that the type may become operational on an indigenously-designed nuclear submarine, probably derived from the 'Han' class and fitted with six launch tubes, in the mid-1980s to early 1990s.

Strengths: Though few in number, Chinese missiles offer a significant threat to the eastern USSR, and a limited threat to Moscow.

Weaknesses: Missiles are obsolescent, and highly vulnerable to a pre-emptive first-strike attack. However, the Soviets have improved the ABM defences of Moscow to take account of this Chinese ICBM.

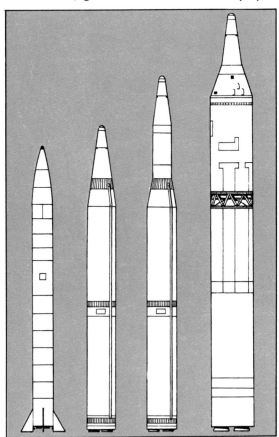

USA **AGM-86B ALCM**

Description: Winged, turbo-fan propelled, to be carried and air-launched from B-52 and other types of bomber aircraft. Nuclear warhead.

Targets: Strategic: industrial areas, weapons complexes, military facilities.

Strengths: Small radar cross-section: flies under ground based radar cover; can be pre-programmed with evasive manoeuvres.

Weaknesses: Slow, flight time to target; vulnerable to detection by look-down radar from aircraft.

History: Project began in 1972 as continuance of various previous cruise missile proposals and was confirmed in 1976 when the B-1 bomber was cancelled. Developed in conjunction with 'Tomahawk' using many common parts. First flight 1976. Now in production but future range and numbers subject to START negotiations.

Dimensions:

Length	19.5 ft/5.94 m
Diameter	25 ins/635 mm
Wingspan	12.0 ft/3.65 m
Weight	2,800 lbs/1,270 kg
Speed	ca 560 miles/900 km/hr
Range	1,555 miles/2,500 km
Accuracy	Not disclosed
Payload	W-80 thermonuclear warhead 300 Kt yield

Guidance: Terrain-comparison aided inertial navigation system (TAINS).

Deployment: To be carried in eight-missile interior rotary launchers in B-52 bombers. Tentative plans are for 165 aircraft to be so fitted, but this number could be reduced in the START negotiations. There has also been a proposal to carry two missiles underwing on the F-111 attack aircraft, and to fit rotary launchers for the B1.

Countermeasures: At present the slow flight time of cruise missiles makes it possible for some of them to be detected by look-down radars on aircraft and to be intercepted with air-to-air missiles. But the large number of cruise missiles anticipated reduces the effectiveness of this countermeasure.

Right: ALCM (AGM-86) air-launched cruise missile

Below: Impression of ASALM (advanced strategic air-launched missile) to be made by Martin Marietta in competition with McDonnell Douglas.
Intended as a possible replacement for the AGM-69 SRAM, currently carried by US strategic bombers, the ASALM is one of the new type of air-to-surface missiles with an air-breathing rather than rocket engine. The use of an external source of oxygen permits more fuel to be carried, increasing range most usefully without any increase in weight or size. No wings will be needed as the body of the missile generates lift at high speeds.

Anatomy of the cruise missile

The key to the cruise missile is a simplicity of concept with extreme sophistication of detail design in areas such as the avionics (flight-control and guidance systems), airframe (flight surfaces folded into the main length of the missile for deployment only after the weapon has been launched), powerplant (miniaturised and de-signed to last for only a few hours to reduce cost and weight), and the compact but effective warhead. The AGM-86 epitomises all these features, which allow many such missiles to be carried by existing platforms (Boeing B-52 Stratofortress and General Dynamics FB-111 and the Rockwell B-1B).

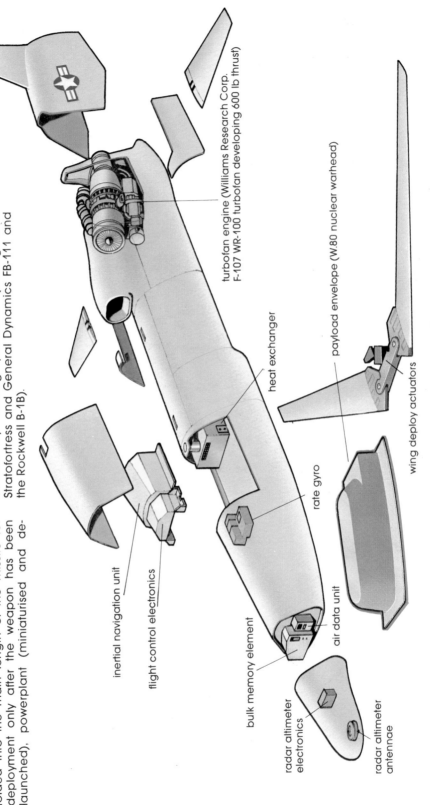

turbofan engine (Williams Research Corp. F-107 WR-100 turbofan developing 600 lb thrust)

payload envelope (W.80 nuclear warhead)

wing deploy actuators

heat exchanger

rate gyro

air data unit

radar altimeter electronics

radar altimeter antennae

bulk memory element

flight control electronics

inertial navigation unit

Tupolev Tu-16 Badger

Soviet aircraft contemporary with the B-52; first flight in 1952. It, too, has gone through a number of improvements and there are about 580 deployed with the medium-range squadrons of the Soviet Strategic Bomber Force and Naval Air Force which are likely to remain in service until the end of the century. The basic bomber model is known in the West as Badger A.

Dimensions:

Length	114 ft 2 in/34.8 m
Wingspan	108 ft/32.92 m
Max take-off weight	Over 158,000 lbs/72,000 kg
Max speed	616 mph/992 km/hr
Max range	3,580 miles/5,760 km
Armament	7 x 20 mm cannon. Bomb load of up to 19,800 lbs/9,000 kg in weapons bay. Some versions can carry missiles on wing pylons
Crew	6

Rockwell International B-1 B

This design is the outcome of several studies begun in 1962 for a supersonic strategic bomber to replace the B-52 by 1980. The programme was cancelled by President Carter in 1978 but testing was permitted to continue until all the technical evaluation was completed. In 1981 authorisation was given for the revival of the project in the revised form of a low-level penetration bomber, with up to 100 B-1B bombers to be acquired. The full specification of the B-1B is not yet known, but the following estimate is believed to be generally accurate.

Dimensions:

Length	146 ft 8 in (44.7 m)
Wing span, fully spread	136 ft 8 in (41.7 m)
Max take-off weight	477,000 lbs/216,370 kg
Max speed	Mach 1.2
Max range	6,100 miles/9,815 km
Armament	Up to 115,000 lbs/56,160 kg of SRAMs or ALCMs, or of nuclear or conventional bombs
Crew	6

Boeing B-52 Stratofortress

Development of this bomber began as far back as 1944 but constant improvements in technology led to radical redesigns and the first flight did not take place until 1952. Since that time there have been several improved models. The final, the B-52H, entered service in 1962. It is anticipated that about 315 will remain in US service for the remainder of this century.

Dimensions: B-

Length	157 ft/47.85 m
Wingspan	185 ft/56.39 m
Max take-off weight	505,000 lbs/229,066 kg
Max speed	630 mph/1,014 km/hr
Range with max fuel	Over 10,000 miles/16,000 km
Armament	20 mm multi-barrel cannon in tail. ALCMs up to 20 short-range attack missiles, or bomb load of 60,000 lbs/27,215 kg
Crew	6

Rockwell International B-1

Boeing B-52, Stratofortress

Tupolev Tu-95 Bear

These aircraft form the principal strength of the Soviet long-range bomber force. First flown in 1954, there have been several improved models of which Bear A is the strategic bomber and Bear B is the cruise missile carrier. There are believed to be about 105 Bear A and B in existence and they are likely to remain in service for many years.

Dimensions:

Length	162 ft 5 in/49.5 m
Wingspan	167 ft 8 in/51.1 m
Max take-off weight	340,000 lbs/154,000 kg
Max speed	540 mph/870 km/hr
Max range	7,800 miles/12,550 km
Armament	6 x 23 mm cannon. Bomb load 25,000 lbs/11,340 kg
Crew	6

Tupolev Tu-22 Blinder

Supersonic strategic bomber which entered service in 1960. Two principal versions exist, Blinder A which carries gravity bombs in an internal bay, and Blinder B which carries a Kitchen stand-off cruise missile under the fuselage. About 165 of both types are believed to be in Soviet service.

Dimensions:

Length	133 ft/40.53 m
Wingspan	90 ft 10 in/27.7 m
Max take-off weight	185,200 lbs/84,000 kg
Max speed	Mach 1.4
Max range	1,400 miles/2,250 km
Armament	1 x 23 mm cannon. 20,000 lbs/9,070 kg of internal bombs, or one Kitchen missile
Crew	3

Tupolev Tu-16, Badger

Tupolev TU-95, Bear

Tupolev TU-22, Blinder

95

Tupolev Tu-26 Backfire

The Tu-22 Blinder failed to live up to its promise, particularly in lacking the necessary range for a strategic bomber, and in 1971 flight-testing of a variable-geometry ('swing-wing') design began. The first version (Backfire A) apparently failed to reach its design parameters, and several design changes were made for the eventual production model, Backfire B. Over 180 are now in service of which about half are deployed by the medium-range bomber force opposing NATO in Europe and the remainder with the Soviet Navy. Production was to be limited to 30 aircraft a year by the SALT 2 agreement, but it is said to have gone up to 42 a year after the failure of the USA to ratify that treaty. It is expected that production will continue until a force of about 400 aircraft is operational.

Dimensions:

Length	132 ft/40.23 m
Wingspan, fully spread	113 ft/34.45 m
Take-off weight	270,000 lbs/122,500 kg
Max speed	Mach 2
Max range	5,530 miles/8,900 km
Armament	2 x 23 mm cannon 22,046 lbs/10,000 kg bombs, or one Kitchen missile
Crew	5

Blackjack

Blackjack is the NATO code name for the latest Soviet bomber. The design bureau is probably Tupolev. Blackjack began flight trials in 1982, and is a strategic bomber in the mould of the US Rockwell B-1B bomber. It has a variable geometry (swing) wing, and is estimated to be capable of long range subsonic cruise with supersonic dash at high altitude, and subsonic/transonic low-level flight profiles for penetration to target. The Blackjack is anticipated to be a multi-role aircraft capable of delivering nuclear or conventional bombs and air launched cruise missiles to intercontinental range. Like the American B-1, the Blackjack may be very expensive to produce in quantity and will be subject to limitation in the START negotiations. It could enter service by 1987.

Dimensions: (estimated)

Length	180.5 ft/55 m
Wingspan, fully spread	140 ft/42.7 m
Take-off weight	580,000 lbs/263,100 kg
Max speed	Mach 2.3
Max range	9,075 miles/14,600 km without inflight-refuelling
Armament	Air-launched cruise missiles or free-fall nuclear or conventional bombs
Crew	4-5

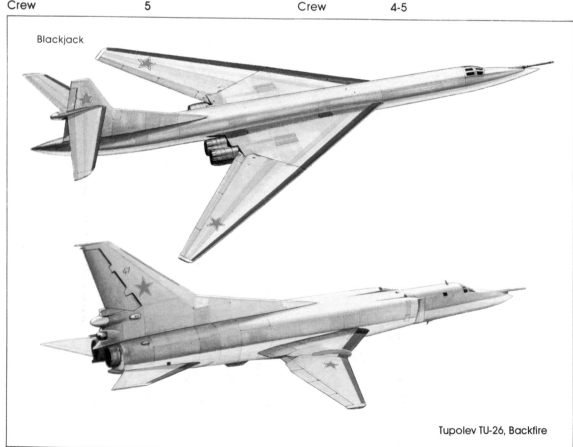

Blackjack

Tupolev TU-26, Backfire

USA **POLARIS**

Description : Polaris is a submarine-launched solid-propellant, two-stage rocket, steered by thrust vector control (TVC) and fitted with three multiple re-entry vehicles or up to six independently targetable re-entry vehicles.

Targets: Strategic: cities, manufacturing areas, other large area military, political, economic targets.

Strengths: The strength of this system lies in the mobility of the submarine, which limits countermeasures against the launching system. Once in flight the inertial guidance is invulnerable to electronic jamming.

Weaknesses: U.K. deployment of 1-3 SSBN vulnerable to Soviet hunter-killer subs.

History: Development began in the mid-1950s and was thought extremely ambitious at the time. Became operational in 1960. Original missile was Polaris A-1 with single 0.5 Mt warhead; in 1962 the A-2 missile was produced, with more powerful rockets and better in-flight control; the A-3 appeared in 1974, with more powerful fuel, better guidance, and multiple warheads. In the late 1970s a 'Polaris Improvement Program' in the U.K. developed a new warhead, and re-entry vehicle which together with other modifications to the missile permits 2-4 warheads with decoys and penetration aids, or 6 MIRV.

Dimensions: (Polaris A-3)

Length	32.3 ft/9.85 m
Diameter	54 in/1.37 m
Weight	35,000 lbs/15,876 kg
Range	2,880 miles/4,635 km
Accuracy	CEP 875 yds/800 m for triple warhead. MIRV can separate each warhead by up to 44 miles/70 km; CEP no estimate, but improved. In the region of 500 metres.
Payload	MRV 3 x 200 Kt, being replaced by UK Chevaline modification in 1983 up to 6 re-entry vehicles, mix of warheads and decoys. Likely configuration 3 x 120 Kt plus decoys and penetration aids.

Guidance: Inertial guidance system linked, for targeting, and updating, to Ships Inertial Navigation System (SINS) in submarine.

Deployment: Originally in 41 submarines of US Navy, each carrying 16 missiles, based on Charleston, SC; Holy Loch, Scotland; Rota, Spain; and Apra Harbor, Guam. Became operational in Royal Navy in 1968; currently four British submarines with 16 missiles each are in service. No Polaris SLBMs are now operated by the US Navy.

Countermeasures: The only countermeasure is the trailing of the submarine from harbour by hunter-killer submarine.

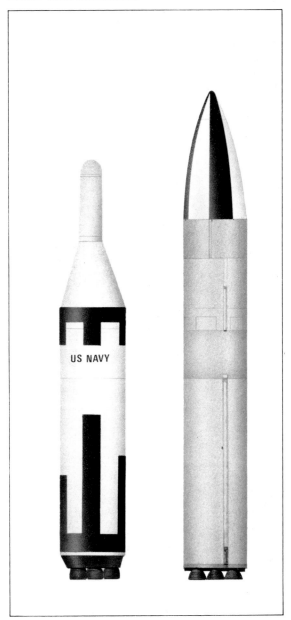

Right: Polaris A-1   *Far right:* Polaris A-3

USA **POSEIDON**

Description: Design evolved from Polaris; two-stage solid-propellant rocket carrying 10-14 re-entry vehicles each of 50 kt yield. Improvements in accuracy and payload give an eight-fold increase in military effectiveness over Polaris.

Targets: Strategic: cities, defence complexes manufacturing areas, other area military targets.

Strengths: Submarine launch vehicle can be concealed. Use of multiple independently-targeted warheads gives potential to handle up to 14 targets per missile.

Weaknesses: Complex command and control for submarine; relative loss of accuracy due to submarine launch platform.

History: Tests in 1960-62 showed that it was possible to modify the Polaris launch tubes and use a fatter missile, which would permit a bigger payload and improved guidance. First flight 1968; first underwater launch 1970; in service 1971.

Dimensions:

Length	34 ft/10.36 m
Diameter	74 in/1.88 m
Weight	65,000 lbs/29,485 kg
Accuracy	492 yds/450 m nominal CEP given by some sources
Range	2,880 miles/4,635 km
Payload	(1) 14 Mark 3 MIRV of 50 kt to maximum range of 2,485 miles (4,000 km).
	(2) 10 Mark 3 MIRV of 50 kt to maximum range of 2,880 miles (4,635 km).

Guidance: Inertial, linked to SINS for location of initial launch position.

Deployment: Replaced Polaris in 31 616-class submarines of the US Navy, based at Charleston, SC; Holy Loch, Scotland; and Rota, Spain. The latter squadron were withdrawn to be refitted with Trident in 1979-84 and will then be based at King's Bay, Georgia.

Countermeasure: The only effective counter-measure lies in anti-submarine warfare or effective ABM defence, neither of which is currently available.

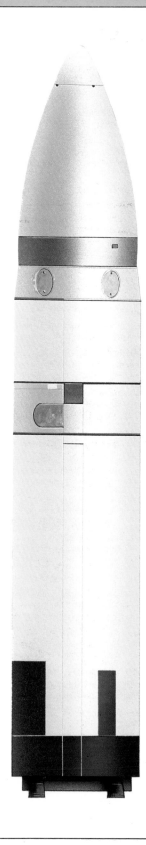

Right: Poseidon missile, submarine-launched, capable of attacking up to 14 targets.

USA **TRIDENT**

Description: Evolved from Poseidon; three-stage solid-propellant rocket, carrying multiple independently-targeted thermonuclear warheads. There are two versions: the C-4 and D-5.

Targets: Strategic: defence complexes, missile sites, command centres, manufacturing areas, other military targets.

Strengths: Submarine launch vehicle can be concealed. Use of multiple independently-targeted warheads give potential to attack up to 14 targets per missile.

Weaknesses: Complex command and control for submarine; relative loss of accuracy due to submarine launch platform.

History: Project began in 1971 as the 'Undersea Long Range Missile'. Intended to be in service by 1976, delays have been due to technical problems and lack of money. First launch 1977. Although the C-4 version of the missile could have been retrofitted into modified Polaris submarines of the UK fleet, a new class of submarine has been designed for the development missile D-5 which will replace existing C-4s in the US SSBN fleet.

Dimensions: (Trident 1) C-4

Length	34 ft/10.36 m
Diameter	74 in/1.88 m
Weight	32,000 lbs/14,515 kg
Accuracy	383-437 yds/350-400 m nominal CEP given by some sources.
Range	About 4,350 miles/7,000 km
Payload	8, 10 or 14 multiple re-entry vehicles each of 50 kt yield, plus varying numbers of penetration aids, and decoys.

Guidance: Inertial, with stellar sensor which takes at least one star sight during flight to check and refine the course. initial launch position is set by the submarine's SINS system.

Deployment: The C-4 has been retrofitted to 12 US submarines formerly fitted with Poseidon. The D-5 will be fitted into a totally new Ohio class of which 9 have so far been ordered. The first entered service in 1981 with C-4 missiles. The older boats carry 16 missiles, the Ohio class, 24 missiles each.

Countermeasures: As with other missiles of this type, the only effective counter is anti-submarine warfare.

Right: *Trident, the replacement for the Poseidon missile.*

USA **BGM-109A** *Tomahawk* **SLCM**

Description: Winged cruise missile of enormous versatility, capable of being launched from submarines, surface ships, land or aircraft. Launched by rocket booster (except when air-launched) and propelled in flight by a turbo-fan engine it can be fitted with conventional or nuclear warheads.

Targets: Depend upon deployment; in naval use, against either other surface ships or for strategic targets and land bombardment. When land or air deployed, fixed strategic or tactical targets.

Strengths: Guidance system permits high accuracy. Small radar cross-section makes missile difficult to detect and therefore to destroy.

Navstar satellite. Anti-ship role: pre-programmed flight path into target area, followed by active radar homing.

Deployment: Not completely decided; will be used by all types of fleet submarine, by surface ships, and from land-based mobile launchers.

Countermeasures: Can be detected by low level radars, and airborne look-down radars. But difficult to engage and destroy especially when used in large numbers.

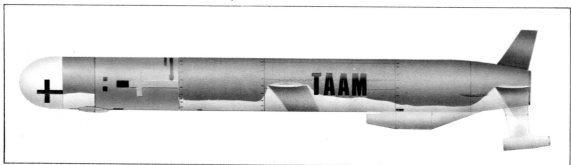

Weaknesses: Guidance system in anti-ship role does not provide same degree of accuracy. Slow flight times to target.

History: Begun in 1974 as US Navy's 'Sea-launched Cruise Missile' (SLCM) and was developed in tandem with the USAF ALCM, with several common components. First flights took place in 1976 but there were delays in perfecting the underwater launch system which did not succeed until 1978. Currently development and flight testing is continuing.

Dimensions:

Length	21 ft/6.40 m
Diameter	21 in/530 mm
Wingspan	8.3 ft/2.54 m
Weight	3,181 lbs/1,443 kg
Speed	About 545 miles/880 km/hr
Range	1,988 miles/3,200 km (land attack); 311 miles/500 km (anti-ship)
Accuracy	Not disclosed
Payload	W-80 thermonuclear warhead, 300 Kt yeild, or conventional antiship high explosive.

Guidance: Strategic role: terrain-comparison inertial guidance, with the possibility of linking to

Above: *A truly versatile weapon system, the Tomahawk cruise missile is being developed in several forms to suit it for a variety of operational tasks and deployments. In its SLCM (Sea-Launched Cruise Missile) form, the Tomahawk is to be used by surface vessels and submarines of the US Navy: as the **BGM-109A** land-attack missile with the W-80 nuclear warhead; the **BGM-109B** conventional anti-ship missile; and the **BGM-109C** conventional land-attack missile. In its GLCM (Ground-Launched Cruise Missile) form the Tomahawk is to be deployed as the **BGM-109G** with the W-80 nuclear warhead under the control of the US Air Force; and in its MRASM (Medium-Range Air-to-Surface Missile) form the Tomahawk will be bought by the US Air Force as the **AGM-109H** conventional anti-airfield missile. Illustrated here is an aerodynamic and systems test prototype.*

Right: *The Russians have not standardised SLBM launch tubes per submarine as much as the Americans, as indicated by this diagram, with the Yankee I class carrying 16 SS-N-6s, the Delta II class 12 SS-N-8s and the Hotel III class six SS-N-8s.*

Description: SS-N-6 is a two-stage liquid-fuelled rocket which uses storable fuel and carries either single or multiple nuclear warheads. It uses the 'cold launch' gas ejection system to discharge it from the submarine's launch tube, but instead of having the gas generator on a discarding section of the missile, as in previous models, the system forms part of the submarine launching system.

SS-N-8 was first thought to be simply an improved N-6, but was later decided, by Western agencies, to be a completely different weapon. Few details have emerged, but it appears to be another two-stage storable liquid-fuelled rocket, cold-launched, and with single or multiple independently-targeted warheads.

Targets: Strategic: defined in Soviet doctrine as enemy nuclear forces and their command and control systems as a first priority, with military stockpiles, training facilities and depots as the second.

Strengths: The range of this rocket is such that any part of the globe can be reached by a submarine from the 100-fathom contour around any shore. This, combined with the MIRV warheads, gives it immense potential.

Weaknesses: SLBMs are generally insufficiently accurate to be used against 'hard' point targets and would probably only be used against area targets such as cities, or large military facilities.

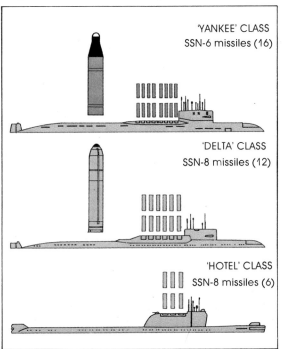

'YANKEE' CLASS
SSN-6 missiles (16)

'DELTA' CLASS
SSN-8 missiles (12)

'HOTEL' CLASS
SSN-8 missiles (6)

History: Development is presumed to have begun in the early 1960s; the first SS-N-6 to be identified by the West was seen in 1967. This was subsequently known as the 'Mod 1' and had a single warhead. The Mod 2 was tested in 1972 and deployed from 1973; this had improved propulsion giving longer range. Mod 3 appeared shortly afterwards and had two MIRVed warheads. The SS-N-6 Mod 3 was the first Russian MIRVed SLBM.

SS-N-8 first appeared in 1971 and became operational in 1973. Test firings in 1975 demonstrated its ability to fire from the Barents Sea against targets in the Pacific Ocean, over 5,590 miles/9,000 km further off. It has been identified in three forms: Mod 1 has a single warhead, Mod 2 has three manoeuvrable independently-targeted warheads.

Dimensions:
SS-N-6
Length	42.6 ft/13 m
Diameter	6 ft/1.8 m
Weight	41,900 lbs/19,000 kg
Range	1,865 miles/3,000 km
Accuracy	(Mod 1) CEP 985 yds/900 m
	(Mod 2) CEP 985 yds/900 m
	(Mod 3) CEP 1,530 yds/1,400 m
Payload	(Mod 1) Single, 1 Mt
	(Mod 2) Single, 1 Mt
	(Mod 3) MIRV, 2 x 200 Kt

SS-N-8
Length	56 ft/17 m
Diameter	6 ft/1.8 m
Weight	88,100 lbs/40,000 kg
Range	5,700 miles/9,200 km
Accuracy	(Mod 1) CEP 1,420 yds/1,300 m
	(Mod 2) CEP 985 yds/900 m
	(Mod 3) CEP 490 yds/450 m
Payload	(Mod 1) Single, 1 Mt
	(Mod 2) Single, 800 kt
	(Mod 3) MIRV, 3 x 200 kt

Guidance: S-N-6; inertial, SS-N-8; stellar-inertial.

Deployment: SS-N-6 is installed in 34 'Yankee' class nuclear submarines, each boat carrying 16 missiles.

SS-N-8 required a new class of submarine to accommodate its great bulk. These are the 'Delta' class, of which there are two types: the 'Delta I' class, built 1973-77, carries 12 missiles; there are 15 boats. The 'Delta II' class, begun in 1976, is longer and has 16 missiles. There are 8 boats in this class.

Countermeasures: As with all submarines, the primary counter is anti-submarine warfare.

USSR **SS-NX-17 and SS-N-18**

Description: These are the most recent Soviet submarine-launched ballistic missiles and relatively few details have been made public. So far as is known, SS-NX-17 is a solid-fuelled two-stage missile with post-boost propulsion, a feature which adds velocity to the warhead during the final stages of flight and also, usually, indicates the ability for the MIRV-bus to manoeuvre.

SS-N-18 appears to be a parallel development, much the same but using storable liquid propellant.

Targets: Strategic: defined in Soviet doctrine as enemy nuclear forces and their command and control systems as priority, with other military targets as secondary.

Strengths and Weaknesses: Insufficient is known of these weapons to assess any particular strength or weakness, but the limited number of SS-NX-17 missiles in use suggests that there are technical problems connected with it.

History: Both these missiles began testing during 1975 and entered service in 1977. The programme of submarine building to adapt to these missiles is not expected to be complete before 1985.

Dimensions:
SS-NX-17
Length	36.25 ft/11 m
Diameter	5.5 ft/1.65 m
Weight	Not known
Range	2,700 miles/4,400 km
Accuracy	1,640 yds/1,500 m
Payload	Single, ? Mt

SS-N-18
Length	46.25 ft/14.1 m
Diameter	6 ft/1.8 m
Weight	Not known
Range	5,000 miles/8,000 km
Accuracy	CEP 1,530 ft/1,400 m
Payload	(Mod 1) 3 x 200 Kt
	(Mod 2) 1 x 450 Kt
	(Mod 3) 7 x 200 Kt

Guidance: Guidance in both missiles is believed to be inertial, assisted by stellar observations.

Deployment: SS-NX-17 is carried on the Yankee II class submarines, 12 missiles being mounted. So far as is known, only one submarine of this class has been launched, SS-N-18 missiles are fitted to the Delta III class, of which there are 13 in service. These carry 16 missiles each.

Countermeasures: Anti-submarine warfare; early warning and anti-missile system.

Below: *SS-NX-17. Fired from Yankee II submarine — carries only single re-entry vehicle (RV) to date.*

Bottom: *SS-N-18. Fired from Delta III submarine — Mod. 1 carries 3 MIRVs*

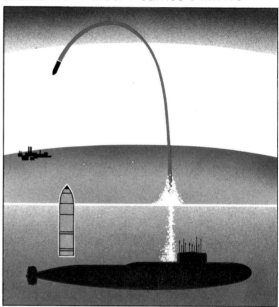

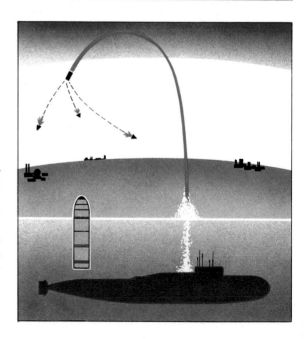

Description: MSBS (Mer-Sol-Ballistique-Strategique) is a medium-range, three-stage, submarine-launched, solid propellant missile carrying a nuclear warhead. The M.20 version is essentially the earlier M-2 with an improved warhead (originally the penaids-equipped and hardened MR-60, replaced from 1980 with the lighter MR-61). The M-2 was an improved version of the original M-1 with a more powerful second stage to increase range.

Targets: Strategic: cities, industrial areas, military complexes.

Strengths: As with all submarine-launched missiles, the main strength of the M-20 lies in the concealability of the submarine.

Weaknesses: Complex command and control for SSBN; relative loss of accuracy for being submarine launched.

History: Project began about 1963; first test vehicles flown 1967; complete missile tested in November 1968; first submarine equipped with the M-1 was Le Redoutable in December 1971; the M-2 improved version had an uprated second stage developing more power for a longer burn period, so extending range considerably; the improved M-20 version of the M-2 entered service in 1977, and was really the M-2 fitted with a more powerful warhead incorporating penetration aids and hardening against ABM detonations; from 1980 a lighter version of this warhead was installed; an M-4 is currently under development, to enter service in the late 1980s.

Dimensions:

Length	34 ft/10.4 m
Diameter	4.9 in/1.5 m
Weight	44,091 lbs/20,000 kg
Accuracy	Not disclosed
Payload	Single nuclear warhead 1 Mt, with penetration aids, anti-ABM hardening, etc.
Range	1,926 miles/3,100 km (M-2) 1,925 miles/3,100 km

Guidance: Inertial, using technology licensed from USA.

Deployment: Carried by five SNLE (Sous-Marine Nucleaire Lance-Engins) missile submarines of the French Navy, S610 to S614. Each carries 16 missiles in two rows of eight, aft of the sail. The latest SNLE (L'Inflexible) is the lead craft of a new improved class and a seventh boat (S655 Gymnote) is fitted out as an experimental vessel for

trials of various missile features for the SNLE force, and has two tubes for trials of the larger-diameter (6.3 ft/1.92 m) M-4. When this M-4 reaches service, it can be retrofitted to the existing SNLE force with the aid of an extensive modification programme, though it is more likely that the new class will use the M-4. All the SNLEs are based at the Ile Longue near Brest.

Countermeasures: Anti-submarine warfare against the carrier is the only effective countermeasure.

Below: MSBS M-1

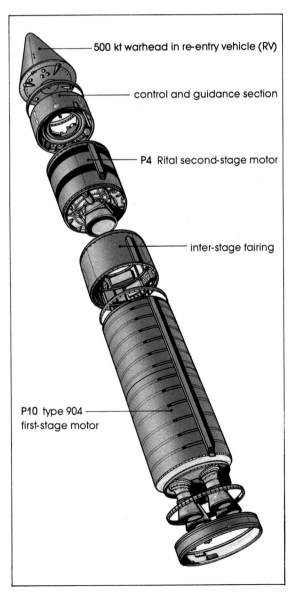

- 500 kt warhead in re-entry vehicle (RV)
- control and guidance section
- P4 Rital second-stage motor
- inter-stage fairing
- P10 type 904 first-stage motor

USSR **ABM-1B, GALOSH**

Weight	72,000 lbs/32,700 kg
Range	200 miles/325 km
Accuracy	Not known
Payload	Single manoeuvrable warhead, nuclear, 2-5 Mt

Description: 'Galosh' is the only anti-ballistic missile in use, the comparable American system having been abandoned. It is a three-stage solid-propellant rocket carrying a multi-megaton warhead designed to detonate outside the earth's atmosphere and destroy incoming ballistic missiles.

Targets: Re-entry vehicles.

Strengths: Its existence means that it must be accounted for in the calculations of Western and Chinese deterrent systems. Latest versions are said to have a manoeuvrable warhead which can 'loiter' in space until warheads are distinguished from decoys, re-starting its propulsion unit several times to maintain speed, and then accelerate for the final home and kill.

Weaknesses: Its principal weakness is that there are not enough installations to safeguard a large scale attack against Moscow, the only area that may be protected under the provisions of the ABM agreement.

History: The missile, in its transport container, was first seen in 1964, and the ABM system was operational by 1968.

Dimensions:

Length	65 ft/19.8 m
Diameter	8.3 ft/2.57 m

Guidance: Linked to Moscow ABM radars.

Deployment: There were originally four sites distributed around Moscow with a total of 64 launchers. Two sites have been deactivated to leave only 32 missiles operational. There are also 'Dog House' 'battle management' radars, 'Triad' engagement radars, and 'Chekhov' target/missile tracking radars forming part of the control system for this complex, and there are a number of 'Hen House' early warning radars as far away as Irkutsk, Latvia, and near the Barents Sea. Although permitted by the terms of the SALT agreement to deploy up to 100 launchers of this type, the Soviets appear not to have taken up the option; research and development of ABM systems is permitted and actively pursued by both Superpowers.

Countermeasures: Since this is a purely defensive system, a counter-countermeasure is the appropriate term. Since the technology of the system is now nearly twenty years old it seems safe to assume that modern sophisticated decoys and penetration aids could defeat the missile, whilst homing anti-radar weapons could deal with the fire control part of the system. This remains true even if parts of the Galosh have been significantly improved.

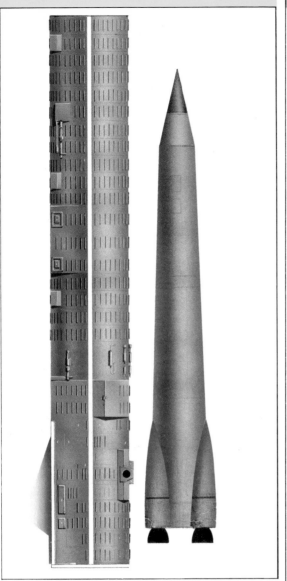

Above: ABM-1 Galosh anti-ballistic missile missile and missile launch tube

Left: ABM-1 Galosh anti-missile system on its transport container

FRANCE **PLUTON**

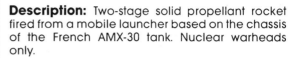

Description: Two-stage solid propellant rocket fired from a mobile launcher based on the chassis of the French AMX-30 tank. Nuclear warheads only.

Targets: Rear area tactical targets-HQs, railheads, troop or vehicle concentration areas; or battlefield tactical targets — troop concentrations, HQs, communications centres.

Strengths: Mobility. Wide variation in trajectory to permit covering the battlefield area.

Weaknesses: Comparable to those for Lance.

History: Became operational in 1974, and is the only missile of its type ever successfully developed by a Western European country; 120 launchers were originally planned, but this was cut to 42 on economic grounds. A 'Super Pluton' is said to be under development for the late 1980s.

Dimensions:

Length	25 ft/7.64 m
Diameter	25.6 ins/650 mm
Fin span	55.7 ins/1.41 m
Weight	5,340 lbs/2,423 kg
Range	6-75 miles/10-120 km
Accuracy	CEP 164-328 yds/150-300 m
Payload	(a) Nuclear, 25 Kt, for rear area targets.
	(b) Nuclear, 10-15 Kt, for battlefield targets.

Guidance: Inertial, fed with target data from the computer which controls the central firing system.

Deployment: Five Pluton regiments have been formed: 3rd Regt, Mailly-le-Camp; 25th Regt, Suippes; 32nd Regt, Hagenau; 60th Regt, Laon-Couvron; 74th Regt, Belfort. Each is dispersed through a 4,000 sq miles/10,000 sq km area, and each launcher is programmed with several firing positions.

Countermeasures: The only effective countermeasure for supersonic short-range battlefield missiles is to find and attack the launcher, which is relatively simple unless the number of launchers is large.

Left: Pluton

USA **PERSHING**

Description: Pershing is a two-stage solid-fuelled rocket carrying a nuclear or conventional warhead. It is mobile and air-transportable and is deployed in Europe by the US and West German armies.

Targets: Battlefield tactical targets — troop and equipment concentrations, headquarters, communications centres etc.

Strengths: Mobility, accuracy, very high probability of penetration to target.

Weaknesses: Command and control complex and vulnerable under some circumstances.

History: Development began 1958 and was the first time the US Army had assigned a whole weapon system to an outside contractor (Martin-Marietta). First flight 1960, in 1967 production changed to Pershing 1A, the same missile but on a new launch system based on wheeled vehicles instead of tracked carriers, which made the system air-mobile in a C130 aircraft. Pershing 2 is now appearing in service for the USA, using improved guidance and extended range. Studies are also under way to use Pershing as the proposed 'conventional airfield attack missile' for cratering airfields at long range.

Dimensions:

Length	34 ft 9 in/10.6 m
Diameter	39.5 in/1.0 m
Weight	10,141 lbs/4600 kg
Range	100-450 miles/170-720 km
	Pershing 2 800 miles/1500 km
Accuracy	Pershing 1: CEP 400 m. Pershing 2: CEP 40 m
Payload	(a) Nuclear: 400 kt
	(b) Nuclear: 60-100 kt; 250 kt (Pershing 2)
	(c) High explosive/fragmentation

Guidance: Inertial. Pershing 1A had an improved system which allowed three missiles to be programmed and launched at once. Pershing 2 could use a video area-correlation system for the terminal part of the trajectory which compares the view of the oncoming target with a stored picture and corrects trajectory until the two match.

Deployment: 108 missiles are deployed by the US 7th Army in Germany, 72 by the Federal German Army, with nuclear payloads under US control.

Countermeasures: As with all mobile missile launchers, the only effective countermeasure is to find and destroy the launch unit.

Below: The Pershing 2 is due to enter service in the mid-1980s to provide the US Army in Europe with a more capable theatre nuclear weapon than the shorter range and comparatively inaccurate Pershing 1. One of the keys to the type's survival is its mobile deployment with a transporter/erector and support vehicles for movement and then rapid deployment in firing mode with accurate launch and target data.

The key to the Pershing 2's accuracy lies in the Goodyear-manufactured RADAG (Radar Area Guidance) system. This becomes operational in the terminal phase of the flight, and compares active radar returns from the target area with stored images of the area; computer correlation of the two then generates steering commands for the re-entry vehicle, resulting in so great a degree of accuracy that only a modest nuclear warhead need be fitted. The use of an earth-penetrator warhead permits the destruction of targets such as command bunkers up to a depth of 100 ft/30 m underground.

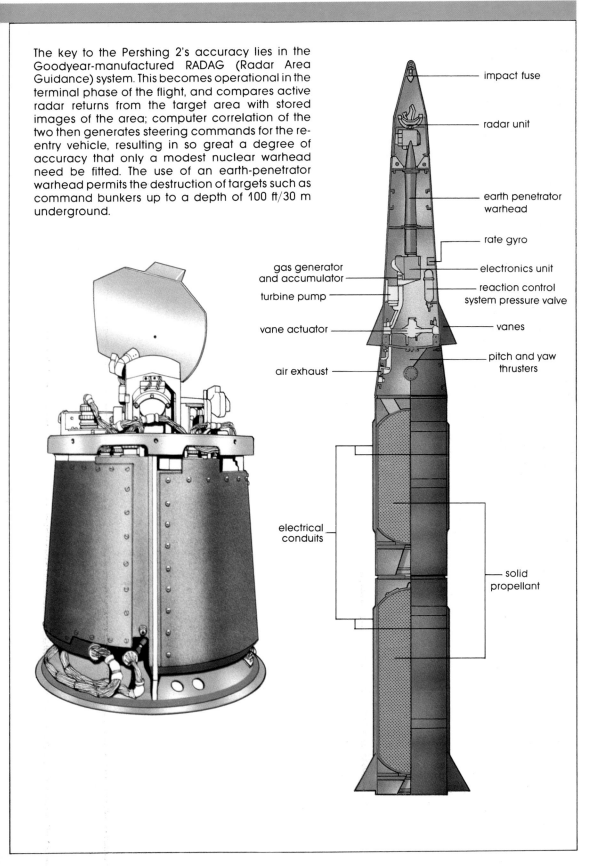

impact fuse

radar unit

earth penetrator warhead

rate gyro

gas generator and accumulator

electronics unit

turbine pump

reaction control system pressure valve

vane actuator

vanes

air exhaust

pitch and yaw thrusters

electrical conduits

solid propellant

USA **LANCE**

Description: Two-stage rocket using storable liquid propellent, designed as a battlefield support system. The system is dispersed to launch positions during crisis; the nuclear warhead is under American custody by crews from the Special Ammunition Storage sites.

Targets: Tank formations at the rear of the first echelon of attacking Warsaw Pact forces with low yield nuclear weapons, or conventional high explosive warheads.

Strengths: Its major strength is that the threat of its possible use forces tank groups to maintain dispersed formations from which it is difficult to concentrate firepower to effect a breakthrough of NATO conventional defences.

Weaknesses: High vulnerability to destruction in launch position through action by special forces, air strikes, artillery or surface to surface missiles.

History: Developed during the mid-1960s, entering US service in 1972. Adopted by many NATO armies under the dual-key arrangement for control of the nuclear warheads. Over 2000 have been built. Modifications are recurrent.

Dimensions:

Length	20.25 ft/6.17 m
Diameter	22 ins/560 mm
Weight	2,900 lbs/1,315 kg with nuclear warhead
Range	.75 miles/120 km with nuclear warhead 45 miles / 70 km with conventional warhead
Accuracy	Varies with warhead and range. CEP 164 ft/50 metres given as nominal figure by some sources.
Warheads	(a) Low yield nuclear fission 10 kt range Fission-fusion (Enhanced Radiation) 10 kt
	(b) Conventional high explosive
	(c) Terminally-guided-submunitions (not deployed)

Guidance: Inertial

Deployment: 36 launchers with US forces in Germany, 26 launchers with forces of the Federal Republic of Germany, 12 launchers with the British Army of the Rhine, 6 launchers with the Netherlands Army, 1 launcher with the Italian Army. Also supplied to Israel, though quantities undisclosed.

Countermeasures: Destruction by special forces.

Below: Lance on towable unit transported by CH-47 Chinook helicopter

USSR **FROG/SS-21 SERIES**

Description: The FROG (Free-flight Rocket Over Ground) is the NATO designation for a series of Soviet missiles which have solid propellant rockets designed to deliver nuclear, conventional high explosive, or chemical/biological agent warheads. The original series of FROG missiles has been superseded by the recent introduction of a new missile designated SS-21.

Targets: Troops, command centres, supply lines.

Strengths: Deployed in large numbers.

Weaknesses: Target acquisition and command, control, and communication problems.

History: The FROG series first appeared in the late 1950s the latest version (FROG 7) began deployment in 1965. Deployed throughout the Warsaw Pact armies, though nuclear warheads are retained under strict Soviet control for use by their forces only. No dual-key arrangements comparable to NATO are known to exist. Later versions have been supplied to the armies of Iraq, Egypt, North Korea, Syria, and Libya. The SS-21 is currently replacing the FROG 7 in the Western Theatre. The system has considerably improved accuracy and increased range over its predecessor.

Dimensions: (FROG 7)

Length	29.5 ft/9.0 m
Diameter	23.6 in/600 mm
Weight	5,500 lbs/2,500 kg
Range	45 miles/70 km
Accuracy	varies with warhead and range. CEP 248 ft/400 metres given as nominal figure by some sources.
Warhead	(a) nuclear, low kiloton range yield, fission
	(b) conventional high explosive 450 kg/TNT equivalent
	(c) chemical agent

Guidance: FROG 7, simplified inertial SS-21, inertial.

Deployment: Some 500 FROG 7 have been deployed. But if comparable numbers of SS-21s are to be expected as replacements some 400 would be deployed in the Western Theatre facing NATO, 100 deployed against China.

Countermeasures: Destruction by special forces.

Below: Frog-7 battlefield support missile on 2IL-135 vehicle

USSR **SS-20**

Description: The SS-20 is a two-stage solid-propellant missile, and was developed as a replacement for the SS-4 and SS-5 missiles. The SS-20 is a land-mobile weapon system, intended for widespread deployment as an IRBM, though its excellent range performance takes it almost into the bracket of a lightweight ICBM. The missile is carried on a wheeled transporter-erector-launcher, and each launcher is accompanied by another vehicle for control and launch. Reloads are available from central deployment locations. The type is designed for use from pre-surveyed sites, which provide a relatively low CEP. Three versions have been observed during development; the deployed model being configured for the delivery of three multiple independently-targetable re-entry vehicles.

Targets: Theatre/Strategic, defined by the Soviet armed forces as enemy nuclear forces (in this instance anywhere in Western Europe, South West Asia and China) and their command and control

Dimensions
SS-20

Length	34.5 ft/10.5 m
Diameter	4.5 ft/1.4 m
Weight	28,600 lbs/13,000 kg
Range	about 4,600 miles/7,500 km for the SS-20 Model 3
Accuracy	(Model 2) CEP 440 yds/400 m
Payload	(Model 1) Single, 1.5 Mt
	(Model 2) MIRV, 3 x 150 kt
	(Model 3) Single, 50 kt

Guidance: Inertial

Deployment: The SS-20 is a fully mobile system, and is widely deployed on both the eastern and the western border regions of the USSR. Some 315 are estimated to be deployed; 330 or more launchers anticipated by the end of 1983; and a possible maximum of 465 launchers towards the second half of the 1980s.

Below: SS-30 on transporter erector launcher.

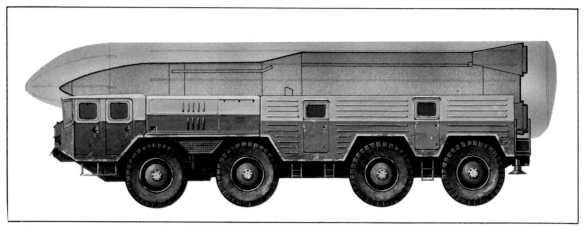

systems as priority, with other military targets as secondary.

Strengths: The SS-20 with three MIRVs is capable of dealing with three major targets in a single launch. The SS-20 is also easily concealed and capable of rapid redeployment, and reloading.

Weaknesses: The system is highly effective and has few obvious weaknesses.

History: Developed in the early part of the 1970s, the SS-20 began to enter service in 1977, and since that time the system has been widely deployed with about two-thirds targeted against Western Europe and the remaining one-third against China, South Korea and Japan. It is believed that the Soviet forces will deploy a maximum of about 465 launchers by the time production is complete.

Countermeasures: There is no effective countermeasure available for the threat posed by the SS-20, which is very difficult to detect except during the short period necessary for deployment and firing. Thus the only response to the the SS-20 is early warning and, perhaps, an anti-missile defence system.

USA **ASROC**

Description: An all-weather ship-launched ballistic missile consisting of an acoustic homing torpedo or a nuclear depth charge attached to a sold-propellant rocket motor. It is fired from an eight-tube launcher or from a Terrier missile launcher.

Targets: Submarines.

Strengths: Rapid attack against located targets.

Weaknesses: The weapon is totally dependent upon accurate location of the target.

History: Developed in the mid-1950s, entered service 1960, has been periodically improved by better torpedoes. In service and likely to remain so for several years. But nuclear depth charges have been reduced in number and could be phased-out of service.

Dimensions:

Length	15 ft 1 in/4.60 m
Diameter	12.6 in/320 mm
Weight	959 lbs/435 kg
Range	6 miles/10 km
Accuracy	Not known
Payload	(a) Honeywell Mark 46 torpedo
	(b) Nuclear depth charge low kiloton range.

Guidance: Semi-active acoustic homing (on submarine noise) torpedo. No guidance in the case of depth charge.

Deployment: In use in US Navy on 27 cruisers, 87 destroyers and 65 frigates; also in use by navies of Japan (15 destroyers, 11 frigates); Spain (5 destroyers, 5 frigates); Greece (4 destroyers); Taiwan (4 destroyers); Canada (4 frigates); West Germany (3 destroyers); Turkey (3 destroyers); Italy (1 cruiser), Brazil, South Korea and Pakistan (2 destroyers each). Only the US Navy has nuclear capability.

Below: Asroc

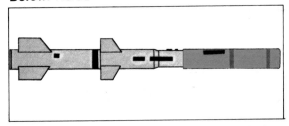

Countermeasures: No effective counter-measure exists against a nuclear depth charge. Acoustic decoys and other countermeasures available against torpedoes.

Below: Diagram showing Asroc in action

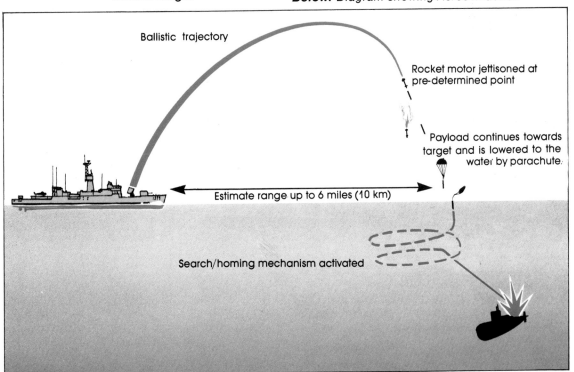

Ballistic trajectory

Rocket motor jettisoned at pre-determined point

Payload continues towards target and is lowered to the water by parachute.

Estimate range up to 6 miles (10 km)

Search/homing mechanism activated

USA **SUBROC**

Description: A submarine-launched missile which follows a short underwater course before transferring to an air trajectory for the major portion of its journey to the target. It is essentially a nuclear depth charge propelled by a solid-fuel rocket motor. At the determined point the depth charge separates from the rocket and follows a ballistic trajectory to enter the water close to the target, after which it sinks to a pre-determined depth and detonates.

Targets: Submarines, particularly those carrying SLBMs.

Strengths: Effectiveness of weapon depends on accurate location of target.

History: Development began in 1955, weapon entered service 1966. Still in service and likely to be replaced only by advanced conventional alternative with similar characteristics.

Dimensions:

Length	20.5 ft/6.25 m
Diameter	21 ins/533 mm
Weight	4,085 lbs/1,853 kg
Range	35 miles/56 km
Accuracy	Not known
Payload	Nuclear, low kiloton range.

Guidance: Inertial.

Deployment: Four to six Subroc are carried in all US nuclear submarines and in some fleet attack submarines (approximately 75 in all). The missile is launched from the standard torpedo tube and can be carried in readiness for long periods of time without inspection or maintenance.

Countermeasures: There is no counter to a nuclear depth charge.

Right: Subroc

USA **NEW JERSEY**

Description: After the two units of the 'Yamato' class, the four members of the 'Iowa' class were the largest battleships ever built, their hallmarks being good firepower and protection (with a high level of internal compartmentalisation and damage-control capability), high speed (33 knots) and excellent range (15,000 miles/24,140 km at 17 knots). Basic physical characteristics are an overall length and beam of 887.2 ft/270.4m and 108.2 ft/33 m respectively, and a full-load displacement of 58,000 tons. The four ships, all laid down and commissioned in the Second World War, are **Iowa, New Jersey, Missouri** and **Wisconsin**. All four ships were operational during the Korean War (1951-1953), and **New Jersey** served as a shore-bombardment vessel in 1968 and 1969 during the Vietnam War.

It is now planned that all four ships be brought back into active service as multi-role combat vessels, **New Jersey** having been recommissioned in 1983, to be followed in 1985 by **Iowa** and later in the decade possibly by **Missouri** and **Wisconsin**. Each recommissioned vessel is to have much revised armament and electronics installed in two phases, the first on recommissioning and the second during a later overhaul. The recommissioned vessel will be suited to several roles, including co-operation with the task forces centred on the US Navy's attack carriers in high-threat areas, semi-independent operations in medium-threat areas and fully independent operations in support of amphibious landings in low-threat areas.

Strengths: The main assets of the recommissioned vessels will be their versatile armament fit, with nine 16-in/406-mm guns firing out to a range of 23 miles/37 km, four SUBROC launchers for defence against submarines, four quadruple Harpoon missile launchers for attacks on enemy shipping, and four launchers with a total of 32 Tomahawk cruise missiles for attacks on land and sea targets. The defence of the ship against sea-skimming missiles is entrusted to four 20-mm Phalanx close-in weapon systems (CIW), while anti-submarine capability is enhanced by the provision of four LAMPS helicopters. The Phase II update will provide hangarage and a flightdeck for 12 V/STOL AV-8B Harrier II aircraft (by the removal of the after main-armament turret) and the replacement of all surviving 5-in/127-mm twin mounts with VLS (vertical launch system) Tomahawk provision.

Weaknesses: These include high overall cost for each refitted ship, and the possible operational problems attendant upon specialisation.

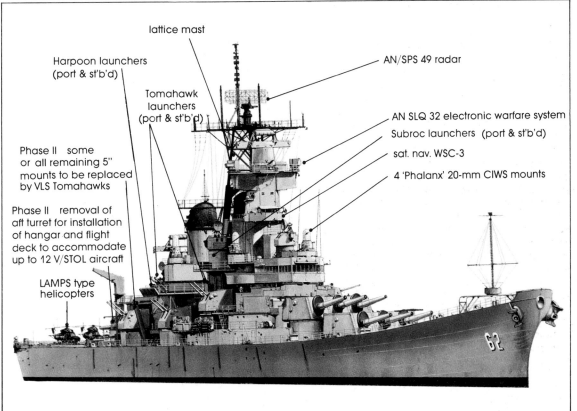

lattice mast

Harpoon launchers (port & st'b'd)

Tomahawk launchers (port & st'b'd)

Phase II some or all remaining 5" mounts to be replaced by VLS Tomahawks

Phase II removal of aft turret for installation of hangar and flight deck to accommodate up to 12 V/STOL aircraft

LAMPS type helicopters

AN/SPS 49 radar

AN SLQ 32 electronic warfare system

Subroc launchers (port & st'b'd)

sat. nav. WSC-3

4 'Phalanx' 20-mm CIWS mounts

USSR **SHADDOCK**

Description: Winged ram-jet cruise missile boosted at launch by two rocket units. Carried by submarines (for surface firing only) and cruisers, and also used on land mountings for coast defence. Largest Soviet cruise missile.

Targets: Surface craft and land bombardment from sea.

Strengths: Powerful warhead could cause great damage with one shot; long range.

Weaknesses: Requires an aircraft to give over-the-horizon information and look after mid-course guidance; believed to be relatively inaccurate. Vulnerable to electronic counter-measures.

History: Development believed to have begun in 1957, in service 1958. Soviet Navy. Several variant models have been developed.

Dimensions:
Length	42.5 ft/13.0 m
Diameter	3.2 ft/1.0 m
Wingspan	7.2 ft/2.2 m
Weight	9920 lbs/4500 kg
Speed	Possibly Mach 2.0
Range	280 miles/450 km
Accuracy	Not available
Payload	Nuclear, 350 Kt

Guidance: Command, by radio. May have equipment for mid-flight guidance; terminal guidance by infra-red or active radar. It is believed that variant models have different types of guidance.

Deployment: In 'Kresta I' and 'Kynda' class guided missiles cruisers (total of 8 ships) and submarines of classes W (10 boats), J (16 boats) and E2 (29 boats). Outfit varies between 4 and 16 missiles according to type of vessel, for a total of 356.

Countermeasures: Vulnerable to electronic jamming during guidance and possibly during terminal homing. Also open to infra-red and radar decoys.

Below: The long range performance of the SS-N-3 Shaddock requires a double and perhaps operationally ineffective guidance sytem: from launch to the horizon the missile is guided by the launch ship's Scoop Pair radar, and from the horizon to the target guidance is assumed by the radar of a Kamov Ka-25 Hormone-B targeting helicopter.

The Kynda class cruiser carries a four-round Shaddock launcher.

TORPEDOES - MINES - DEPTH CHARGES

In no field of nuclear weaponry is so little made public as in undersea warfare. America, Britain, France and Soviet Russia have carried out studies on nuclear devices as purely naval weapons, but the rest is assumption. It is likely that the Soviet Union has nuclear depth charges and torpedoes, but the only public information is of American weapons and even that is sparse.

the nuclear naval arsenal is certainty. A conventional torpedo might miss, or it might detonate, by a proximity device, just too far away to do serious damage. Where the target is a submarine carrying twenty or more ballistic missiles, a near miss is not good enough, whereas a nuclear torpedo, mine or depth charge can be detonated some considerable distance away and yet

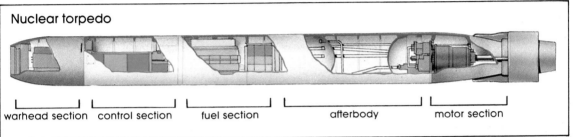

Nuclear torpedo

warhead section   control section   fuel section   afterbody   motor section

American weapons include a nuclear depth charge (used with the Asroc and Subroc weapons) and a nuclear torpedo, the Mark 45 Astor. This is provided for use in all nuclear and fleet submarines. It is 18.9 ft/5.76 m long, 19 ins/483 mm in diameter, and weights about 2,800 lbs/1,300 kg, nuclear yield unknown. The Astor is believed to travel at high speed to a maximum range of about 7 miles/11 km. The primary targets are submarines but it can be used against surface ships.

Relatively small charges of conventional

thoroughly wreck the target.

Secondary effects of a nuclear explosion probably include an electromagnetic pulse effect, which wipes out the control system on missiles and submarines too far away to be directly damaged, and leaves them militarily ineffective.

A 20 Kt nuclear mine will probably seriously damage surface warships at 875 yards/800 m range from the point of burst and cause moderate damage out to 1,640 yards/1,500 m radius; the figures for nuclear depth charges are probably

Nuclear depth bomb

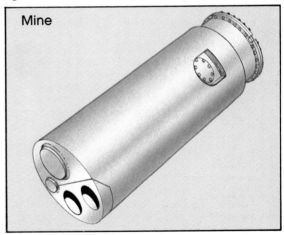

Mine

explosive can do enormous damage, bearing in mind that the submarine is operating in an already hostile environment. The conventional American Mark 46 torpedo uses a mere 97 lbs/44 kg of high explosive, for example, and this is sufficient to open up the submarine's pressure hull, leaving the water forces to do the rest. A conventional depth charge or mine measures its charge in hundreds of pounds of TNT only and yet does immense damage to underwater hulls, whereas nuclear charges are usually measured in kilotons. The reason for

similar; nuclear torpedoes may use a lower yield and inflict a smaller radius of damage.

Nuclear mines are particularly attractive when laid in a choke point, a narrow channel through which target shipping must pass — such as the entrance to a harbour or a channel between islands. Here the effect would be confined and magnified, so that upon the detonation of the mine virtually anything in the channel would be destroyed.

It is a truism of statesmanship that the effort devoted to treaty negotiations increases proportionally with the severity of the crisis to which the proposed treaty is relevant. By this yardstick the nuclear confrontation between the USA and USSR is in the middle 1980s particularly severe, with both parties actively involved in a series of negotiations designed to stabilise the balance of nuclear forces in Europe, and to reduce the enormous stockpiles of nuclear weapons held by the two superpowers. The negotiations pertinent to the two series of talks are the Intermediate Nuclear Forces (INF) talks and the Strategic Arms Reduction Talks (START). The negotiations for the former had formerly opened in 1981, and were joined in 1982 by the latter. At the same time a United Nations' initiative was launched with a second Special Session on Disarmament, which opened in Geneva during June 1982 as a proposed means to produce confidence-building measures between the two superpower blocs and to promote reductions in conventional force levels within the European continent.

Much could come of these talks (particularly INF and START), for the Americans have entered into them under considerable West European and domestic pressure for an effective agreement. The result of the earlier negotiations was a nominal reduction in superpower tensions which was then counter-balanced by Soviet development and deployment of new missiles that defeated the spirit if not the letter of agreements such as SALT I.

Relations between the Americans and the Soviets were easier after the SALT I agreement, matters only taking a strong turn for the worse after the Soviet invasion of Afghanistan in 1979. But while the US Administration began to realise the inadequacy of the previous agreements for promoting long-term equality between the two blocs, it was frustrated in its efforts to capitalise on the invasion of Afghanistan by a lack of consensus between the USA and Europe over the implications of Soviet policy. This concern has had strong political repercussions in the USA, and has certainly played a part in determining American and European approaches to negotiations.

With a few exceptions, earlier negotiations in the field of strategic weapon limitations had been broad-based, with the intention on the part of the USA of securing a wide-ranging limitation of all strategic weapons as the cornerstone of improved East-West relations. The flaws in these good intentions were revealed by US satellite reconnaissance, which revealed the full extent to which the Soviets were developing a new generation of weapons. Thus the period leading up to and immediately following the Soviet invasion of Afghanistan has been marked by a return to confrontation. Superpower relations have returned to an antipathetic position reminiscent of the mid-1960s, in which both sides stand to gain from a realistic settlement but yet seem unprepared to pay the political price.

The INF talks are concerned with the European theatre, in which the large-scale introduction of new Soviet weapons (notably the SS-20) has produced so strong a Soviet nuclear preponderance that a US-sponsored programme for the modernisation and enlarging of the European theatre nuclear arsenal has been proposed and accepted by NATO, the object being to deploy in Europe between 1983 and 1990 some 464 ground-launched cruise missiles and 108 Pershing II ballistic missiles to counter the Soviet force of SS-4s, SS-5s and SS-20s.

The first political move in respect of this proposed balancing of theatre nuclear forces was President Reagan's offer of the so-called 'Zero Option' in November 1981: if the Soviets would agree to dismantle their entire force of SS-20s, the Americans would not deploy to Europe any GLCMs or Pershing IIs. This offer was made with the full support of the European NATO powers, but the American bargaining position had no sooner been postulated than it was undermined. As the first portion of the talks (30 November to 17 December 1981) got under way with Soviet offers of a missile deployment moratorium (rejected by the Americans) while discussions took place on the exact weapons to be included in the negotiations, European support for the American position was eroded by public opposition and a Soviet diplomatic offensive designed to persuade the Europeans that they were being more flexible than the Americans.

The second round of talks (12 January to 16 March 1982) was marked by the proffer of an American draft treaty and the issue of Soviet counterproposals in a speech by President Brezhnev on 3 February 1982: this latter called for a ban on the introduction of new theatre nuclear weapon systems in Europe and for the freezing of number and capabilities among systems and aircraft already deployed in the theatre, followed by a slow reduction in numbers to a maximum of 600 systems apiece by 1985 and to 300 systems apiece by 1990. The problem lay not so much with these basic propositions but steadily increasing differences between the Americans and the Soviets as to the scope of any possible agreement. The Americans (supported by NATO) wanted the agreement to cover land-based weapons on a world-wide basis, to take account of systems' mobility, while the Soviets wanted to include all systems 'intended for use in Europe'; conversely the Soviets also wanted to include in the process all American nuclear weapons based in Europe and the British and French independent nuclear deterrents. There was some legitimacy to this, but the British and French could not find an acceptable basis to negotiate a ceiling for their deterrent forces. Also serious problems arose in relation to the nature of the weapons under discussion, for though the Soviets wished to include the British and

French forces (with strategic weapons such as SLBMs to count), they were not prepared to take into the reckoning nuclear-capable tactical fighters such as the Mikoyan-Gurevich MiG-27 and Sukhoi Su-24 recently introduced into the Soviet inventory and capable of reaching targets in Britain and France.

It was now becoming clear that the Soviet Union was seeking to turn what had begun as bilateral talks into multilateral talks, and were proposing an extreme counterproposal to the Americans' admittedly extreme initial proposal: acceptance of the Brezhnev position would have required the Soviets to have reduced their forces only very slightly while the Americans would have been compelled to withdraw all their forward-based nuclear systems in Europe, and to cancel the development of any new systems. The chances of such an acceptance were about as likely as a Soviet acceptance of the initial US position, which would have forced the USSR to scrap all its SS-4s SS-5s and SS-20s merely for the removal of the US threat to introduce new weapons to Europe.

Soviet attention was now turned to fostering an attitude of antipathy towards Intermediate Nuclear Forces among Western European populations: in March Brezhnev called for a scaling down of military activities and announced a Soviet freeze on the deployment of additional theatre weapons (though US reconnaissance showed that three new SS-20 bases, including one in western USSR, were commissioned shortly after the announcement of the 'freeze'), and in July he announced that the USSR would never be the first to use nuclear weapons. Other aspects of the Soviet campaign were more threatening: if the USA deployed new nuclear systems to Europe, the USSR would be forced to put the USA under similar threat (raising once again the spectre of Soviet land-based missiles in Cuba), additionally, because of the short flight time of the Pershing II the Soviets would have to adopt the 'launch on warning' policy with all the risks associated including accidental war.

In Geneva, meanwhile, the third session of talks (20 May to 20 July 1982) was seeking to define Europe for INF purposes, the Soviets claiming somewhat vaguely that 60° East of the crest of the Urals was the border between Europe and Asia, and the deployment of the SS-20 to the east of this line would remove the threat from Europe. The entire session begged the question of the SS-20's mobility, and the fact that the Americans claimed for it a greater range than the Soviets would concede, so that even if the SS-20s were based east of the Urals and not moved west at a later date, they could still strike into Europe (and on the Russians' own data, the missile could reach Turkish and Norwegian targets from east of the Urals).

The resumption of talks on 30 September 1982 was marked by a reversion by both sides to their initial positions, and by the collapse of the West German administration of Chancellor Schmidt. The Soviets then offered to reduce their total of SS-20s to match the British and French weapons (reckoned at 162 missiles). Then the rise to power of Yuri Andropov on the death of Brezhnev paved the way for a further Soviet move in a campaign becoming increasingly one of propaganda rather than of military reality, and on 2 December 1982 Andropov made a public announcement to this effect, though his delegation at Geneva had previously intimated that the Soviet deal would entail the cutting back of the current 600 SS-4s, SS-5s and SS-20s to about 250 SS-20s, only 150 of which would be based west of the Urals. And this proposal had the benefits of squaring with Brezhnev's ceiling offers of 3 February and, if accepted, of detaching Europe as a nuclear power from the USA. The Soviet proposal was interpreted as being an attempt to split European and American positions and was rejected by the UK and France instantly and by NATO as a whole in February 1983. The Andropov proposal nevertheless made limited concessions and it is more difficult for NATO to maintain its support for the 'zero option', for the Soviet offer met with some public acclaim in the West.

With the initiative in his hands, Andropov maintained pressure on NATO as the crucial West German elections approached on 6 May 1983: on 6 January 1983 the Warsaw Pact called for a non-aggression treaty with NATO, Soviet hints of a reduction in the SS-20 force were dropped, and tempting offers of a treaty to ban tactical nuclear weapons in West Germany were broached. All these ideas had been mooted at INF talks, but were now made public to suggest the flexibility and willingness to negotiate of the Soviets at a time when the Western position was one of some discord, exacerbated by the sacking of the chief American negotiator at the INF talks for too great a degree of compromise with the Soviets. The Western position was further troubled by suggestions by British, Italian and West German authorities that Europe could perhaps 'go it alone' to secure an interim INF agreement for a reduced deployment of GLCMs and Pershing IIs in return for a smaller Soviet deployment of SS-20s.

The Geneva talks had restarted on 27 January 1983, but little real effort was made until the election of Chancellor Kohl in the West German elections of 6 March. This strengthened the Western position somewhat, and a certain solidarity was given to NATO's position by a consensus on a proposal by Kohl that the Americans negotiate with the Soviets on the basis that NATO would agree to peg deployments of the GLCM and Pershing II to the level of Soviet SS-20 deployments. This proposal was turned down by the Soviets, and matters were effectively back to their starting point when the sixth round of talks began on 17 May 1983. At the time of writing (June 1983) it appears that the Americans have shifted away from the 'zero option' as a short-term aim, realising that a less ambitious but nonetheless worthwhile reduction of INF in Europe is better than a stalemate and that such a reduction may offer better chances for a future return to the 'zero option'. The basis for such reductions may well lie with the personal proposal of the two main negotiators (Yuli Kvitsinsky for the USSR and Paul Nitze for the USA), reached during an informal meeting on 16 July 1982. This 'joint exploratory package for the consideration of both governments' was later turned down by the Americans and Soviets, but proposed among other items a balance of 75 SS-20s with 225 warheads against 75 GLCMs with 300 warheads, 150 medium-range nuclear bombers on each side, Soviet Badger, Blinder and Backfire bombers against American F-111s, and a freeze on Soviet IRBM deployment east of the Urals.

At an altogether different level are the START negotiations, also held in Geneva. These began on 30 June 1982 and the avowed American intention was the reduction of the so-called 'window of vulnerability' that made American ICBMs vulnerable to a first strike from Soviet SS-18s. Thus the Reagan Administration was committed to securing a considerable reduction in Soviet strategic systems while securing the right of the Americans to improve their own forces so as to close the 'window of vulnerability'. There was considerable delay before the talks started, partially as a result of US reaction to the situation in Poland, and partially an inexplicable hesitancy on the part of the Administration casting doubt upon the credibility of the Americans' oft-repeated claim to want strategic arms reduction negotiations. But then President Reagan announced the American position during a speech at Eureka College on 9 May: the Phase I proposal was that both sides should reduce their strategic forces from the 1982 levels permitted under the SALT II agreement (unratified by the U.S.): the permitted levels were 1,572 launchers with 7,920 warheads (2,152 of them on ICBMs) for the USA, and 2,367 launchers with 8,395 warheads (6,170 of them on ICBMs) for the USSR; the Phase I proposal of Reagan demanded a reduction by both parties to a parity position of 850 launchers with 5,000 warheads, of which not more than half were to be on ICBMs. Reagan also proposed a Phase II in which throw-weight would be reduced to figures below the current American total (this would be of particular benefit to the USA as the USSR has always enjoyed the advantages of superior throw-weight from its ICBMs), and negotiable reductions in cruise missiles and long-range strategic bombers. The package was hardly one that would appeal to the Soviets, for the Phase I proposal demanded that while the USA reduced its launcher strength by only 722 and its warheads by 2,930, the USSR would have to axe 1,517 launchers and 3,395 warheads, 3,670 of them on ICBMs, and the Americans would lose no ICBM warheads.

Despite the fact that the proposal clearly favoured the Americans, the Soviets did not immediately reject Eureka Phase I, for it was assumed tacitly that the US proposal was more a declaration of intent that an immovable bargaining position. On 18 May 1982 Brezhnev called for a freeze on superpower nuclear arsenals, and later backed up this indication of willingness with a suggestion that the Soviets would contemplate a reduction in launcher strength to 1,800. (Oddly enough, this was close to the figure first suggested by President Carter in his first SALT II proposal in 1977.) But the Soviets insisted that any such ceiling would have to be accompanied by a ban on long-range cruise missiles, and the Soviets reserved the right to choose their own 'mix' of strategic launchers. A rider was added to the effect that any American bolstering of the intermediate nuclear forces in Europe would jeopardize any strategic limitation between the USSR and USA.

While there was general agreement within NATO that the American proposal was worthwhile, there were fears that it was too bold for any realistic chance of success. The major obstacle, it was believed, was that the turning of the emphasis from ICBMs to SLBMs was hardly calculated to appeal to the Soviets, who currently deployed about three-quarters of their warheads on ICBMs and were loath to switch to SLBMs in the face of the Americans' far superior anti-submarine warfare capability and technology. Even so, the Americans had put forward a solid basis for negotiation, and the Reagan Administration added to this with further proposals for items such as measures to reduce the chances of an accidental outbreak of nuclear war, notification of strategic missile tests, and notification of manoeuvres using strategic forces.

While these preliminary proposals were being made, both sides accepted that the terms of the unratified SALT II be followed. The USA, for example, dismantled Polaris missiles and their submarines so as to be able to introduce Trident missiles and their submarines, while the Soviets did the same to their 'Yankee" class boats in preparation for the deployment of the 'Delta' and 'Typhoon' classes. There were also accusations of violations, such as the continued Soviet encryption of missile-test telemetry, specifically limited as one of the verification measures of SALT II, and the testing of more missile types than was permitted.

So far, however, the START negotiations have produced no proposal of significance. Despite the initial optimism of the chief American negotiator, General Edward Rowny, that some success might be expected in 1983, the talks are currently deadlocked on preliminary matters such as definitions and the scope for verification measures. Various initiatives have been made, the most recent being the Reagan Administration's offer to scrap two older missiles for each new launcher deployed, and to limit each ICBM to one warhead, but there can be little doubt that the Soviets are deliberately stalling matters until some progress is made with the INF talks. As a counter the Americans have stopped further talks towards a Comprehensive Test Ban Treaty, shelved in 1980 because of doubts over the verification procedures required. As noted above, the desire for co-operation that was a characteristic of the negotiations in the 1970s, has recently been replaced by an apparent desire for competition, and this is reflected by a lack of real progress with either INF or START negotiations.

There have been other attempts to bring the two superpower blocs to a less acute political and military confrontation, some of them under the auspices of the United Nations, but these too appear to have failed: the most important of these have been the second Special Session already mentioned, which bogged down in talk that was

---

Restrictions on nuclear weapon testing

Treaty banning nuclear weapon tests in the atmosphere, in outer space and under water (Partial Test Ban Treaty — PTBT).
> Signed Moscow 5 August 1963: entered into force 10 October 1963

Treaty between the USA and the USSR on the limitation of underground nuclear weapon tests (Threshold Test Ban Treaty — TTBT).
> Signed Moscow 3 July 1974: not in force by 31 December 1981

Treaty between the USA and the USSR on underground nuclear explosions for peaceful purposes (Peaceful Nuclear Explosions Treaty — PNET).
> Signed Moscow & Washington 28 May 1976; not in force by 31 December 1981

---

general to current realities and was suspended; the Conference on Security and Co-operation in Europe, which attempted to deal with confidence-building measures and human rights at Madrid, without any real success; and the Mutual Balanced Force Reduction talks at Vienna, which strive to reduce manpower in the European theatre to 700,000 men per side and which have been ongoing for many years without success. Unofficially, an Independent Commission on Disarmament and Security Issues under the Swedish prime minister, Olaf Palme, was designed to produce a better machinery for crisis management in Europe, and also proposed a nuclear-free zone stretching for 150 km/93 miles on each side of the border between East and West Germany. This latter was seized by the Soviets as a chance to disengage West Germany from the American 'nuclear umbrella', and the USSR suggested that East and West Germany both become nuclear-free countries. The idea was rejected by Chancellor Kohl.

Strategic Arms Limitations

SALT 1

Treaty between the USA and the USSR on the limitation of anti-ballistic missile systems (ABM Treaty).
> Signed Moscow 26 May 1972: entered into force 3 October 1972

Protocol to the US-Soviet ABM Treaty.
> Signed Moscow 3 July 1974: entered into force 25 May 1976

Interim Agreement between the USA and the USSR on certain measures with respect to the limitation of strategic offensive arms.
> Signed Moscow 26 May 1972: entered into force 3 October 1972

Memorandum of Understanding between the USA and the USSR regarding the establishment of a Standing Consultative Commission on arms limitation.
> Signed Geneva 21 December 1972: entered into force 21 December 1972

SALT II

Treaty between the USA and the USSR on the limitation of strategic offensive arms (SALT II Treaty).
> Signed Vienna 18 June 1979: not in force by 31 December 1981

Protocol to the SALT II Treaty.
> Signed Vienna 18 June 1979; not in force by 31 December 1981

Joint Statement by the USA and the USSR of principles and basic guidelines for subsequent negotiations on the limitation of strategic arms.
> Signed Vienna 18 June 1979

Non-proliferation of nuclear weapons

Treaty on the non-proliferation of nuclear weapons (NPT).
> Signed London, Moscow & Washington 1 July 1968: entered into force 5 March 1970

Convention on the physical protection of nuclear material.
> Signed Vienna & New York 3 March 1980: not in force by 31 December 1981

UN Security Council Resolution on security assurances to non-nuclear weapon states.
> Adopted 19 June 1968

The 1950s were the first full decade of the 'cold war'; 10 years of hectic development of the first true strategic weapons in which it became vital to accurately assess what the Soviet Union was achieving. The best source of information proved to be aerial reconnaissance, but in May 1960 Gary Powers's U-2 was shot down on a reconnaisance mission, and it became necessary to establish less vulnerable means of surveillance.

A solution was at hand in the form of the earth-orbiting satellite: the Soviets had launched their Sputnik 1 in October 1957, the Americans following with their Discovery in February 1959. These were primitive platforms, designed primarily for experimental purposes. The prospects for reconnaissance satellites could only be assessed as the payload increased and photography could be returned to earth, by capsule. The Discovery series had a 300 lb/146 kg re-entry vehicle designed to be retrieved in mid-air by specially equipped aircraft, which then rushed the satellite's film to land for assessment.

Improvements in this field were already under development, as indicated by the success of the American SAMOS satellite in January 1961. In SAMOS the reconnaisance photographs were scanned electronically and the encoded data radioed down to a receiver station in the USA for retranslation into pictorial form. Though still not a real-time system for tactical purposes, it was a very distinct improvement over the film-recovery technique of the Discoverer. Items of interest revealed by the SAMOS could then be followed up in detail by an updated Discoverer. The Soviets were content with the delay system offered by their Cosmos series, based on the Vostok manned orbiter. In this system exposed film was returned to earth in a spherical re-entry vehicle, but the whole cumbersome arrangement required large numbers of Cosmos vehicles for worldwide coverage. Improvement came in 1962 with the development of a high-resolution type, the Cosmos 22 satellite being the first of this series.

The Americans were already moving on to a more sophisticated type of satellite system, with considerably more capable photographic equipment and associated scanning gear. The result was the evolution of 'ferret' subsatellites, which were carried into orbit on piggyback on the basic satellite. These piggyback satellites were designed to separate from the mother satellite in space for the recording of Elint (electronic intelligence) information such as radio and radar transmissions.

With the launch of between 20 to 30 satellites per year the US Air Force had almost completely covered the USSR by the mid-1960s.

Information was provided by an Itek multi-spectral item carried by close-look satellites launched by the powerful Titan/Agena combination. The Itek camera could 'see' through most types of camouflage and natural cover, securing the detail whose outline had been detected by area-coverage satellites.

In the early 1970s the 13,000 kg/28,660 lb Big Bird was launched by the Titan 3D, and payloads were area-coverage and high-resolution cameras (with scanning equipment and six re-entry vehicles for the electronic and physical return of information to earth) and side-looking radar. The Big Bird series was partnered by improved close-look satellites, but these were launched in fewer numbers as the USA had covered most of the USSR and thus needed only comparatively infrequent monitoring passes.

Information on a continuous level was provided after 1976 by the KH-11 series, with information from the camera digitalized for transmission to earth. Although this cannot produce as accurate a picture as earlier methods, it is less prone to scrambling in transmission and is more useful for real-time coverage of important targets. Other information, in which interpretation was important, was produced by scientific satellites and manned spacecraft, and it is believed that the Soviet Salyut series has played a very considerable part in the USSR's orbital reconnaissance effort. The military effort continued with small radar satellites pioneered by the US Navy in the 'White Cloud' and 'Clipper bow' programmes, a set of three satellites spaced round the earth providing comprehensive coverage of the world's oceans. The Soviets have a comparable system, but they use single short-lived platforms with powerful radar to watch the US Navy carrier task group deployments.

Early warning of Soviet ICBM tests and launches is provided by the Rhyolite class of satellite, which is a geostationary type. Four are currently in space, two operational over the Indian Ocean and the Horn of Africa, and the other two in reserve. Further information comes from the MIDAS series, which preceded the Rhyolite series. Considerable technical problems have been encountered with the MIDAS type, and only nine of the planned satellites were flown between 1960 and 1963. The idea was sound, and in 1966 it was revised in the form of three synchronous satellites with television equipment, paving the way for the fully operational Block 647 satellites in 1968. Also known as Defense Support Program (DSP) satellites, these carry some 2,000 infra-red cells and a special Schmidt telescope for visual observation of ICBM/ SLBM launch areas. Such satellites can provide confirmation within 90 seconds of a Soviet ICBM launch, and have proved this in the successful monitoring of all Soviet test launches. Additionally they guard against the possibility of a surprise first strike. Comparable capability is offered to the USSR by its Cosmos 775 satellite over the Atlantic, which is designed to watch for SLBM launches, and by the Molyina and Electron class satellites, which observe the continental United States.

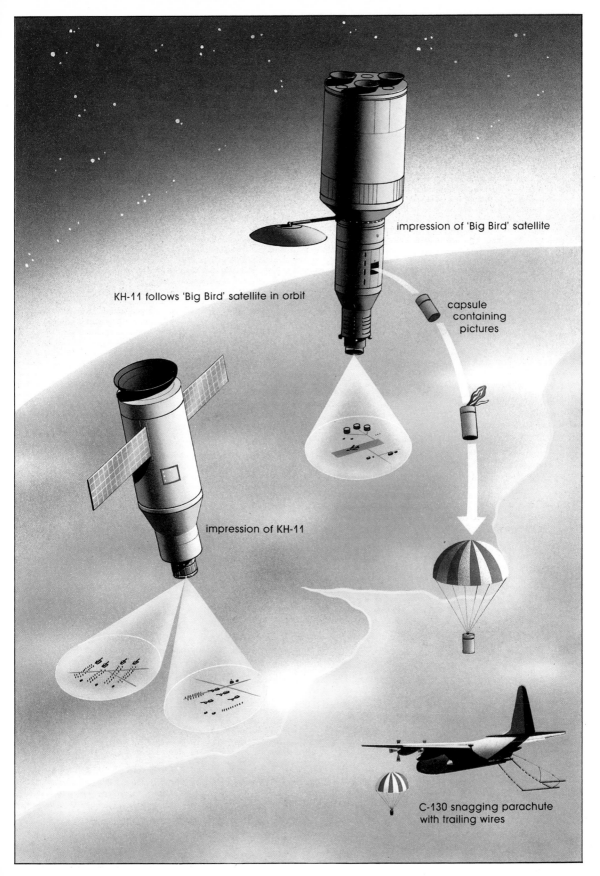

impression of 'Big Bird' satellite

KH-11 follows 'Big Bird' satellite in orbit

capsule containing pictures

impression of KH-11

C-130 snagging parachute with trailing wires

Spy satellites have many functions, ranging from the determination of potential enemies' grain production; the building up of a detailed topographical picture of hostile terrain as an element in the guidance of cruise missiles, to intelligence gathering about the build-up and location of forces, both conventional and nuclear. Many satellites have a specific function. The US 'Vela Hotel' series, for example, were launched into 60,000 mile/96,560 km high orbits during the 1960s purely as detectors of nuclear explosions. Others can be programmed from the ground-control station to cover a specific area or target. Information received from other sources, can be verified or disproved by satellite reconnaissance. The orbital parameters of the various moving satellites can be determined with considerable accuracy for several passes ahead, allowing the controller to query the satellite about the status of its various sensors, set up a monitoring programme, and then institute a search of the target area at the right moment. The US intelligence apparatus places great reliance on satellite reconnaissance, and all four basic types (imaging reconnaissance, electronic reconnaissance, ocean surveillance and missile warning) contribute to the overall assessment of the Soviet development, testing, production and deployment of nuclear weapons. The types of information are graded into estimated confidence levels of how accurate and full the information is believed to be. Exceptional levels are generally obtained from satellites (especially the imaging and electronic reconnaissance models) for the counting of all types of nuclear delivery system; moderate to high levels for the evaluation of delivery system tests (to determine factors such as physical size and weight, general configuration in terms of number of stages and number of warheads, and re-entry vehicle

performance); high to moderate for the detection and evaluation of atmospheric nuclear tests; low to high for the monitoring of warhead production, and low to high again for the monitoring of nuclear weapons development.

US and Soviet reconnaissance satellites have been used to monitor most of the major armed conflicts in the world in recent times. The USSR launched two manoeuvrable satellites in December 1971 to observe the conflict in East Pakistan (later Bangla Desh). The USSR also orbited a series of Cosmos photographic reconnaissance satellites during the Middle East War of 1973. The army coup of Cyprus on 15th July 1974 and the subsequent Turkish invasion of Cyprus on 20-22 July were observed by both the USA and the USSR by means of reconnaissance satellite orbits over Cyprus, Greece and Turkey. The conflict between Iran and Iraq which commenced on 22 September 1980 had been anticipated by the Soviet launch of Cosmos 1210 on 19 September. Cosmos 1211 was launched the day after the conflict began, closely

Right: *The diagram shows the variety of military surveillance satellites and their characteristic orbits. Nuclear detection sensors are placed on many satellites, but those specifically assigned roles for detection of nuclear explosions on the surface, in the atmosphere and in space are placed in distant (near geo-synchronous) orbits. Photo-reconnaissance satellites have low orbits whereas early warning satellites have geosynchronous or geo-stationary orbits for the United States and an eliptical orbit for the Soviet Molyina series.*

Below: *The diagram shows the regular pattern of surveillance conducted by photo-intelligence satellites.*

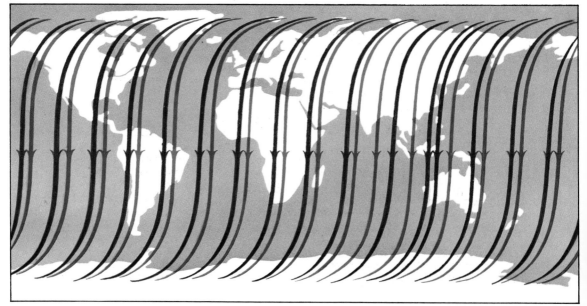

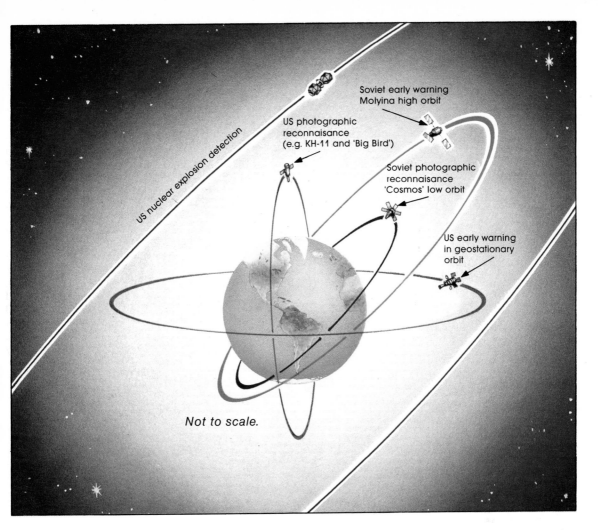

US nuclear explosion detection

US photographic
reconnaisance
(e.g. KH-11 and 'Big Bird')

Soviet early warning
Molyina high orbit

Soviet photographic
reconnaisance
'Cosmos' low orbit

US early warning
in geostationary
orbit

Not to scale.

followed by Cosmos 1212 on 26 September.

Reconnaissance satellites are obviously extremely useful for the monitoring of conflicts and crises in the world, but at the moment only the USA and the USSR have the capability to do so and are reluctant to relinquish this monopoly. The establishment of an international satellite monitoring agency to observe the implementation of international disarmament and security agreements, originally proposed by France during the first United Nations Special Session on Disarmament, would be of considerable assistance to the UN in its peace-keeping role.

Natural disasters can also be monitored by satellite, and Canada, France, Norway the USA and the USSR have been involved in a joint feasibility study on a Search and Rescue Satellite System (SARSAT).

The ground station for the SARSAT will be located in Canada and it will be used to pick up marine and aviation distress signals from all over the world.

US satellites also played a decisive part in assessing the extent to which the USSR complied with the terms of the SALT I treaty between 1972 and 1975. Assuming that the Soviets used hot-launch techniques only, the Americans were content to allow missiles to be characterized by their silo diameters. A hot-launch system limits the diameter of the missile and thus its weight, payload and range. But the Soviets had under development the cold-launched SS-17, SS-18 and SS-19, and were thus able to exploit the constraint of the SALT I agreement by installing these missiles in the silos designed for the less capable hot-launched SS-9. American satellites watched the whole process evolving. At the same time new excavation was observed and this was raised in the standing consultative committee formed to discuss issues of treaty compliance and the issue was resolved.

Satellite reconnaissance thus continues to play a decisive part in the evolution of nuclear strategy by the Americans and it must be assumed that the Soviet Union have a similar capability to monitor American and other developments. This is the essence of the present systems, for both nations have built up comprehensive reconnaissance pictures of their primary opponents, and now maintain a relatively small number of advanced satellites to monitor changes in the status quo.

It is arguable that bomb tests were necessary in the early days of the nuclear weapon age to verify that such weapons actually worked, but that once the principles on which nuclear weapons (fission and thermonuclear) operate had been validated such tests might have been prohibited. This view received concrete endorsement in the signing of a Partial Test Ban Treaty by the USA, UK and USSR. But subsequent progress towards a Comprehensive Test Ban Treaty has not been so forthcoming. The General Assembly of the U.N. adopted three resolutions in December 1982 calling for a comprehensive ban on all nuclear tests (at the same time urging a freeze on the production and deployment of nuclear weapons) expressing the frustration of many nations at the lack of progress towards a CTBT. Such resolutions are frequently made by the UN, but the body has no jurisdiction to impose such a ban (or virtually any other arms control measure for that matter), and even UN-controlled bodies such as the International Atomic Energy Authority, which among other concerns monitors the safeguards built into the Non-Proliferation Treaty of 1968, can operate only with the co-operation of the parties involved. And in the matter of nuclear weapons, some of the parties have a tendency to be less than fully co-operative.

In historical terms, therefore, it must be conceded that the early nuclear powers needed bomb tests to prove the effectiveness of the weapons on which their national securities would increasingly rest, and highlights of this early period were the detonation of the first atomic and thermonuclear devices in tests by the USA (July 1945 and November 1952), the USSR (September 1949 and August 1953, the latter date indicating how rapidly the USSR was able to close the 'nuclear gap' between itself and the USA), the UK (October 1952 and May 1957), France (February 1960 and August 1968) and China (October 1964 and June 1967). Bomb tests at these times proved that the weapons actually worked, while other tests (such as the celebrated American series at Bikini Atoll in July 1946) were designed to evaluate the effect of such weapons on armoured vehicles, warships and the like when deployed in an operational manner.

A clearer indication of the manner and objectives of such tests can be obtained by an examination of a typical series, in this instance the Chinese programme between 1964 to 1976, when the country progressed from simple fission — based devices to powerful warheads for long-range ballistic missiles, and also towards weaponised devices for carriage by aircraft. The Chinese series began on 16 October 1964 with the detonation of a primitive U-235 implosion device located on a tower, this 20-kiloton explosion confirming that Chinese scientists and technicians had been working along the right lines. The country moved a step further in 1965 with the explosion of two semi-operational air-dropped weapons: the first, on 9 May, was a development towards more powerful weapons, and was a U-235 fission weapon with some thermonuclear elements, and dropped by a Tupolev TU-16 jet bomber for an air burst with a yield in the order of 200-300 kilotons; the second, on 14 May, was a less ambitious weapon, being a pure fission device of U-235 dropped by a Tu-4 bomber and producing an air-burst yield in the order of 20-40 kilotons. Two more tests were detected in 1966: on 27 October a Soviet-supplied SS-4 missile delivered a warhead of the U-235 fission type for a ground-burst yield of 20-30 kilotons, while on 28 December a tower-mounted explosion of some 300/500-kiloton yield indicated that China was progressing with the upgraded fission type of device made up of U-235 with some thermonuclear material.

That these experiments were fast moving towards the next step up the nuclear ladder was indicated on 17 June 1967, when China detonated her first true thermonuclear device only three years after her first nuclear test — the shortest transition of any of the nuclear powers. The test was of an air-burst device of about 3-megaton yield dropped by a Tu-16 bomber; this was a U-235 bomb working on the fission-fusion-fission principle. A considerably more powerful device was tested on 24 December of the same year, in the form of an air-burst thermonuclear bomb dropped by a Tu-16, despite the fact that the estimated yield was between 20 and 25 megatons. The year 1968 was characterized by only a single test, an air-burst 3-megaton device delivered by Tu-16 bomber and comprising a U-235 weapon with some plutonium. The two tests of 1969 took place in September, and were markedly different from each other: on 22 September a fission device of about 25 kilotons was detonated under the ground, and on 29 September a prototype warhead for the CSS-2 missile was dropped by a Tu-16 for a 3-megaton air-burst yield. In 1970 and 1971 there were only single tests in each year, that of 14 October 1970 being a 3-megaton thermonuclear air-burst device, and that of 18 November 1971 being a ground-burst device of less than 20-kiloton yield, the U.235/plutonium thermonuclear explosion being a partial failure.

The pace was stepped up again in 1972 with two tests, that of 7 January being a partial failure of a U-235/plutonium thermonuclear device that was air-burst after drop from the aircraft, while that of 18 March was again apparently a partial failure, with an air-burst yield of between 20 and 200 kilotons from the thermonuclear device possibly intended as a trigger for a larger weapon. Single tests of thermonuclear devices were conducted in the years 1973, 1974 and 1975, and in 1976 there were no fewer than four tests: that of 25 January was a ground-burst, that of 26 September an air-burst, that of 17 October an underground test and that of 17 November again an air-burst.

The pattern is relatively clear: ground bursts of

Right above: An atmospheric test of a thermonuclear weapon conducted by the United States at Bikini Atoll in the Pacific Ocean. *Below:* The first test of an atomic weapon conducted near Alamagordo in the New Mexico desert.

prototype devices confirm the working of the type, which is then turned into a weaponised device and dropped from an aircraft for air-burst at the predetermined altitude to cause the optimum damage pattern round ground-zero; further developments of the type are also air-dropped, while trigger devices and 'dirty' weapons which would spread a large amount of radioactive contamination in the form of fall-out are generally tested underground.

Fears about what would now be termed ecological damage were soon voiced about such tests, especially in the light of damage and disease associated with exposure to radioactive fall-out from the numerous tests of the 1950s. On 31 March 1958 the USSR announced a unilateral suspension of tests though it reverted to testing with the first of a series on 30 September of the same year, while the USA followed with its own unilateral suspension on 31 October 1958, initially to last for one year, and, having completed its own tests, the USSR joined the USA in a moratorium on bomb tests in December 1958.

During 1959 talks between the USA, USSR and UK failed to reach agreement about comprehensive Test Bans, but the USA announced that it would undertake no bomb tests so long as the USSR did not. This was thought to be most important as a way of preventing massive atmospheric tests, with all their dire consequences in terms of fall-out. However, on 7 May 1960 the USA announced its intention of resuming underground tests (as a means of building up the information bank for the detection of such tests), and on 1 September the USSR began a series of atmospheric tests (following the successful French first test), to which the USA responded with the start of its own series on 5 September.

Such was the outcry engendered by this 'tit for tat' nuclear 'diplomacy' that the superpowers were forced to start negotiations for a partial Test Ban Treaty, which was signed between the USA, USSR and UK in Moscow on 5 August 1963, from 10 October of the same year banning bomb tests in the atmosphere, in space and underwater, and also banning any tests that might deposit radioactive material outside the territory of the detonating power. France and China are not signatories, but the French ended atmospheric tests in 1975.

The Partial Test Ban Treaty was followed by the Threshold Test Ban Treaty, which was signed between the USSR and USA in Moscow on 3 July 1973, even though this has not been ratified by the U.S. Congress the Treaty is observed by both parties. This banned the testing underground of weapons with a yield in excess of 150 kilotons, and urged both parties to keep the number of underground tests to a minimum. From time to time considerable doubt exists as to the yield of certain Soviet tests particularly during the later 1970s but in general the observance of the threshold has been good. The Threshold Test Ban Treaty covered only military tests, and peaceful underground nuclear explosions were limited to the same kilotonnage by a further unratified treaty, the Peaceful Nuclear Explosions Treaty signed between the USSR and USA in Moscow and Washington on 28 May 1976. Further proposals about the limiting of underground nuclear tests have been proposed for the 1980s further reducing the threshold yield to perhaps 75 kt per explosion, but both the utility for arms control and the verification problems posed have not been particularly conducive to significant progress.

Peace Movements

In the late 1950s and early 1960s, the UK Campaign for Nuclear Disarmament (CND) attracted a very considerable popular following and gained a measure of respect in that it also attracted eminent intellectuals, scientists, religious leaders, educationalists and writers to its cause. Mass rallies and carefully conceived propaganda helped to get the CND message over to the public, and the movement spawned comparable (but generally less effective) movements in Europe and the USA. The reasons for this initial success are not hard to find: the sudden and virtually total annihilations of Hiroshima and Nagasaki were still in everyone's mind, new intercontinental ballistic missiles with immensely powerful thermonuclear warheads were under development and deployment, the new breed of submarine-launched ballistic missiles was reaching widespread service, and atmospheric tests of massive weapons (brought to public attention by films and television) confirmed the destructive potential of such weapons while adding to fears about the long-term health and environmental hazards of fallout from the tests. But then the nuclear arms race began to settle down as the sides switched their main efforts to qualitative improvements of their nuclear arsenals, and to development of the current weapon generation; the result, so far as the anti-nuclear movement was concerned, was a dwindling of popular support as people moved away from a cause that had begun to lose its immediacy as the threat from fallout was resolved, and the fear of war between the Superpowers receded.

There remained a dedicated core to the movement, and it was this that began to build up the movement again in the late 1970s, offering the new generation of weapons as the threat to be countered. The anti-nuclear effort fell on fertile ground, for a new generation of the concerned public had emerged. These people had grown up in an era in which dispute with authority and an espousal of minority causes seemed to have become the norm, and in which youth had been taught to think more for itself. To such a public, with a strong sense of ideals but perhaps without enough thought for political realities, the possible deployment among the civil populations of the UK, West Germany, Belgium, the Netherlands and Italy of a new generation of weapons was a move that seemed unnecessary and increased the chances of a nuclear war. Thus the anti-nuclear campaign began a remarkable renaissance in 1979, the year in which NATO decided to improve its theatre nuclear capability by the deployment of cruise and Pershing II missiles. Fears about the new generation of weapons combined with a lack of appreciation for the massive deployment of Soviet SS-20 missiles (which are potentially far more devastating than the cruise and Pershing II missiles, and are the stimulus for the NATO decision), combined with an apparently hopeless domestic economic future produced a considerable wave of protest.

By the autumn of 1981 this protest was extremely vociferous, to the extent that very large demonstrations took place in many European and, to a lesser extent, American cities. President Reagan's 'zero option' proposal helped to quieten matters at the end of 1981, but it was possible to see that the protest movement was gathering strength, much encouraged by increasing demands in the USA for a nuclear 'freeze'. This strength was evident in a series of demonstrations, in every capital visited by Reagan during his European tour of May 1982, and realisation that the bolstering of the theatre nuclear forces in Europe would have to take into account the twin factors of popular (and political) opposition, and of the degree to which governments would bow to such opposition, even if it was from a very vociferous minority.

The anti-nuclear party also gained in strength during 1982 by an accession of political support from parties which had lost power since the autumn of 1981: in September 1981 the Labour party lost the Norwegian general election, in December 1981 the Socialist party left the Belgian administration, in September 1982 both the Danish and the West German Social Democratic parties lost power, and in October 1982 the Labour party failed in its attempt to be included in the Dutch coalition government. All these parties had hitherto supported (or at least not opposed) the decision to bolster Europe's theatre nuclear forces, but now saw the chance to make some political capital from opposition. The political opposition also grew with the British Labour party's incoherent opposition to nuclear weapons, with a portion objecting only to the increase in nuclear forces represented by the proposed deployment of GLCMs in the UK, another portion wishing to see the closure of all American nuclear bases in the UK, and a third portion wanting unilateral nuclear disarmament for the UK. The general conclusion of this political shift was the polarisation of the anti-nuclear lobby as left-wing and of the pro-nuclear lobby as centre/right-wing.

The whole of the opposition to INF deployment has clearly paid much less attention to the Soviet developments which brought it about. Although claims that the opposition has been fermented by Soviet 'fronts' such as the World Peace Movement in Vienna remain unproved, and in any case the results were ambiguous from a Soviet view, the solidarity of NATO on this major issue has withstood enormous pressure, if somewhat shakily at times. The strength of NATO's position has been increased first by the success of the Christian Democrat and Christian Socialist Alliance in the West German elections of March 1983, and secondly by the poor showing of the defeated Labour party in the British elections of June 1983.

Nevertheless, it cannot be imagined that the anti-nuclear lobby has failed, for the popular campaign has gained considerably in the first half

of 1983, particularly in the UK, Norway, Denmark, the Netherlands, Belgium and, to a smaller degree, West Germany. The only countries not to have developed a strong anti-nuclear lobby are Italy and France, and in June 1983 President Mitterand of France committed his administration firmly to a support of the orthodox NATO position on the Intermediate Nuclear Force issue, and Italy is committed to accepting cruise missiles.

To be expected, therefore, is a stepping-up of the popular opposition, especially as preparations for the deployment of cruise and Pershing II missiles approach completion and the first weapons begin to appear in Europe late in 1983. And while it is on the cruise and Pershing II missiles that the popular opposition is centred, there are strong indications that the movement is being expanded to encompass American nuclear weapons of all types in Europe, as indicated by the CND blockade of the American base for General Dynamics F-111 nuclear-capable strike aircraft at Upper Heyford in Oxfordshire in June 1983. NATO governments have pledged their full support for the deployment of the Intermediate Nuclear Forces, but the growth of popular opposition, as yet relatively peaceful and well ordered, may spur problems in the immediate future: the Danish parliament has already voted, against the wishes of the minority government, to curtail expenditure necessary for the development of the basic infrastructure for the deployment of cruise and Pershing II missiles; and a similar move by the Norwegian parliament was defeated by a single vote. It may fairly be said, therefore, that while the popular movement in Europe is perhaps waning a little, it is still able to secure increasingly powerful political support, and the campaign may become more bitter as the first of the American missiles arrive.

The opposition in the USA is different, for though there is an anti-nuclear lobby, it is comparatively small. Such opposition as there is in the USA wants a freeze on the development, testing and production of new nuclear weapons, and thus to fix the current balance in nuclear weapons between the USA and USSR as adequate for the security of the USA without the additional expense of new programmes. To this extent, therefore, some of the anti-nuclear Europeans may be regarded as wishful thinkers, the implementation of whose unilateralist desire would destabilise the balance of European nuclear forces. The Americans against the development of new weapons may be regarded as just the opposite, a lobby dedicated to the preservation of the equilibrium currently dominating relations between the East and West which would be upset by the introduction of new weapons into Europe by the Americans. While the European movement may rightly be called radical, and possibly a minority movement, the American freeze movement has very pronounced establishment roots, and by June 1982 enjoyed the support of very slightly under three-quarters of the US population according to opinion polls. This popular strength was confirmed by the fact that some three-quarters of a million Americans demonstrated against the Administration's nuclear weapons policy in rallies to mark the opening of the UN's Second Special Session on Disarmament.

Perhaps the most important part of the American freeze dilemma is that the American public also believes that the USA's defences should be maintained, and while sympathetic to European concerns finds the complexity and contradiction in the European debate difficult to support.

Professional armies have for many years relied on peacetime exercises or manoeuvres to provide the individual soldier and unit with experience of protracted military operations under the most realistic circumstances possible outside a real war. At the same time these exercises provide commanders and their staffs with invaluable chances to put into action the command and control functions which might otherwise remain theoretical and, perhaps, inadvertently inadequate to the test of real war. Exercises thus hone the military towards the pitch required for combat operations, and also provide commanders with experience in the real-time control of large bodies of men and material. Protracted exercises also test the stamina of men and machines, the capabilities of the supply organisation, and the flexibility of the communications system. This last is of particular importance in the modern battlefield, which has become much more complex than could have been imagined only 25 years ago.

Such exercises are essential not only for the honing of men and systems, but also for the revealing of problems that are mere inconveniences in peace but decisive in war. At the same time such exercises are extremely expensive, and it is frequently felt that such expense would be better used for new equipment or an improvement in the men's conditions. This is not a new factor, and over the years there has evolved the war game, in which an exercise is played out on paper, either in real time, to allow the 'players' to become fatigued, or in accelerated time so that the implications of the game can be approached as rapidly as possible. The development of the computer since the Second World War has increased the scope and capability of the war game enormously, allowing complexities approaching those of genuine combat operations to be built into the war game scenario.

The combination of war game and exercise is also an invaluable planning tool for actual military operations, either offensive or defensive. In such defensive operations, such as the containment of a major Soviet drive through the Fulda Gap towards Frankfurt, NATO planners start with the known dispositions of Warsaw Pact troops, their known capabilities and equipment, possible reinforcements, psychological profiles of the relevant Soviet commanders and what is known of Soviet assault tactics. From these can be postulated the likely nature of the Soviet assault, in such terms as ratio of armoured vehicles to men to artillery, speed of advance and frontage of the assault. Then, given comparable information about the NATO forces in the area, the planners can work out the likely course of events, and make alterations to the NATO forces and equipment until they have the best chance of holding and defeating the Soviet thrust. Once this has been worked out on paper, the planners can then computerize the war game to

be played out at accelerated time first, and then in real time. Both computer war games inevitably reveal the need for further modifications to the NATO plans, and the process is continued until the planners come up with a proposal that seems likely to succeed in most possible eventualities in the notoriously unpredictable conditions of real warfare.

With the teething problems worked out of the plan, it is then possible and desirable to stage the scenario as an exercise. Here the actual movements of men and equipment reveal further flaws, often significant, in the basic premise, and the planners go back to the beginning of the process so that account can be taken of factors such as higher levels of motor transport unserviceability then had been anticipated. And all this is two-sided to the extent that the planners can better perform their function while combat troops learn from experience where their procedures need to be tightened up. The result, it is hoped, is a plan that takes into account the many possible critical factors, and thus gives the troops on the ground the optimum chance of defeating such a major Soviet thrust. But of course the Warsaw Pact forces go through a similar process, honing their assault plans to provide the best chances of breaking through the NATO forces in the anticipated battlefield of the Fulda Gap to break through to Frankfurt and so down the Main to the Rhine.

War games and exercises both individually and in combination with each other, are vitally important in conventional warfare, but take on a yet more threatening role when the prospects of nuclear warfare are included, as indeed they must be in any scenario that is intended to have relevance to the current European battlefield. Both sides hope that the use even of tactical nuclear weapons (artillery, battlefield missiles and free-fall bombs delivered by fighter-bombers) can be avoided, but must inevitably plan for the use of such weapons should the other side first use them, or should the military situation so demand. Also to be taken into account is a comparable situation with biological and chemical weapons, and the need to plan for the possibility of NBC (nuclear, biological and chemical) warfare has produced what is now termed the integrated battlefield. What complicates matters so imponderably is the fact that while conventional weapons can be used as and when required without threat of escalation, the use of NBC weapons (and particularly nuclear weapons) raises the spectre of escalation so massively that it is vital to plan as thoroughly as possible for their use, offensively or defensively. The trouble is that nuclear weapons are almost 'wild cards' inasmuch as they can be used at any time or place, and are sufficiently powerful that they will totally destroy the previous situation prevailing on the battlefield. This makes it exceptionally difficult to assess the effect of such weapons on the overall

Above: A Soviet Bear reconnaissance aircraft is intercepted by Phantoms and escorted away from the area of a NATO exercise.

military picture. In conventional warfare, for example, units may suffer heavy casualties and so require reinforcements from the rear, and particular lines of communication may be damaged or removed by enemy action and the activities of saboteurs; in nuclear warfare whole units of battalion size or larger may be destroyed, requiring the bringing up of far larger bodies of men than would ever be required in conventional warfare, and whole areas may be rendered impassable by radiation and physical damage, requiring the large-scale restructuring of battle contingency plans. Other features of nuclear warfare which have to be taken into account in the planning of operations that may 'go nuclear' are the overloading of medical facilities with men suffering from radiation and burns, the incapacitation of the communications net by the ionisation of the atmosphere as a result of a nuclear explosion, and the destruction of much electronic equipment by the electro-magnetic pulse emanating from the nuclear explosion. The degree to which the complexity of planning is increased can only be imagined, but the combination of war game and exercise can at least acquaint troops and planners alike with the problems, even if detailed contingency planning is impossible in the circumstances.

The complexities added to warfare at the tactical level by the possibility of nuclear weapons are thus enormous. At the operational and strategic levels they are greater still, though it might be more accurate to describe the problems at these levels as being of greater importance but comparable technical difficulty from the commander's point of view. For in the mathematics of strategic planning it is, in comparative terms, no easier to deal with the destruction of a complete unit or even formation. At the higher command levels the inevitability of casualties on a possibly massive level is always taken into account, and 'broad-brush' planning must allow for this inevitability. But while the planning may be easier in military tacticians' terms, it is immeasurably more difficult in terms of national survival, calling for extreme caution allied with assessment of the enemy's intentions and capabilities to match just the right force to any degree of aggression. At this level warfare is more a matter of planning and producing the right strategic weapons and assessment of the enemy. Computer assessment of a host of plans, modifications of plans and constantly reviewing the perceptions of the possible enemy is the norm, but it is virtually impossible to test these war games under anything approaching an operational reality, for the ICBMs and SLBMs must never be fired if they are to be successful deterrents.

Bombers can indeed be sent on realistic exercises, but in general the strategic triad is more dependent than ground forces or naval units on the computer for the development and assessment of war plans.

Accidental War

Everyone rightly fears the possibility of nuclear warfare, the outcome of which must surely be the end of our present civilisation. But within this overall fear there lie deep-seated and somewhat irrational fears that nuclear war might break out as a result of an accident or as a result of illicit authorisation. As with all human endeavours, it is not absolutely impossible for either of these two events to occur, but the possibilities have been reduced to miniscule proportions by careful analysis and planning, the objects of which are the prevention of any accidental or illicit nuclear weapon discharges and the maintenance of each possessor country's ability to restrict the launch of such weapons to the necessary military and political crises.

The starting point for any such system of nuclear weapons safety measures must be the personnel directly involved with the launch of weapons, such as commanders, weapons system officers, and technicians in missile silos, ballistic missile submarines, nuclear bombers and surface-to-surface missile launchers. Under the US Personnel Suitability Program, men in these key positions are subjected to an investigation comparable to the UK's Positive Vetting technique to confirm the candidate's emotional and political suitability for the role, and also his freedom from the 'contamination' of possible links with the potential enemy. No such human process can be anything like 100 per cent accurate, but it does weed out those who are fundamentally unsuitable for positions of such responsibility. Those passed by the process are then checked at intervals (not necessarily regular) to establish that the responsibility or new external factors have not interfered with the original situation.

Thereafter, the initiation of an accidental nuclear war is made all but impossible by the use of a comprehensive system of physical and electronic safety measures, which ensure that before the weapon is actually committed, the requisite authority for launch has been received. The process is started (in the case of the USA, with comparable systems being used by the other nuclear powers) by the President, who has with him at all times an officer with a locked case containing the necessary codes for the start of any nuclear weapon launch sequence. These codes are chosen at random by computer, and changed at frequent intervals. The Presidential issue of the code starter merely gets the process under way. Thereafter the sequential system demands that the right ancillary codes be supplied in the right sequence and within specified time limits for each code group; any failure at this stage demands that the sequence be restarted at a high level. Through what is in effect a filtering system, therefore, the code necessary for the weapon launch crew to arm their weapon is received only after it has been checked and verified at various levels, and even then the prevention of single-man

launch of strategic weapons is ensured by the need for two or more physically separated operations to be performed simultaneously before the weapon can be launched. In the British V-bombers of the 1960s, for example, it was necessary for each of the crew to undertake a specific action in precisely the right sequence before a nuclear bomb or missile could be armed and released. The physical separation of the crew stations made it impossible for any one man to perform all four or five sets of actions in the short time involved.

Further security is given to the system by the physical separation of the nuclear warhead from the delivery system as much as is practical, with missiles and aircraft armed only at the last minute. The warheads are guarded by special troops at their secret dumps and en route to the launcher site, and a measure of additional security is provided to many tactical weapons in the NATO arsenal in Europe by the provision of two-nation launch crews: the Pershing IA surface-to-surface missiles operated by the West German air force, for example, are useless without the warhead which can be supplied only by the Americans, who control all the tactical nuclear warheads in Europe apart from those of French and British ownership. The U.S. warheads are stockpiled in Turkey, Greece, Italy, West Germany, Belgium and the UK. But by bilateral agreements under agreed NATO guidelines for use of nuclear weapons the United States has undertaken to use the weapons only with the consent of the host-nation.

The Soviets employ a comparable physical security system, for while the launchers may be in the hands of Soviet troops or those of other Warsaw Pact countries, the nuclear warheads are stockpiled and guarded by the KGB (state security police), and will only be released to operational units on receipt of orders from the Soviet political authorities. The Soviet system thus provides for political security of nuclear warheads (in effect a dual-key system), which are generally transported to the launch site by helicopter with a powerful escort of helicopter gunships.

It is clear, therefore that all possessors of nuclear weapons are vitally concerned with the prevention of accidental war, and protect their nuclear weapons most carefully with complex and constantly monitored systems of electronic and physical safeguards. It is just conceivable that a well organised and well funded conspiracy might be able to get through to such a weapon, but there is no way in which such a group of conspirators (let alone a deranged individual) could detonate a nuclear weapon even with the most unlikely collusion of individuals in the highest command echelons. To all practical intents, therefore, the possibility of nuclear war caused by unauthorised action can be ruled out.

Comparable safeguards protect the nuclear warfare systems from being triggered by a false alarm. Such public fears are raised by not infrequent press reports about the issuing of an alarm based on radar returns that turn out to be the result of bird migration, freak climatic conditions or meteorite showers. But in fact such alarms should rather give confidence to the public, for they indicate that the early warning systems on which deterrence depends are functioning well. No attack can be launched on the unsupported

the region of 40 over a period of 23 years, ten of which were serious in that the warheads were lost at sea or broke up, spreading radioactive contamination over a significant area. Of the serious accidents some six were with systems of the western powers and four with the Soviet Union. The RAF Vulcan shown has been one of the most reliable systems in service. Submarines by comparison have had roughly the same overall

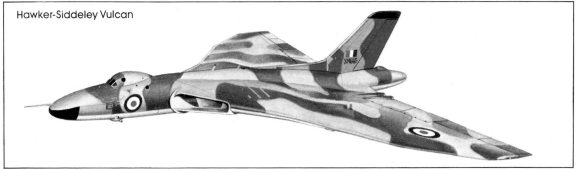

Hawker-Siddeley Vulcan

evidence of a single radar station: both sides realise full well that such stations can be 'fooled' under certain circumstances, and therefore the initiation of any nuclear attack inevitably awaits the verification of an incoming attack from other sources, preferably working on a different system or, if radar, on different wavelengths not susceptible to the types of 'electronic hallucination' that can be suffered by the initial warning equipment. For example, radar warning could be verified by infra-red or optical tracking of the incoming missiles by satellite-based systems after an initial alert had been ordered after radio monitoring had detected a considerable increase in the communications traffic associated with missile and bomber operations. The whole system is given greater speed and verification by the provision of special computer programmes constantly updated with the latest information about aircraft movements, meteorological conditions, and factors such as bird migrations, orbital patterns and analysis of previous false alarms.

In such circumstances it is highly unlikely that nuclear war could come about as a result of an unverified warning, and even policies adopted to 'launch on warning' are backed up by the fact that there is a hot-line connection between Washington and Moscow for continuous consultation in crisis. The whole system is loaded with redundancy features and failsafe mechanisms both on the weapons themselves and the procedures associated with arming them, and situations of tension and crisis are dealt with by continuous consultation and by a graded system of alert measures designed primarily to avert the possibility of a nuclear conflict, but especially one that could be initiated by accident.

A separate concern to the possibility of accidental nuclear war is that of an accident with a nuclear weapon system such that an accidental explosion or extensive radiation damage might result. The record is good but far from perfect. The number of accidents involving aircraft has been in

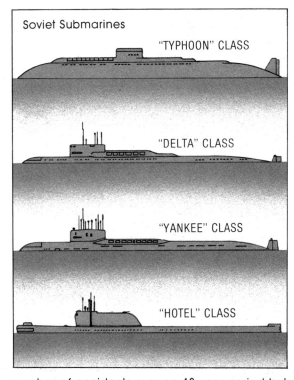

Soviet Submarines

"TYPHOON" CLASS

"DELTA" CLASS

"YANKEE" CLASS

"HOTEL" CLASS

number of accidents over an 18 year period but with only four serious accidents where nuclear warheads were lost. The majority of these more serious accidents have involved Soviet submarines which are considered to have a much poorer safety record than their western counterparts. The full series of Soviet nuclear missile submarines is illustrated. It was one of the earlier Hotel Class Soviet submarines that the CIA reportedly tried to recover in the Pacific a few years ago. All reports of accidents involving nuclear weapons systems are given by western sources; the Soviet Union very rarely acknowledges nuclear accidents as ever having taken place with their weapon systems.

The considerable size of nuclear arsenals can only cause considerable anxiety to the civilian populations of the world. In particular, the Soviet development and deployment of a new generation of nuclear weapons together with the continual updating and growth of their conventional forces, highlights the inadequacy of NATO civil defence provisions for its peoples. Opponents of civil defence have argued that they may be destabilising, and that the implementation of a comprehensive protection scheme could be interpreted by the Soviets as provocative, as a deliberate preparation for war. It is also argued that any civil defence programme would be hopelessly inadequate against the ferocity of modern weapons. These arguments, together with economic considerations, have contributed to the start-stop character of many national programmes in recent years.

At first the technological lead enjoyed by the West over the Soviet Union allowed NATO to keep a low profile in civil emergency planning, on the assumption that deterrence would work. For many years the concept of MAD which reckoned on the destruction of half the USSR's industrial concerns and up to a quarter of its population, has put an effective restraint upon civilian defence planning in NATO thinking. But the Soviet Union's progress towards both a theatre weapons and a strategic weapons superiority in recent years offers a new challenge to the complacency inherent in the concept of deterrence. In a nuclear war the victor, if any, will undoubtedly be the country which can recover most quickly, and recovery will depend upon the maximum survival of the able-bodied population. The objectives of civil defence programmes must include not only the continuance of government and of essential services, but the protection of the population to maintain and regulate communication links, and supplies of necessary resources. In a state of war, whether conventional or nuclear, military effectiveness would depend ultimately on civilian support, especially if such a confrontation were long drawn out. Even though the targeting of nuclear weapons has become increasingly sophisticated and accurate, civilians are likely to suffer immense casualties in the event of war. Unlike weapons systems, shelters and evacuation plans do not require a constant injection of capital. Once established, they will last for years to provide protection against the horrors of war, whether nuclear or conventional.

Civil defence can and should be justified upon humanitarian grounds alone. Yet the West, which prides itself upon its civilisation, individual freedom and democratic governments, could be thought extremely negligent in taking the risk of consigning millions of its populations to needless suffering and death through the lack of adequate provisions for their protection. However, the task of implementing civil defence and/or evacuation programmes in many Western nations is one of truly mammoth proportions. By comparing the nations' land mass with population densities, the accompanying chart shows the magnitude of the problem to which there can be no easy answers however much money is made available. Shelter and evacuation programmes are most feasible in those countries which have low density target areas, and a high proportion of hospitable land mass relative to its population density. Sweden is one example of such a country; having a population of only eight million in the fourth largest country in Europe, evacuation is clearly a practicable option. In Britain, which stands to lose between 20 and 40 million people in a nuclear exchange, the situation is on quite a different scale. Nowhere else in the world is there so high a density of potential targets concentrated in so small a land area, and only The Netherlands have a higher density of people per square mile. The consideration that the population of London alone is roughly equivalent to the population of Belgium highlights the difficulty of implementing an effective evacuation scheme, and the government's recommendation that people stay put is based on the assumption that in a country so stiff with potential nuclear targets no one place can be guaranteed to be safer than any other. The cost of providing mass shelters for the population of the UK has been estimated to be in the region of £10,000 million per 10 million people, and the government assess the risk of a nuclear war to be "very limited" so that such expenditure cannot be justified. The responsibility of finding a shelter has therefore been thrown on to the individual, who can take small comfort from the fact that in the UK Warning and Monitoring Organization, (for detecting fallout) Britain has the best warning system of any country.

The neutral countries, Sweden and Switzerland have the best protection schemes, with provision for between 90-98% of their populations. Per head, the Swiss spend over ten times as much on civil defence as the Americans, whose civil defence budget is barely 1% of the total defence budget.

The Russians currently have shelters for between 11% and 24% of their population and civil defence expenditure represents some 5% of the total defence budget. They have an extensive scheme of self-help training in schools and industries for the widespread teaching of emergency and first aid skills. It is likely that the Soviet Union will continue to expand its civil defence programmes as a back up to its prodigious nuclear arsenal. In such circumstances, deterrence may fail if the Soviets come to believe that the outcome of a nuclear war would leave their population relatively unscathed.

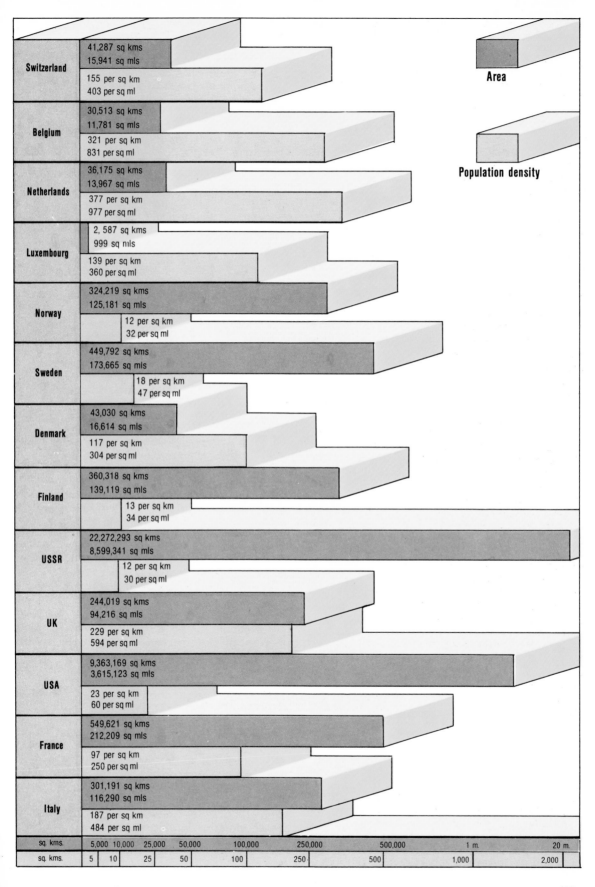

Area

Population density

	Area	Population density
Switzerland	41,287 sq kms / 15,941 sq mls	155 per sq km / 403 per sq ml
Belgium	30,513 sq kms / 11,781 sq mls	321 per sq km / 831 per sq ml
Netherlands	36,175 sq kms / 13,967 sq mls	377 per sq km / 977 per sq ml
Luxembourg	2,587 sq kms / 999 sq mls	139 per sq km / 360 per sq ml
Norway	324,219 sq kms / 125,181 sq mls	12 per sq km / 32 per sq ml
Sweden	449,792 sq kms / 173,665 sq mls	18 per sq km / 47 per sq ml
Denmark	43,030 sq kms / 16,614 sq mls	117 per sq km / 304 per sq ml
Finland	360,318 sq kms / 139,119 sq mls	13 per sq km / 34 per sq ml
USSR	22,272,293 sq kms / 8,599,341 sq mls	12 per sq km / 30 per sq ml
UK	244,019 sq kms / 94,216 sq mls	229 per sq km / 594 per sq ml
USA	9,363,169 sq kms / 3,615,123 sq mls	23 per sq km / 60 per sq ml
France	549,621 sq kms / 212,209 sq mls	97 per sq km / 250 per sq ml
Italy	301,191 sq kms / 116,290 sq mls	187 per sq km / 484 per sq ml

sq. kms.	5,000	10,000	25,000	50,000	100,000	250,000	500,000	1 m.	20 m.
sq. kms.	5	10	25	50	100	250	500	1,000	2,000

Shelters can be improvised indoors from household materials, or constructed out of doors by digging a shelter of the covered trench type. Purpose built shelters of various kinds are available, but for most people their cost is likely to be prohibitive. Shelters can only reduce the dangers of a nuclear explosion; they cannot guarantee the safety and survival of the inhabitants. It has been estimated that an attack on London similar to the one postulated in the government war exercise 'Square Leg', of 1980 of between one and three megatons, would result in the collapse of the government-advised shelter described in 'Protect and Survive' in 85% of the Greater London Council area, and that government-advised kit shelters would have collapsed within a radius of 6½ miles/ 10.5 km of a three megaton airburst and within 3½ miles/5.6 km of a two megaton groundburst.

Survival will depend not only upon the type of and size of the explosion, but also upon chance conditions of weather and wind direction. In addition to a great deal of forethought and careful planning, stockpiling water and food and other essential supplies, survival will require very great determination and will to live. Even if no physical injury is sustained, the distress and psychological stress resulting from the nuclear attack itself and the subsequent prolonged stay in the shelter are likely to be enormous.

Once the all clear is given and it becomes relatively safe to come out from the shelters, emergence will be to a world so dramatically changed, so unimaginably devastated, that great courage and fortitude will be required for the prosecution of even ordinary human affairs. With the disruption of those services which we now all take for granted, electricity, and gas supplies, transport and communications, people will be thrown back on their own resources of ingenuity to an extent never previously experienced, and it may be necessary to re-learn skills all but forgotten by post Industrial Revolution generations. Survival will also depend very greatly upon community cohesion; the only way in which people will be able to rebuild a future for themselves will be to rebuild the country and its economy quickly, even if it is only at a fairly simple agrarian level, and for this the mutual co-operation of all survivors will be crucial.

Improvised shelters in the home

This type of shelter is shown under construction in the top picture opposite. It is best situated in the innermost part of the house and may give a little protection against blast and, provided the building remains largely intact, some protection from fallout. The doors or other boards should be placed at an angle of approximately 60 degrees from the floor and propped up against a strip of wood nailed to the floor to prevent them from sliding. One door per person is the very minimum amount of tolerable space and many more will be required to protect water and other supplies from fallout. Heavy furniture, boxes of books, bags of earth and sand or other dense materials should be piled up to absorb radioactive dust. The ends should be closed off as much as possible, though it will be necessary to leave some space for the air to circulate; steel wool could be used to make a rudimentary air filter. Large stout tables enclosed and covered with heavy dense materials could also be used as an inner refuge and might be more practical if there is only a short time available for construction and assembly of supplies.

Covered Trench Shelter

If there is sufficient time and many helpers available, a covered trench shelter built out of doors well away from any buildings, will be much more effective against blast, heat and fallout than an indoor refuge. Its construction will have to be thorough however, as in addition to the nuclear effects, an underground shelter will be susceptible to damp, water seepage and earth movement. To counteract these, the shelter should be well lined with waterproof materials and floorboards. Doors well covered with waterproof sheeting can be used for a roof which should then be covered with a minimum of 18 in/46 cm of earth. A sloping earth roof is best and will permit rain water to drain away more effectively. Entrances should be covered with sandbag barriers, and should be as long as possible to give the maximum protection from fallout. A covered trench shelter such as the one shown in the middle picture opposite could well survive up to 7 psi of blast and withstand a ten megaton bomb at 5-7 miles (8-11 km) from ground zero.

Purpose built shelters

One of the many types of purpose built shelters available is shown in the bottom picture opposite. If it is well-constructed, it may remain intact at less than two miles from a one megaton airburst. In the shelter shown, the entrance leads down into a decontamination area and a specially constructed blast door. Other refinements include a vent, a periscope and a chimney for a gas stove.

Whatever the type of shelter chosen, cleanliness and hygiene will be of paramount importance. Painting the walls of the shelter white will help to show up any leaks or seepages and will show up the dust which may be radioactive, and should be cleared away. In addition to other supplies, clean water for drinking is essential. Provision should be made for each person to have a minimum of 3½ pints (2 litres) for drinking alone for each day of the proposed stay in the shelter.

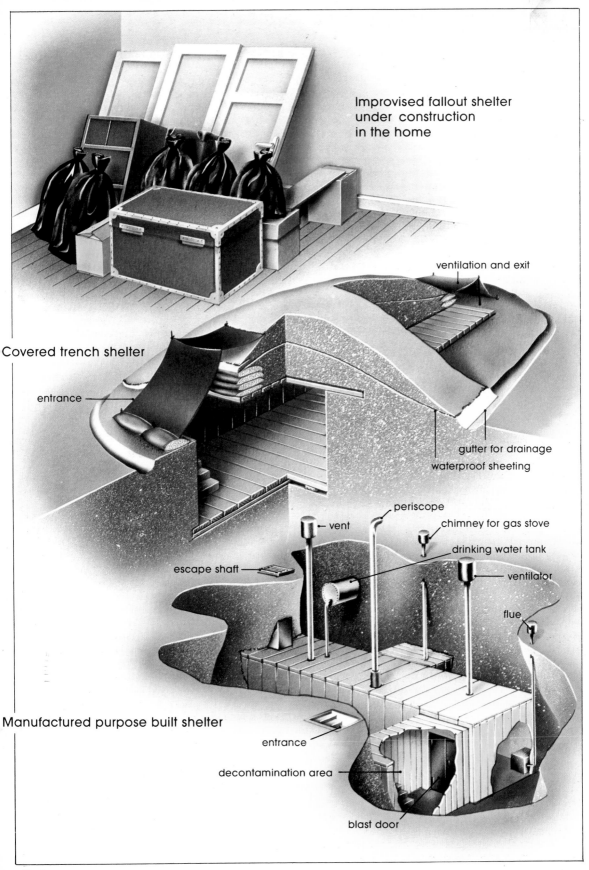

Improvised fallout shelter
under construction
in the home

Covered trench shelter

ventilation and exit

entrance

gutter for drainage

waterproof sheeting

Manufactured purpose built shelter

periscope

vent

chimney for gas stove

drinking water tank

escape shaft

ventilator

flue

entrance

decontamination area

blast door

An enormous flash of light signals the detonation of a nuclear weapon. Within a millionth of a second of the detonation very large temperatures and pressures are created. The maximum temperatures attained by a fission weapon are in the order of several tens of million degrees. This enormous heat converts all the bomb material into gaseous form. At the instant of the explosion the gases are confined to the area originally occupied by the constituents in the weapon, as a result huge pressures of over a million times the atmospheric pressure are produced.

The extremely hot weapon residues radiate large amounts of energy, primarily as X-rays which are absorbed in the immediate atmosphere of the weapon. This leads to the formation of an extremely hot, incandescent spherical mass of air known as the 'fireball'. The fireball from a IMT nuclear weapon would appear to an observer 50 miles away as very much more brilliant than the mid-day sun. Because of the characteristics of the transmission of light in the air, the flash of an atmospheric nuclear explosion can be seen some 400-700 miles away.

Immediately after its formation the fireball grows in size and its temperatures drop due to the increasing mass. At the same time the fireball rises upwards. Within a millisecond of being detonated, the fireball from a IMT weapon is roughly 500 feet/ 180 metres in diameter and increases to about 6,000 feet/1,800 metres within 10 seconds. All the while it is rising upwards at a rate of 250 feet/90 metres per second.

As the fireball increases in size and cools the vapours condense to form a cloud containing solid particles of weapon debris as well as droplets of water from the air sucked into the rising fireball. The upward movement of the fireball through the atmosphere causes it to change its shape from its spherical form to a dome or mushroom shape. The circulation moves more air through the bottom of the mushroom. A strong updraught with inflowing winds is produced in the immediate vicinity of an 'air-burst' detonation. These winds cause varying amounts of dirt and debris to be sucked up from the earth's surface into the radioactive cloud.

The speed with which the radioactive cloud continues to ascend depends on the weather and the size of the explosive yield. For a IMT explosion the cloud would be 3 miles high in 30 seconds, and reach 5 miles in about a minute. When the mushroom cloud reaches the upper limit of the atmosphere it tends to spread out laterally but if the explosive yield was large and sufficient energy remains, it will push through to the stratosphere.

At present the fissile material necessary for nuclear weapons is drawn entirely from isotopes of uranium and plutonium. There has been some speculation about the existence of superheavy isotopes but if these exist it is unlikely that they can be found in sufficient quantity and at an acceptable cost to make them available for nuclear weapons use.Therefore it is probable that the fundamental processes involved in nuclear weapons design will remain unchanged for the foreseeable future. These processes utilize fissile material and the burning of thermonuclear fuel in the form of deuterium, deuterium-tritium mixture, and lithium deuteride, and these fuels appear to be the only ones available. They have over the years been used in various combinations to refine the types of nuclear explosives that can be made and the effects can be tailored to a considerable extent to suit the type of target being considered. But there is no reason to suppose that any significant new combination can now be found which could dramatically change the general range and type of nuclear weapons already available. It is only possible to envisage improvements, adaptations, and modifications rather than fundamental changes.

The design of nuclear weapons today seeks to utilize nuclear fissile material more efficiently and to produce specific destructive effects while minimising those that serve to cause unintended damage to nearby non-targets. Thus one direction has been to obtain 'more bang for the buck' while another has been to reduce the size and weight of the warhead making it suitable for use with specialised delivery systems such as artillery, small missiles, and on ICBMs and SLBMs where such savings allow more warheads to be carried per missile. Both of these are close to the practical limits achievable in the case of the superpowers, but it is likely that both China and France will continue to strive to improve the weight to yield ratios for their nuclear warheads. Other areas of nuclear weapons design concern the development of weapons with special effects such as the neutron bomb. Here the possibilities are more politically charged than technically novel and most of the possibilities are known and have been exploited at least experimentally. It was once thought that nuclear explosives might be applied to peaceful purposes such as excavating harbours or canals. But nuclear devices do not lend themselves to this type of peaceful application; there are always cheaper and less politically problematic methods of achieving the same result, without the additional hazard of radioactive contamination.

The last important feature of continuing nuclear weapons design is concerned with making the systems safe in peacetime by proofing the arming systems against accidental triggering or unauthorised arming. But the work here too is not of a fundamental type but one requiring the application of existing techniques or new developments from other scientific areas in rather specific ways.

The first manifestation of a nuclear bomb is a blinding flash of light.

Simultaneously there is a release of initial radiation, lethal up to 1.5 miles (2.4 km).

Air heats to 10,000,000°C. The fireball can reach a maximum diameter of 1.4 miles (2.24 km).

The bomb's energy converts to a blast wave travelling outwards at the speed of sound.

The fireball rises at a rate of 250 mph as the hot gases expand outwards.

The fireball diminishes as dust and debris is caught up in the chimney of smoke and hot gases.

Air rushes to fill the vacuum left by the rising fireball to create the mushroom cloud.

The radioactive cloud may rise up to 15 miles (24.1 km) and penetrate the upper stratosphere.

The radii of destructive effects for a 1 Mt weapon are shown here in concentric rings from 'ground zero', (the point on the earth over which the weapon detonates.) The climatic and atmospheric conditions at the target, the height of the explosion and the geographical features of the target will all influence the degree of destructiveness, so the information given can only be regarded as very approximate.

Light flash

The first manifestation of a nuclear explosion is a blinding flash of light. Anyone looking directly at the flash would be temporarily blinded as far as 100 miles/160 km. away, especially if the explosion occurred at night when the pupils are at their most widely dilated.

Heat

The detonation of a nuclear weapon gives rise to temperatures as great as the centre of the sun, and 35% of the bomb's energy is given out in the form of this very intense heat, particularly during the early stages of the fireball's formation. This heat travels outwards at a speed of 186,000 miles per second, or 300 million metres a second, and will vaporize almost all substances immediately below the point of detonation and up to 3 miles/4.8 km. from ground zero. Many materials up to 8 miles/13 km. away will ignite spontaneously in the resulting firestorm. Severe burns would be sustained by those caught out in the open up to 11 miles/17.8 km. away and first degree burns and skin reddening would afflict people as far as 20 miles/32.4 km from ground zero.

Blast

The main destructive effects for weapons of this size are due to the enormous overpressures causing blast or shock waves. Approximately half the total energy of the explosion is dispersed by the blast which travels outwards at a speed greater than the speed of sound. At a distance of 1.5 miles/2.2 km from ground zero the overpressure would be roughly 30 times greater than the normal atmospheric pressure of approximately 15 lbs to the square inch. Under these pressures only underground facilities specially protected with concrete reinforcements could possibly escape a high level of damage. Almost all brick structures would be completely destroyed up to a radius of 4 miles/6 km. This high level of destruction would all take place in the 15 seconds it takes for the blast from a 1 MT weapon to travel 4 miles.

Wind speeds of up to 700 mph/1120 km per hour exacerbate the damage caused by the blast by hurling wreckage and people about in the air. Blast and wind effects will cover a larger area if the bomb is detonated high up than if it is detonated close to the ground, and the blast wave may be reflected back from the ground as a kind of 'echo', known as the 'Mach' effect. These two blast waves arriving simultaneously at the same place would roughly double the overpressure at that point. In nuclear test explosions, it has been found that on some occasions, the blast initially passed into the upper atmosphere. Some minutes later the blast was then reflected back to the earth shattering windows some hundreds of miles away. This highlights the difficulty of predicting the precise range of damage from a nuclear weapon.

Electromagnetic pulse

The electromagnetic pulse (EMP) produced by the nuclear explosion would cause extreme chaos in our modern civilisation. Telephone communications systems, radios and televisions, radars, computers and power supplies would be severely damaged. If the explosion is ground burst, damage would be confined to a relatively small area, but with an airburst, the strength of the pulse is so powerful that these facilities could be damaged over enormous distances.

Fallout

In addition to the immensely powerful pulse of initial radiation consisting mainly of neutron and gamma rays given out at the moment of detonation, there is still deadly danger persisting from residual radiation, even when all other effects of a nuclear explosion have ceased. This fallout is caused by the materials vaporized by the intense heat condensing back into solid particles of radioactive dust as the fireball cools. The larger, heavier particles fall back to earth within a few hours and are most likely to fall locally or a little downwind of the target area, but the remaining dust, which consists of microscopic particles, may take weeks or even months to descend, depending upon the prevailing wind and weather conditions.

There are some two hundred types of radioactive elements in fallout dust. These are known as radioisotopes, and may be stored by the body which mistakes them for elements necessary for sustaining life. For example, strontium-90 which occurs in beta particles and gamma rays, is very similar to calcium which is necessary for the growth and maintenance of healthy bone structure. If strontium-90 is absorbed and stored by the body instead of calcium, it may cause cell mutations and cancers. In addition to their effect on bones and the respiratory tract, uranium and plutonium isotopes, carried by alpha particles, affect other vital organs such as liver, kidneys and lymphnodes. These isotopes are particularly dangerous in that they emit their radiation over an extremely protracted time span of up to thousands of years.

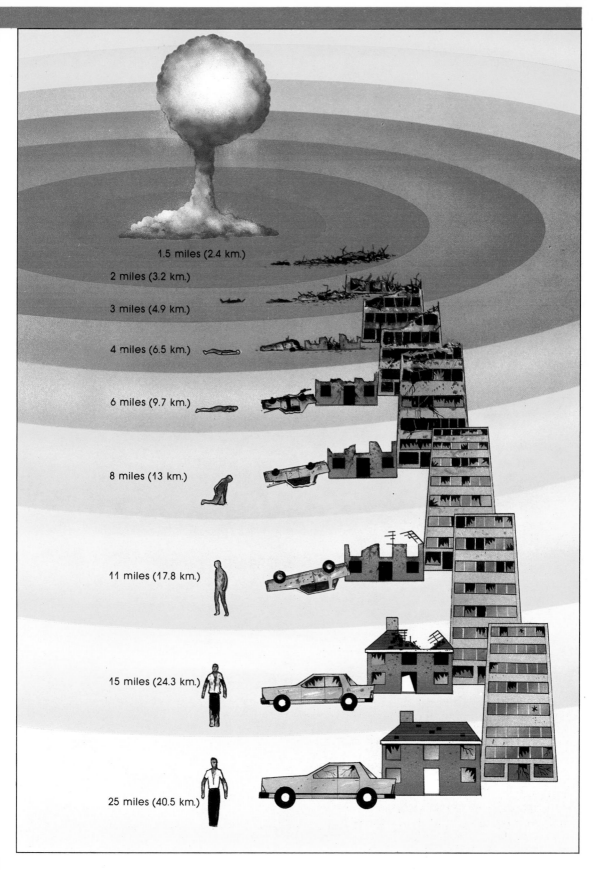

1.5 miles (2.4 km.)

2 miles (3.2 km.)

3 miles (4.9 km.)

4 miles (6.5 km.)

6 miles (9.7 km.)

8 miles (13 km.)

11 miles (17.8 km.)

15 miles (24.3 km.)

25 miles (40.5 km.)

The medical effects of radiation vary according to the combination of particles contained within it. There are four main types of radiation: alpha, beta, gamma and neutron.

An Alpha particle consists of two protons and two neutrons. It is identical to a helium nucleus in that it has a mass of four units and an electrical charge of two positive units. Although they are heavy, alpha particles deteriorate rapidly when passing through the air so it is unlikely that particles would travel the 1,600 feet/500 metres from the point of detonation of an airburst to the ground. A ground-burst explosion would be much more dangerous because, although alpha particles can only penetrate about 1mm of body tissue, they are damaging when inhaled or ingested.

A Beta particle has mass and an electronic charge equal to an electron. Like alpha particles, they have a limited life when passing through the air and they are most dangerous when inhaled or ingested, but they can also cause beta burns to the skin.

Gamma rays are electromagnetic radiations of high photon energy, having no mass or charge. They are not unlike x-rays, but as their wavelength is shorter, they are much more energetic. Concentrated gamma rays can penetrate several inches of concrete so they are offered little resistance by living tissues in which they cause a release of electrons from the atoms of the body. The fireball of a nuclear explosion gives out an intense pulse of gamma rays and fallout dust releases gamma radiation continuously.

A Neutron is a neutral particle with no electrical charge. Neutrons can pass through flesh, interacting with the atomic particles of the body as they do so to cause further radiation.

Ionizing radiation

Radiation is a continual presence in the world. In addition to the cosmic rays from the stars and the radioactive elements in the earth which affect food resources, nuclear tests and nuclear power stations release radioisotopes into the atmosphere. This background radiation is neglible compared to the huge pulse of radiation that is released at the moment when a nuclear device detonates, and the resulting prolonged dangers of skin contact or inhalation of fallout and from irradiated food and water. The danger persists for the half life of the radioactive material which can vary enormously.

Radiation is a slow, stealthy and insidious killer. As it is undetectable by any of the five senses, a human being may receive a mortal dose within a few seconds and yet not be aware of it. Death may be instantaneous, or follow only after days of painful suffering.

Because radiation changes the electrical charges of elements contained in the body tissues, creating positively or negatively charged ions, it is sometimes called 'ionizing radiation'. Radiation alters the nature of the enzymes, those chemicals, which initiate and sustain the vital chemical reactions in the body necessary to maintain life. The immediate effect of ionizing radiation is the injection of excessive energy into living cells. Most particularly it affects those cells which reproduce themselves rapidly; the cells lining the digestive tract are continually multiplying at a great rate so the gut is immediately affected. Initial symptoms which include nausea, vomiting and diarrhoea may occur within the first few hours of receiving a dose of ionising radiation.

If the dose has been intense, the radiation sickness causes rapid weakening and exhaustion. Fever and delirium follow leading to death within a week.

If the dose has been small and the initial symptoms disappear, the person affected may feel moderately well, but tired, listless and without appetite. Two weeks later new symptoms occur including hair loss, and haemorrhages in the skin, especially in the mouth. There is a tendency to bruise easily and there may be bleeding from the gums. The mouth, throat and gut may become ulcerated and loss of appetite, rapid weight loss and fever will follow.

Bone marrow, essential to the manufacture of the blood, is particularly sensitive to radiation. Anaemia results from the diminuition of red blood cells, while the manufacture of white blood cells is also impaired. The loss of white blood cells which help to combat infection and which are also necessary for the manufacture of platelets which cause blood to clot and so prevent haemorrhage, leaves the victim susceptible to the danger of bleeding to death. Lymphocytes manufactured in the lymph nodes and spleen, the organs which produce antibodies, are also diminished by radiation. With the body's natural defences against disease dramatically reduced, the victim of radiation who appears to have made a good recovery from the initial symptoms may be vulnerable to sudden death from an infection that would cause only a very minor illness in a healthy person.

The most significant longterm effect however is probably an increased incidence of leukaemia, a progressive and normally fatal disease in which the body's white blood cells become more and more numerous. Victims within half a mile of the hypocentre at Hiroshima were 60 times more likely to suffer from the disease than the general population. The incidence of this disease increases rapidly in all those exposed to more than 100 rem.

Right: The areas of the body in which cells are rapidly multiplying continuously are most susceptible to the effects of radiation. The accompanying diagram opposite indicates these areas in descending order of susceptibility.

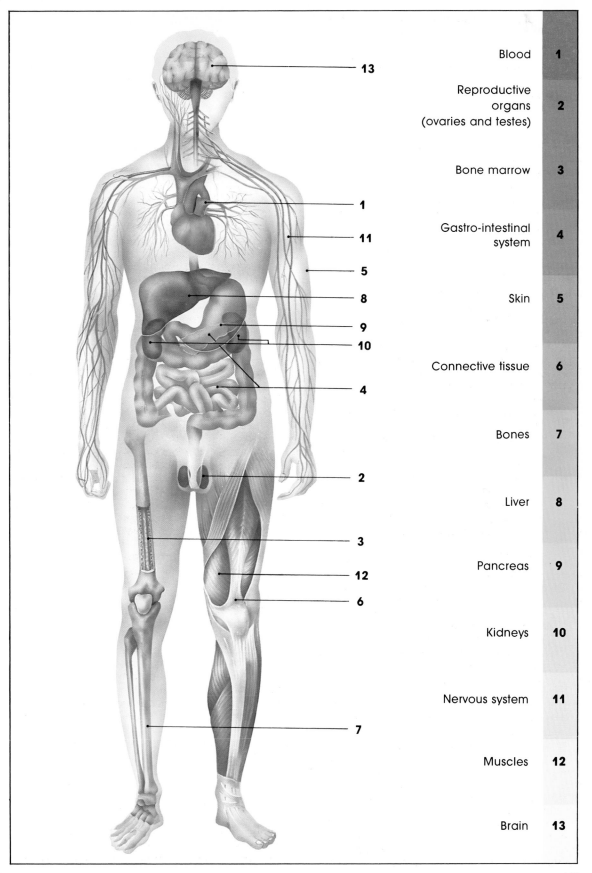

Blood **1**

Reproductive organs (ovaries and testes) **2**

Bone marrow **3**

Gastro-intestinal system **4**

Skin **5**

Connective tissue **6**

Bones **7**

Liver **8**

Pancreas **9**

Kidneys **10**

Nervous system **11**

Muscles **12**

Brain **13**

The nuclear arms race is essentially a technological battle, which has since the early 1950s been characterized by American efforts to capitalize on the USA's technological lead to produce decisive weapons, and by Soviet attempts to counter this lead first by 'brute force' weapons produced in prodigious numbers and second by eroding the American technological lead, which in many sensitive areas is now thought to be not much more than two years. Many developments have been of Soviet origin, but the Soviets have also relied heavily on the clandestine purchase of Western technology and, failing this, outright theft of advanced technology by espionage.

The consequence of this technological and intelligence battle has been a gradual narrowing of the physical differences between the two sides' weapons: whereas American weapons have generally been smaller than their Soviet counterparts, relying on greater reliability, systems integration and accuracy to achieve the same effect as the massive Soviet weapons relying on huge and not very accurate thermonuclear warheads. But while Soviet technology in the field of rocket motor design and solid propellants has not yet allowed a reduction in size comparable to that achieved by the Americans with missiles such as the Minuteman and Peacekeeper, developments in guidance and warhead miniaturization have reached a point at which CEP (and thus counter-military potential) is not significantly worse than that attainable by the Americans.

The combination of increased accuracy and smaller yield warheads has by the mid-1980s made possible a strategic scenario in which the possible destruction of military point targets predominates over that of civilian area targets. And in the foreseeable future this tendency will become more pronounced, increasing terminal accuracy making possible yet further reduction in warhead yield. This must spell the end for the silo-launched missile, for sufficient physical and electro-magnetic hardening to survive the latest generation of super-accurate warheads will run into the twin problems of prohibitive cost and a physical unwieldiness that will make rapid response all but impossible. The alternative is the mobile ICBM, and this has been made technologically feasible by the improvements in propellant and guidance technology mentioned above. As a successor to the Peacekeeper, now regarded to be deployed in an interim basing mode, the Americans are considering the development of a fully mobile ICBM, a lightweight weapon nicknamed 'Midgetman'. It would be very hard for the Soviets to target their ICBMs on such a system (just as it is in the present with mobile systems such as the GLCM and Pershing II intermediate nuclear weapon systems), which will have a phenomenal accuracy and carry only a single low-yield warhead. Present ICBMs have to be fed extremely accurate launch and target co-ordinates to ensure that the inertial navigation (even in its satellite or stellar-updated form) can function adequately, and this could not be achieved in a mobile system with current guidance packages. However, three important developments are under investigation by the Defense Advanced Research Projects Agency in the USA. These three systems, which could be used individually or in conjunction with each other to ensure an extremely low CEP in mobile ICBMs are much improved inertial navigation (using low-viscosity or ring-lasergyroscopes), pre-launch or mid-course guidance using the Global Positioning System based on a satellite net scheduled for completion in 1988, and terminal guidance such as RADAG (radar area guidance) already in service with the Pershing II and requiring only one prominent geographical feature in the area of the target. DARPA confidently expects that these three systems can provide lightweight mobile ICBMs with CEP capability measures in metres rather than tens of metres after launch from anywhere on the earth.

The lightweight ICBM will be partnered by a new generation of cruise missiles using 'stealth' technology to reduce the radar signature of the missile and so enhance its survivability while crossing enemy territory at high subsonic speed. This technology is based on the reduction of areas which return radar echoes, and on special surface finishes which are radar ablative, to 'soak up' radar emissions and so weaken the return echo. A new generation of fuel-miserly turbofan engines will provide greater range, and guidance systems will be improved from the already formidable standard attained in cruise missiles.

Vital to the adequate control of strategic forces equipped with such weapons is a more comprehensive, flexible and survivable C^3 system. This whole aspect of battlefield management, surveillance, targeting and C^3 is being much improved at the moment with the development, production and constant updating of aircraft such as the Boeing E-4 advanced airborne command post, the Boeing E-6 TACAMO flying communication-relay station for the control of missile-armed nuclear submarines, and the Boeing EC-135 series for the control of the USA's ICBM force. Further improvements are expected in the later 1980s with the development of a new generation of computers, which will use high-speed integrated circuits using 1-micron silicon chips (and sub-micron chips later in the programme) to produce much faster computation speeds allied with greater 'intelligence'. The result will be a quantum advance in battle staffs' ability to control ever more complex strategic, operational and tactical battlefields, and also the possibility of developing guidance packages able to 'think' for themselves in a limited fashion. Besides offering a considerable advance in operational capability, these advanced computer packages will also be smaller than current systems, and possess greater reliability. The next decade will probably see a useful improvement in reliability of all components of nuclear weapons systems, which in the early 1980s have a reliability index ranging from 0.6 for the elderly SS-N-5 Serb SLBM to 0.8 for more advanced weapons such as the SS-20 and Pershing II. Increased reliability means that the 'overkill' factor can be reduced, with spin-off advanced computers have been greatly aided by a massive espionage effort in Europe and the USA. There are certain of these areas, indeed, in which there is evidence of a Soviet lead, and this is particularly true of the Soviet use of spacecraft for military purposes. The overall effect of these developments, it should be noted, may be to alter the balance of forces in such a way that it favours the offensive rather than defensive military

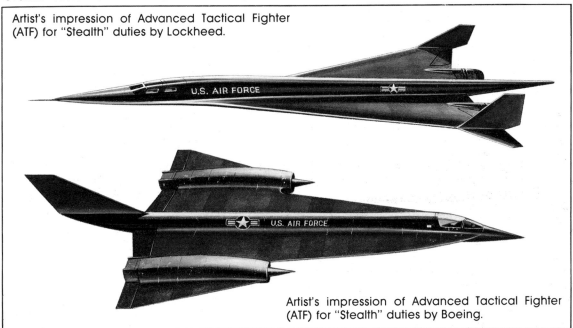

Artist's impression of Advanced Tactical Fighter (ATF) for "Stealth" duties by Lockheed.

U.S. AIR FORCE

U.S. AIR FORCE

Artist's impression of Advanced Tactical Fighter (ATF) for "Stealth" duties by Boeing.

advantages in terms of reduced production and weapon-holdings. This combines with improved accuracy and penetration indices to make possible a considerable reduction in the number of nuclear warheads thought necessary by the superpowers.

Current satellites associated with strategic warfare are concerned mostly with recon-naissance and early warning, but the 1980s are witnessing a slow but important development of satellites for more offensive purposes, and there is the possibility that by the end of the decade US spacecraft will have been developed (in defensive terms by physical and electronic hardening, and in offensive terms by the development of advanced sensors and computers) to the extent that they will be able to undertake real-time retargeting of missiles right up to the moment of launch and, under certain circumstances, during the flight of the missile. Other features of such spacecraft will be orbital manoeuvrability and electronic countermeasures as part of the defensive system, and advanced onboard computers for semi-autonomous operation in the event of the destruction of the control facility on the surface.

It is to be assumed that the Soviets are working along the same lines, and their developments into

Above: "Stealth" is the codename given to a family of technology designed to so dramatically reduce the visibility of an aircraft or missile to radar that it would be effectively invisible. These technologies involve special surface coatings to absorb radar signals and aerodynamic forms that minimise reflectivity to radar. Two possible aircraft shapes incorporating "Stealth" tech-nology are illustrated; both are conceptual realisations of the likely shapes rather than actual designs for prototypes.

doctrine. But advantages also accrue in terms of smaller procurement figures and reduced possibility of collateral damage to purely civilian areas. Both the Americans and the Soviets are keeping abreast of the technology required for improved anti-ballistic missile missile defences, using advanced radar and computers in con-junction with high-acceleration missiles for exo-atmospheric interception, but treaty limitations, exceptionally high costs and only limited effectiveness militate against such a defence, which is all that is possible with current technology. While some developments may appear at first to be destabilising, the same technology can be applied to military problems where its contribution has a positive, reassuring and stabilising effect.

It is likely that offensive weapons will reach a performance and accuracy plateau, and that in the 1990s emphasis will shift towards the defences possible against ballistic missiles. The scope for development is indicated by the current Homing Overlay Experiment (HOE) being undertaken by the US Army as part of its long-term development of effective anti-ballistic missile systems. This uses a combination of spacecraft; aircraft- and ground-based sensors (radar, infra-red and optical) to determine the nature and trajectory of the threat, high-speed computers for assessment of interception parameters, and a mix of missiles for destruction of the incoming target. Missile possibilities are the exo-atmospheric HOE missile carrying a conventional warhead and based on the first two stages of the Minuteman ICBM, and the Update Spartan missile carrying a thermonuclear warhead; and the endo-atmospheric Sentry missile with a conventional warhead and radio command guidance, and the SRHit missile with a conventional warhead and millimetre-wavelength radar guidance. The object of the HOE is to assess such a four-layer system as an effective defence against ballistic missiles, the use of four missile types and three sensor systems helping to ensure that gaps in one system are plugged in another. The sensors would be those in operation at present, plus the Space Infrared Sensor (SIRE, due for launch by a shuttle orbiter in the mid-1980s) and a telescopic infra-red system carried on lengthy flights in the upper atmosphere first by converted airliners, and then at higher altitudes by aircraft such as the Lockheed TR-1A battlefield reconnaissance platform once the size of the system has been reduced.

The Soviets are also working on advanced anti-missile missiles, and two types known to be under development have the NATO reporting names SH-4 and SH-8. Little is known of these weapons, which are probably intended as a complementary pair to replace the ABM-1B Galosh. The SH-4 is an exo-atmospheric weapon, probably with a thermonuclear warhead, and is fitted with a motor capable of being started and stopped up to five times; this permits the missile to loiter in space while the ground-based radars and computers assess the incoming threat, separate the real warhead from the dummies and then call in the missile for the kill. The SH-8 is thought to be an endo-atmospheric missile, and intended for last-ditch defence in much the same way as the SRHit.

Both superpowers are heavily engaged in anti-satellite developments. Indeed, the Soviets have probably had operational since the early 1970s a primitive satellite killer. Such weapons have been tested with regularity for about 10 years, and have proved most effective. They are designed to operate principally against satellites in low orbit, and when required for action are manoeuvred into the same orbit as the victim. Closing up to within short range, the Soviet weapon expels a cloud of small metal pellets at the target; moving at high velocity relative to the target, many such pellets are likely to strike the target with considerable kinetic energy and do vital damage.

American efforts in anti-satellite technology are completely different in concept, as epitomized by the Vought ASAT missile currently under development. This is a three-stage weapon intended for launch within the atmosphere by air-defence fighter aircraft, notably the McDonnell Douglas F-15 Eagle. The missile uses a first stage based on the SRAM missile, a second stage based on the Vought Altair rocket, and a specialized third stage. The missile is launched from the aircraft at the top of a zoom climb, and is then boosted out of the atmosphere under inertial guidance by the first two stages. Outside the atmosphere, the third stage will be able to home on satellites at an altitude of 620 miles/1,000 km, the target being located by eight telescopic infra-red sensors. The third stage homes at a velocity of some 30,680 mph/49,375 km/h, and should strike the target with sufficient kinetic energy to render superfluous an explosive charge. The ASAT is due to begin test firings in 1983, and the type may be given capability against geosynchronous satellites by the addition of booster motors for the third stage, but interception at such long ranges (50,000 km) is very difficult.

Looking further into the future, there are likely to be killer satellites with directed-energy weapons, in the form of lasers and charged-particle team weapons. Both superpowers are heavily involved in research programmes and several experimental 'firings' have been conducted from surface- and aircraft-installed prototypes, though success has been limited. Laser and charged-particle weapons could be deployed in space by about 1990, but these would be experimental models designed to evaluate the concept under operational conditions, and to provide data for the development of combat-capable systems for the end of that decade. Satellites with directed-energy weapons would be nuclear-powered, and considerable problems of control have to be surmounted before these weapons can become operational.

In this artist's representation of the 'Star Wars' concept the following envisaged systems are depicted: The bottom left of the picture shows a ground-based laser defending a ballistic missile silo field and attacking incoming missiles with bursts of laser radiation. Above this are space-based chemical laser battle stations which are attacking launched ICBMs early in their trajectory soon after they leave the earth's atmosphere. To the top right a massive attack of ICBMs is detected and attacked by X-ray laser battlestations. Other satellites are utilising ultra-violet/infra-red telescope sensors for target acquisition and tracking and are armed with casing rods for defence against hunter/killer or ASATs that are approaching in the top left of the picture.

A

AABNCP	Advanced Airborne National Command Post.
AAM	Air-to-Air Missile
ABM	Anti-Ballistic Missile
ABRV	Advanced Ballistic Re-entry Vehicle
ABM Treaty	Treaty between the U.S. and the Soviet Union limiting Anti-Ballistic Missile systems (1972).
Active Homing	Means by which the guidance system of a missile seeks its target. Principally by means of emitting a signal e.g. acoustic or radar, which when reflected by a target is detected by a receiver in the missile homing guidance system. The reflected signal provides the information necessary for the missile guidance to direct the course of the missile to the target.
AEC	Atomic Energy Commission (United States) now part of the Department of Energy.
AFAP	Artillery Fired Atomic Projectiles.
AFBMD	Air Force Ballistic Missile Division (United States).
AFF	Arming, Fusing and Firing System.
AGR	Advanced Gas-cooled Reactor.
Air-Burst	The term given for weapon detonated in the atmosphere above a target at a pre-set altitude to maximise the destructive effective effect.
AIRS	Advanced Inertial Reference System.
ALBM	Air-Launched Ballistic Missile.
ALCM	Air-Launched Cruise Missile.
AMTE	Adjusted Megaton Equivalent: a measure of soft target kill probability.
Anti-Radar	Weapons designed to suppress radar installations.
Apogee	The highest point of a trajectory or orbit.
ASALM	Advanced Strategic Air-Launched Missile.
ASATS	Anti-Satellite Systems.
ASDC	Alternate Space Defense Centre.
ASROC	Anti-Submarine Rocket.
ASW	Anti-Submarine Warfare.
ATF	Advanced Tactical Fighter.
Avionics	The electronic equipment fit for an aircraft.
AWACS	Airborne Warning and Control System.

B

B-	Designation for bomber aircraft, Soviet aircraft identified as bombers are designated with NATO codenames the first letter of which corresponds to the classification of the system e.g. for bombers: Badger, Bear, Blinder, Backfire, Blackjack, etc.
Big Bird	Generic name for a series of U.S. spy satellites.
BMEWS	Ballistic Missile Early Warning System.
Booster	Term generally given to the first propulsion stage of a ballistic missile providing the initial acceleration for the missile flight.
BWE	Boiling Water Reactor. A nuclear reactor in which the nuclear fuel boils water circulating around the fuel rods, the steam thus created driving the turbines which generate electricity.

C

C3	Command, Control, and Communications.
C3I	Command, Control, Communications, and Intelligence.
CADIN/Pinetree	Line Aircraft detection radar network in southern Canada.
CANDU	Canadian Deuterium Uranium reactor.
Cat House	Intermediate-range Soviet radar, associated with the defence of Moscow.
CBW	Chemical, Biological Warfare.

CEP	Circular Error Probable, a measure of the accuracy attributable to ballistic missiles. It is the radius of circle into which fifty per cent of the warheads aimed at the centre of the circle are predicted to fall.
Chaff	Radar reflective material sometimes comprised of fine wire pieces cut to fractions of the wavelength of the radars to be jammed. Chaff operates by obscuring the target from the detecting radar by creating a much larger radar signature due to the reflectivity of the chaff material.
Chain Reaction	A chain reaction results when a mass of fissile material is brought together so that spontaneous fission occurs as in a nuclear explosion.
CIA	Central Intelligence Agency (United States).
CIEW	Close-In Weapons System.
CIWS	Close-In Weapon Systems.
Clipper Bow	The programme name for a U.S. Navy Ocean surveillance radar satellite project.
CMP	Counter Military Potential. A measure of the potential capability for nuclear weapons primarily delivered by intercontinental ballistic missiles to destroy hard targets, i.e. where the accuracy of the delivery system has special significance.
CND	Campaign for Nuclear Disarmament.
Cold Launch	A technique by which a missile is ejected from its silo by compressed air, after which the rocket motor is ignited. The technique slightly enhances the throw-weight of the missile and enables the silo to be reused.
Command Guidance	Control of a missile's flight by commands from ground stations transmitted to the missile by radio signals.
Conventional	Not nuclear — i.e. Chemical high explosive.
Cosmos	Generic name for a series of Soviet satellites some of which are spy satellites.
countermeasures	Measures undertaken by a defender to reduce or eliminate the effectiveness of an attacking weapon system.
Critical Mass	The amount of fissile material needed to be brought together in order to create spontaneous fission and a chain reaction.
Cruise missile	A missile which flies supported by a wing or body lift.
CTBT	Comprehensive nuclear Test Ban Treaty.
Damage radius	The radius of a circle from the centre of which the destructive effects over distance are measured for specific weapons.
DARPA	Defence Advanced Research Projects Agency (United States).
DCS	Defense Communications Systems.
Decoy	Carried as a penetration aid by the MIRV Bus of a missile in order to allow the warheads to reach their targets without interference. Can include decoy warheads and chaff.
Decoy warhead	A warhead replicating some characteristic of a true ballistic missile re-entry vehicle such as radar cross section.
Depressed trajectory	A ballistic trajectory with an abnormally low apogee to reduce the possibility of early detection by radars. Use of such trajectories has the effect of reducing the range of the missile.
Deuterium	Thermonuclear fuel, together with such substances as deuterium-tritium mixture and lithium deuteride. Can be used in various combinations to tailor the type of nuclear blast to the particular target. Deuterium is also a constituent of heavy water.
DEW Line	Distant Early Warning Line detection radars.

D

Discoverer	Series of early U.S. satellites that were the precursors to the first photo-reconnaissance satellites.
Dog House	Intermediate-range Soviet radar, associated with Moscow defence.
DSCS	Defense Satellite Communications Systems.
DSMAC	Digital Scene-Matching Area Correlation.
DSP	Defense Support Program. Project designation for a series of U.S. early warning satellites.
Dual-Key System	The method by which more than one country is included in the final decision to use nuclear weapons during time of war. This allows for consultation among allies as to the decision to resort to a nuclear attack.

E

ECCM	Electronic Counter Countermeasures. A range of measures that can be implemented to counteract or reduce the effectiveness of ECM by improving the resistance of radars to jamming for example.
ECM	Electronic Countermeasures. A range of electronic and other measures (e.g. chaff) used to retard the effectiveness of enemy electronic systems, primarily radars, missile guidance systems and communications and surveillance systems.
Electron Class	Soviet class of satellites aimed at providing coverage of the continental United States.
ELF	Extremely Low Frequency. Frequencies used for communication with submerged submarines.
ELINT	Electronic Intelligence. Refers to detailed information of the characteristics of electronic equipment obtained by means such as monitoring radar transmissions of enemy surface to air missile sites.
EMP	Electromagnetic Pulse. The pulse of intense electromagnetic radiation emitted by a nuclear explosion.
EMT	A measure of the explosive force of nuclear weapons against area targets such as cities or industrial complexes.
ENDO-Atmospheric	Normally used with reference to ABMS designed to intercept ballistic missile re-entry vehicles after they have entered the Earth's atmosphere.
Enhanced Radiation	A nuclear weapon whose design maximises the generation of radiation effects over those of blast and heat.
Enrichment	A process capable of increasing the content of Uranium 235 to a higher level than that found in natural conditions, useful for either nuclear reactors or nuclear weapons.
EUCOM	United States European Command.
Exo-Atmospheric	Referring to ABM intercepts outside the Earth's atmosphere.

F

FAE	Fuel/Air Explosive. A weapon which disperses fuel into the atmosphere above a target prior to detonation. The combustion of the fuel/air mixture creates intense blast and heat.
FBM	Fleet Ballistic Missile (United States).
FBR	Fast Breeder Reactor.
Ferret Satellite	A satellite collecting electronic intelligence.
Fin Stabilised	Missiles whose stability in flight is maintained by aerodynamic control surfaces 'FINS'.
Fireball	The massive, bright, hot spherical mass created immediately after the initial detonation of a nuclear device. As the hot gases within it expand, the fireball moves upwards and its place is eventually taken by a mushroom cloud.
Fissile Material	Either uranium or plutonium that is in a form that can be utilised in nuclear reactors or nuclear weapons. Fissile material for nuclear weapons is referred to as 'weapons

grade'.

Flaming Arrow	American satellite communications link for nuclear command and control.
Flight Profile	The flight path of an aircraft as a function of its altitude at the beginning, middle, and end of its flight to target, i.e. High, High, High (abreviated to HI HI HI) or similarly High Low Low.
FOBS	Fractional Orbital Bombardment Systems. A method of ballistic missile attack over intercontinental distances that involves launching the warhead into a fractional orbit around the Earth so that the warhead arrives over the target from the opposite direction of a direct ballistic trajectory.
Force de Frappe	The French independent nuclear deterrent.
Force Ratio	The ratio of comparable weapon systems in the arsenals of opposing forces.
Free-Fall Weapons	Air-delivered bombs without their own guidance system.
FROG	Free-flight Rocket Over Ground. A rocket without specialised guidance, whose ballistic trajectory is determined by its pre-launch elevation and azimuth.

G

GCR	Gas-Cooled Reactor.
GEMINI	A series of American manned spaceflights.
Geo-Synchronous	Orbits of satellites whose position over a given point on the earth remains the same by synchronisation of the satellites' orbit with the rotation of the Earth.
GIUK	Greenland-Iceland-UK Gap.
GLCM	Ground Launched Cruise Missile.
GPS	Global Positioning System. A system of American navigational satellites.
Ground Zero	The point on the Earth over which a nuclear weapon is detonated.

H

Hard Target	A target protected against the blast, heat and radiation of nuclear explosions: for example, a missile silo.
HE	High Explosive.
Heavy Water	A substance very different from ordinary water due to its containing a hydrogen isotope named deuterium. Used as a coolant in HWRs.
Hen	A long-range Soviet radar providing warning of ICBM attack.
HF	High Frequency.
HOE	Homing Overlay Experiment. An anti-ballistic missile system experiment.
Homing	Guided towards a target by onboard guidance system.
Hot Launch	Launch method for ballistic missiles involving ignition of motors while missile is in silo. The method precludes reuse of the silo for another missile until the silo is repaired.
Howitzer	A weapon designed fo fire shells at a greater trajectory than normal guns and at a lower velocity.
HWR	Heavy Water Reactor.
Hypersonic	Velocities many times the speed of sound e.g. Mach 4 and above.

I

IAEA	International Atomic Energy Agency.
ICBM	Intercontinental Ballistic Missile.
IGS	Inertial Guidance System.
Inertial Guidance	An onboard guidance system, able to steer such machines as missiles over pre-determined courses by measuring factors such as altitude and distance travelled.
INF	Intermediate Range Nuclear Forces.
IR	Infra-Red.

	IRBM	Intermediate Range Ballistic Missile.
J	Jamming	The effect of disrupting or confusing an enemy's communications, radars and allied equipment. This can be done by electronic means, or by the use of such material as chaff or decoys.
	JSS	Joint Surveillance System (United States).
K	Killing Grounds or Zone	Area where weapons are expected to come under attack or troops exposed to fire.
	Kt	Kiloton. An explosive yield equal to 1,000 tons of TNT.
L	LAMPS	Light Airborne Multi-Purpose System. Anti-submarine helicopter equipment, which can comprise search radar, sonar buoy and MAD equipment, plus electronic support machinery. The helicopter so equipped can also have an attack capability.
	Launch Tubes	Torpedo or ballistic missile launchers on board submarines.
	Launch-Under-Attack Policy	A policy of launching missiles under attack conditions to prevent a large number of them being destroyed in their silos.
	LCC	Launch Control Centre. The supporting vehicle for a cruise missile TEL, providing launch capability for the missiles.
	LF	Low Frequency.
	Look-down Radar	Aircraft radar with the ability to distinguish from above airborne targets from the ground clutter produced by the Earth's surface. Cruise missiles are capable of detection in this way.
	Low Level Penetration	Flight profile of aircraft designed to minimise detection by ground based radars.
	LRBM	Long Range Ballistic Missile.
	LWR	Light Water Reactor. The most commonly used nuclear reactor, employing water to prevent the uranium fuel from overheating; can be one of two kinds, either the Boiling Water Reactor, or the Pressurised Water Reactor.
M	MAD	Magnetic Anomoly Detection system, used to detect submerged submarines. A MAD receiver is carried over the sea, for example by an aircraft, and is designed to detect the very small change in the Earth's local magnetic field caused by the submarine.
	MAD	Mutual Assured Destruction. Idea of deterrent consisting in the destruction of a large part of the civilian population and industrial capacity of a country as retaliation. A policy expressed for a time by the United States.
	Main Operating Base	The normal location of a GLCM, such as Greenham Common in England, from which the weapon would be moved to its operational deployment area in time of conflict.
	MaRV	Manoeuvrable Re-entry Vehicle. In this case, the missile warheads can be steered to their targets both by internal or external means.
	MBFR	Mutual and Balanced Force Reductions.
	Mikoyan-Gurevich (MiG)	Soviet designer and manufacturer of combat aircraft.
	Millisecond	One-thousandth of a second.
	Milstar	A series of two-way communications satellites, due for full-scale operation by the late 1980's and including the possibility of unjammable communications.
	MIRV Bus	Multiple Independently Targetable Re-entry Vehicle, carrying the various warheads of the missile back into the atmosphere for dispensing at their independent targets.

MLF	Multi-Lateral Force. A scheme for collective nuclear forces.
Molyina	Soviet class of satellites, providing observation of the continental United States.
Mt	Megaton. The yield of a nuclear weapon, equivalent to 1,000,000 tons of TNT.
MSBS	Mer-Sol-Ballistique Strategique. French term for an SLBM.

N

National Military Command System	The main priority part of the World-wide U.S. Military Command and Control System, providing the necessary information and support for the NCA to make executive decisions regarding the direction of U.S. strategic forces.
NATO	North Atlantic Treaty Organization. A body created by treaty comprising fourteen countries in Europe and North America, guaranteeing mutual assistance and military co-operation. The Warsaw Pact arose in large part as a response to the creation of NATO.
Navstar	Satellite component of the U.S. Global Positioning System (GPS).
NBC	Nuclear, Biological and Chemical. An NBC suit is available for issue to infantry and other fighting men, in the event of the use of any of these three weapon types on the battlefield.
NCA	National Command Authority. The main security officials of any country. In the United States, this consists of the President, together with his senior political and military decision-makers.
NORAD	North American Air Defence Command. The combined U.S. and Canadian command responsible for world-wide surveillance and early warning of air attack on North America by nuclear or conventional means.
NPT	Non-Proliferation Treaty.
Nuclear Artillery Pieces	Tactical battlefield shells armed with nuclear warheads and capable of being fired from ordinary artillery pieces.
Nuclear Burst	The detonation of a nuclear weapon, sometimes referred to as a nuclear Air-Burst when the weapon is detonated at a pre-set distance above the ground.

O

Overkill	The building-up of many more weapons than would be adequate to destroy all specified targets. This ensures that sufficient back-up is allowed for in the event of some weapons failing to function correctly and thus not destroying their targets.
Over-the-Horizon Radar	Surveillance radar whose signals stay near the Earth's surface, for further than the line of sight. The signals bounce off the ionosphere and return to Earth in waves. An Over-the-Horizon Backscatter Radar has a considerable range; any return waves reflected by an airborne target reflect back to a receiver near the original transmitter.

P

PACBAR	Pacific Radar Barrier (United States). Designed to give space surveillance coverage over the Pacific.
PARCS	Perimeter Acquisition Radar attack Characterization System (United States).
pave Paws	A radar system providing warning of a sea-launched ballistic missile attack from either the East Coast or the West Coast against the continental United States.
Payload	Total mass of a missile's warheads, together with their associated arming fuzing and safety systems, penetration aids, and any other device which is carried to the target.

PBPS	Post-Boost Propulsion System.
Penetration Aids	Carried by the Bus containing the warheads of an ICBM, these include decoys and ECM intended to deceive detecting radars and ABMs in order to allow the missile's warheads to reach their targets without interference.
PNET	Peaceful Nuclear Explosions Treaty.
Point Target	A target small enough to be identified by a single co-ordinate on operational maps: for example, a missile silo.
Pre-emptive Attack	An assault started on the basis of evidence that an enemy attack is about to take place.
PWR	Pressurised Water Reactor. A nuclear reactor in which water is circulated around the fuel at very high pressure; the hot, non-boiling water so created is fed into a separate loop of water which subsequently boils, driving the turbines which generate electricity with its steam.
PTBT	Partial Test Ban Treaty.

Q

QRA	Quick Reaction Alert.

R

RADAG	Radar Area Guidance system. The radar guidance system of the U.S. Pershing II missile, resulting in considerable accuracy for this weapon.
Radar Cross-section	The radar picture created by radar waves reflected back from a given target surface. The image so produced is influenced partly, but not wholly, by size: as structural shape can also play an important part, as can the refracting characteristics of the materials from which the target is made.
Real Time	Something instantaneous, like communications with or between military forces, or instantaneous recon-naissance for example by spy satellites.
Re-entry	The act of re-entering the Earth's atmosphere during the flight of a ballistic missile.
Regional Operations Control Centre	One of seven control centres of the JSS, receiving information of intruding aircraft in North America from radar locations.
Rhyolite	A U.S. class of satellite, designed to provide early warning of Soviet ICBM tests and launches.
RV	Re-entry Vehicle.

S

SAC	Strategic Air Command (United States). The U.S. Air Force Command responsible for America's manned strategic bombers and ICBMs.
SACEUR	Supreme Allied Commander Europe.
SALT	Strategic Arms Limitations Talks. Negotiations between the Soviet Union and the U.S. aimed to halt the expansion of strategic weapon systems of both countries, with the possibility of reducing these forces.
SAM	Surface-to-Air Missile.
SAMOS	U.S. spy satellite using radio link with Earth to transmit reconnaissance photographs.
Satellite Link	A satellite link avoids some of the jamming or destruction of Earth-bound communications links, and can include more than one satellite; an example is Flaming Arrow, with back-up communications for GLCM units when deployed away from their Main Operating Base.
SHAPE	Supreme Headquarters Allied Powers in Europe.
SHF	Super High Frequency. Can be used, for example, for communications with satellites.
Shroud	The uppermost part of a missile, protecting the warheads and RV.

Side-locking Radar	A radar that can provide a continuous radar map of the ground on each side of the flight path of the machine carrying the radar.
Silo	The underground base of a nuclear missile, with facilities for the missile's launch. The silo provides protection from nuclear attack, and often a high-precision attack is the only means of destroying it.
SINS	Ships Inertial Navigation System.
SIOP	Single Integrated Operations Plan. U.S. plan for strategic retaliatory strike in the event of nuclear war, including targets, tactics and force strength needed for such a plan.
SIRE	Space Infrared Sensor.
SLBM	Submarine/Sea-Launched Ballistic Missile.
SMW	Strategic Missile Wing (United States).
SNLE	Sous-marine Nucleaire Lance-Engins. French nuclear missile submarines able to carry the MSBS.
Soft Target	A target unprotected against the blast, heat and radiation of a nuclear explosion, such as a major centre of population.
Sonar Buoy	A buoy equipped with sonar equipment designed to detect submerged submarines, that listens for sounds reflected back from the submarine.
SOSUS	Sound Surveillance System.
SPADATS	Space Surveillance System (United States).
SPADOC	Space Defence Operations Centre (United States).
Special Ammunition Storage	A means of storing nuclear warheads, particularly those of tactical weapons; an example is the U.S. Lance tactical missile used by several NATO countries, whose warheads are under U.S. custody by crews of these storage sites.
SRAM	Short-Range Attack Missile. An air-launched nuclear-tipped missile. Now being replaced by ALCM due to the vulnerability of manned bombers in delivering short-range weapons by flying close to the target and its defences.
SS	Designation applied to Soviet nuclear missiles.
SSBS	Sol-Sol-Ballistique-Strategique. French term for IRBM.
SS-N	Designation applied to Soviet sea-launched nuclear missiles.
Stand-Off Bomb	A weapon fired by a manned aircraft some distance from the target, and capable of reaching the target under its own power. This allows the aircraft to stand off from the target, thus avoiding its defences.
START	Strategic Arms Reduction Talks.
Stealth	Aircraft designed so that their radar visibility is considerably reduced; this involves using aerodynamic shapes that minimise reflectivity to radar.
SUBROC	U.S. submarine-launched missile, essentially a nuclear depth charge designed to destroy SLBM-carrying submarines.
Subsonic Cruise	The ability of an aircraft, especially with swing-wings, to cruise at relatively low speed: thus conserving fuel, but being on hand to dash supersonically to deliver its weapons.
Sukhoi	Soviet designer and manufacturer of combat aircraft.
Supersonic Dash	A swing-wing aircraft has the ability to fold back its wings and dash at supersonic speed to its target.
Swing-Wing	Some aircraft, including some projected manned strategic bombers, are designed with variable geometry wings. The main portions of the wings are hinged, and can extend for subsonic flight, while being capable of being folded back to allow supersonic dash.

T

TACAMO	Take Command And Move Out. U.S. Navy means of communicating with submerged submarines when

	necessary by means of specially-equipped communications aircraft.
Tactical Aircraft	Land and Carrier based aircraft capable of carrying out a variety of roles especially in and around the battlefield. This can include the carrying of tactical nuclear weapons.
TAINS	Terrain-comparison Aided Inertial Navigation System.
Tall King	Series of Soviet intermediate-range aircraft-detection and tracking radars.
Teeth to Tail Ratio	The ratio of fighting men (Teeth) to the logistical support personnel and hence non-fighting men (Tail) or armies, especially when deployed in an operational area.
TEL	Transporter Erector Launcher. The combined transporting vehicle and launch platform for a GLCM.
Thermal Shielding	Shielding designed to reduce the effects of heat from nuclear explosions.
Thermonuclear Warhead	The hydrogen warhead commonly known as the H-bomb, which has a much greater power than the earlier atomic weapons.
Throw Weight	A ballistic missile's payload capacity: expressed in terms of the RV, its warhead(s), and associated devices such as arming and fuzing systems, and penetration aids.
TNT	TriNitroToluene. A high explosive, often used as an equivalent measure of the yield of nuclear warheads.
TTBT	Threshold Test Ban Treaty.
Tupolev	Soviet designer and manufacturer of combat aircraft, mainly bombers.
Turbofan Engine	A later powerplant than the earlier turbojet engine, a major advance being its requirement for less fuel. Turbofan engines can thus help provide greater range.

U

UHF	Ultra High Frequency.
US	United States.

V

Vela Hotel	U.S. series of satellites launched to detect nuclear explosions.
VHF	Very High Frequency.
VLF	Very Low Frequency. Capable of use, as with the United States AABNCP, for communication with submerged submarines.
VLS	Vertical Launch System.
V/STOL	Vertical/Short Take-Off and Landing.

W

Warsaw Pact	Military alliance of Eastern Europe comprising some seven countries, which arose in response to the creation of NATO and the re-militerization of West Germany in the 1950's.
Weapons Grade Fissile Material	Uranium or plutonium in a form capable of use in nuclear weapons.
Weapons Mix	The mix of weapons and missiles in a country's arsenal, especially when older and new weapons are in service simultaneously.
White Cloud	A U.S. Navy radar satellite ocean-surveillance programme.
World-wide Military Command and Control System	The operational direction and support of U.S. forces deployed throughout the World is provided through this system, which also contains the National Military Command System.

Y

Yellowcake	Uranium oxide, a bright yellow powder created following the chemical treatment of crushed rock containing uranium.

Yield	The explosive power of a nuclear weapon, expressed as an equivalent in metric tons of TNT.

Z

Zero Option	A proposal for limiting the deployment of nuclear weapons in Europe, put forward by U.S. President Reagan.

Index

A

B

C

O

P

R

S

T

The following authoritative current reference sources have been used for factual material throughout this book:

Official U.S. Department of Defense Data
NATO/Warsaw Pact Force Comparisons
Military Balance (International Institute of Strategic Studies)